Early Praise for *41*

"A good and decent man—part of the Great Generation that saved civilization in World War II, then came home to make the American Century and win the long struggle against the Soviet Union—gets his due in this brisk, bright, insightful volume."

—**Karl Rove**, *The Wall Street Journal*

"Jurdem ably studies the character of George H. W. Bush, a one-term chief executive who accomplished more than most presidents do in two terms. The book traces Bush's political origins, reaching back to Teddy Roosevelt, Colonel Stimson, Eisenhower, and definitely Senator Prescott Bush. In addition to recounting Bush's extraordinary international leadership—in German unification, the peaceful end of the Cold War in Europe, and the coalition that liberated Kuwait—Jurdem fills a gap by pointing to Bush's domestic accomplishments: the Americans with Disabilities Act; major amendments of the Clean Air Act; and his selfless budget deal that cut deficits into the '90s. He also points to Bush's role in shaping America's post–Cold War future through negotiations for continental free trade and the liberalization of global trade. Bush's life was defined by his character, friendships, and competitive drive to serve his country. This book explains the wellsprings of that presidential leadership."

—**Robert B. Zoellick**, former secretary of state and White House deputy chief of staff, author of *America in the World: A History of U.S. Diplomacy & Foreign Policy*

"A lot has been written about the life of the 41st president of the United States, but by examining who were the major influencers and inspirations in George H. W. Bush's life, author Laurence Jurdem's new book manages to give the reader a fresh and fascinating insight into who and what made George Bush...well, George Bush. It's a timely and inspirational read."

—**Jean Becker**, author of *The New York Times* bestseller *The Man I Knew: The Amazing Story of George H. W. Bush's Post-Presidency*

"In *41*, Laurence Jurdem masterfully chronicles the individuals and events that shaped the character of our 41st president, George H. W. Bush. I thought I knew most of what there is to know about President Bush but was proved wrong in reading this book. I highly recommend it."

—**David Q. Bates Jr.**, former assistant to the president and secretary to the Cabinet

"Laurence Jurdem has done a remarkable job researching and explaining the origins and influences on George Bush's life, that shaped an American leader's heartbeat and resulted in the wise leadership and character of President George H. W. Bush."

—**Thomas J. Collamore**, longtime aide and senior government appointee to George H. W. Bush, current senior advisor to the George and Barbara Bush Foundation

"Laurence Jurdem has written an insightful account of the forces and personalities that shaped the nation's 41st president. Despite coming from a privileged background, George H. W. Bush was a man of great humility with a remarkable capacity to grow and to learn. This is a terrific read about an underappreciated president whose decades of public service did the nation proud. It is also a moving glimpse into a time when presidents honored their oaths and served the nation with dignity and integrity."

—**Stephen F. Knott**, author of *The Lost Soul of the American Presidency*

"A good and decent man…gets his due in this brisk, bright, insightful volume."

—**Karl Rove**, *The Wall Street Journal*

"Bush's life was defined by his character, friendships, and competitive drive to serve his country. This book explains the wellsprings of that presidential leadership."

—**Robert B. Zoellick**, former secretary of state and White House deputy chief of staff, Author of *America in the World: A History of U.S. Diplomacy & Foreign Policy*

"A timely and inspirational read."

—**Jean Becker**, author of *The New York Times* bestseller *The Man I Knew: The Amazing Story of George H. W. Bush's Post-Presidency*

"I thought I knew most of what there is to know about President Bush but was proved wrong in reading this book. I highly recommend it."

—**David Q. Bates Jr.**, former assistant to the president and secretary to the Cabinet

"Laurence Jurdem has done a remarkable job researching and explaining the origins and influences on George Bush's life."

—**Thomas J. Collamore**, longtime aide and senior government appointee to George H. W. Bush, and currently senior advisor to the George and Barbara Bush Foundation

"This is a terrific read about an underappreciated president whose decades of public service did the nation proud. It is also a moving glimpse into a time when presidents honored their oaths and served the nation with dignity and integrity."

—**Stephen F. Knott**, author of *The Lost Soul of the American Presidency*

Also by Laurence Jurdem

Paving the Way for Reagan: The Influence of Conservative Media on US Foreign Policy

The Rough Rider and the Professor: Theodore Roosevelt, Henry Cabot Lodge, and the Friendship That Changed American History

GEORGE H. W. BUSH *and the* END *of the* AMERICAN ESTABLISHMENT

LAURENCE JURDEM

Published by Bombardier Books
An Imprint of Post Hill Press
ISBN: 979-8-89565-538-2
ISBN (eBook): 979-8-89565-679-2

41: George H. W. Bush and the End of the American Establishment

Cover Design by Cody Corcoran
Cover Photo by George H. W. Bush Presidential Library and Museum

This is a work of nonfiction. All people, locations, events, and situations are portrayed to the best of the author's memory.

This book, as well as any other Bombardier Books publications, may be purchased in bulk quantities at a special discounted rate. Contact orders@bombardierbooks.com for more information.

Post Hill Press
New York • Nashville
posthillpress.com

Published in the United States of America
1 2 3 4 5 6 7 8 9 10

For Elliot and Jorie,
you are truly my thousand points of light.

CONTENTS

INTRODUCTION

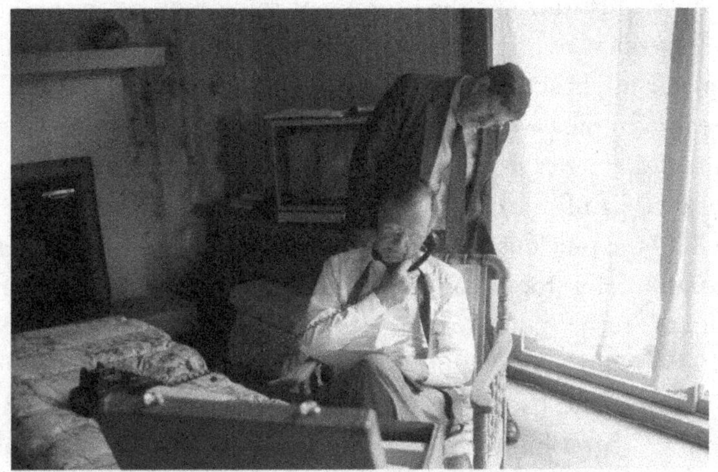

President Bush speaks to King Fahd of Saudi Arabia via telephone from his suite at the Catto Ranch in Aspen, Colorado regarding Iraq's Invasion of Kuwait. August 2, 1990.

August 2, 1990

Just after 10:20 a.m., the twin-engine Gulfstream IV, en route from Andrews Air Force Base in suburban Maryland to Aspen, Colorado, hit its maximum cruising speed of over five hundred miles per hour. With its sleek blue-and-white exterior and small American flag on its tail wing, the aircraft sliced through thick clouds, leaving behind the oppressive humidity and heat of the East Coast as it soared toward the cooler, more temperate air of the American West.[1]

In the aircraft's tight main cabin, President George H. W. Bush sat engaged in intense conversation with National Security Advisor Brent Scowcroft and White House Chief of Staff John Sununu. While many viewed the sleek, elegant craft as a luxurious way to travel, neither the president nor his team viewed it as ideal. The cramped space made any work difficult, and handling multiple phone calls proved a challenge.[2]

Months earlier, Bush had accepted an invitation to deliver an address to the Aspen Institute. As the prominent think tank celebrated its fortieth anniversary, the organization had invited the president to discuss the strategic implications on the Western alliance of the Soviet Union's collapse. But in the past twenty-four hours, the importance of the speech had shifted dramatically from a topic of casual interest to one of critical international significance.[3]

At 8:20 the previous evening, Brent Scowcroft briefed the president that 120,000 Iraqi troops had crossed into Kuwait. The man behind the invasion, the ruthless dictator President Saddam Hussein, had ruled Iraq since 1979. Notorious for authorizing the execution of political opponents, Hussein had used chemical weapons to quell dissent within his own country. After his 1988 sarin gas attack on the city of Halabja, it came as no surprise when *US News & World Report* labeled him "The Most Dangerous Man in the World."[4]

As Bush prepared for his Aspen appearance, he received word that the Iraqi military had not only occupied Kuwait's capital but also seized control of the nation's vital oil fields. When questioned by the media about the administration's response, the president stated that various options were under consideration. However, beneath his confident exterior, Bush recognized the limited means available to compel Hussein to halt his aggression.[5]

Bush had other concerns besides Iraq's violation of Kuwait's sovereignty. The president also had the responsibility for the safety of twenty-five hundred Americans stationed in the Emirate. Additionally, the president recognized the threat Hussein posed to Saudi Arabia's vast oil reserves. If the Iraqi military advanced southward and seized control of

Saudi oil fields, Hussein would dominate 45 percent of the world's oil market, significantly shifting the balance of global power.[6]

The president's concerns about a potential Iraqi incursion into Saudi Arabia also led Bush to consider the possibility of a wider conflict. With Iraq's military possessing greater offensive capabilities than its southern neighbor, he remained uncertain about Saudi Arabia's ability and willingness to resist Iraqi aggression. "God knows...whether they'll stand up," Bush wrote in his diary. As the crisis deepened, he feared that if Saudi Arabia yielded to Iraq, Hussein might set his sights on the next target in the Arab world.[7]

As the plane continued its journey, the president tapped into his extensive international network, built over more than two decades in government, to assess the impact of Hussein's invasion on the Middle East. His first call went to his longtime friend, King Hussein of Jordan. According to a 1990 article by *The Washington Post*'s David Hoffman, the two had first become acquainted in the 1970s when Bush served as director of the CIA. The Jordanian leader—who had ruled from the Hashemite throne since 1952 and served as an American intelligence asset since 1957—shared many common interests with Bush, including a love of speedboats and a deep engagement with the complexities of Middle East diplomacy.

When Bush called, King Hussein was in Alexandria, meeting with Egyptian President Hosni Mubarak. During their conversation, the king informed Bush of his plans to visit both Saudi Arabia and Iraq, hoping to resolve the crisis by working with Saddam to establish "a foundation for a better future." Bush, however, found the king's approach troubling. Taking a conciliatory approach with a leader with little regard for human life or international law would only risk escalating the crisis. Bush remained firm in his stance; Saddam had to withdraw his forces from Kuwait immediately. "I told the king that the world would not accept the status quo now, and that it was unacceptable to the United States." Bush also made sure the Arab leader understood his position clearly, adding, "I'm sure Saddam Hussein knows this, but you can tell him that from me."[8]

Upon arriving in Aspen, the president headed straight to a meeting with British Prime Minister Margaret Thatcher. Thatcher, invited to deliver the conference's closing address, had scheduled the meeting with Bush to coordinate their remarks. However, just that morning, as she prepared to meet with the president, British diplomat Charles Powell informed her of Iraq's invasion of Kuwait.[9]

Gathering at US Ambassador Henry Catto's stone cottage, set on 128 acres just outside Aspen in Woody Creek, Colorado, the two leaders discussed the gravity of Iraq's aggression against its Arab neighbor. Both Bush and Thatcher were shaped by the turmoil of the 1930s, when isolationism had prevented Europe and the United States from responding decisively to Adolf Hitler's growing threat. The vivid lessons of that era led them to the shared conclusion: They could not allow another megalomaniacal dictator to endanger global stability. "If Iraq wins, no small state is safe. They won't stop here," Thatcher warned the president.[10]

Reminiscing about her conversation with Bush years later, Thatcher recognized that the lessons of history resonated deeply with the former World War II naval aviator. "I had no doubt what you had to do to deal with an aggressor. My generation, as indeed President Bush's, knew a terrible world war—which had been caused because we didn't deal firmly enough with Hitler in the early stages, and of course, the Japanese came into Pearl Harbor, so we knew the importance of stopping it quickly and then reversing it," she recalled. As the crisis unfolded, it became clear to Thatcher that Bush saw Saddam Hussein's invasion of Kuwait as equivalent to Hitler's annexations of Austria and Czechoslovakia in 1938 and 1939.[11]

When President Bush addressed the media at the White House on August 5, three days after his meeting with Thatcher, his firm declaration, "This will not stand, this aggression against Kuwait," reaffirmed his determination not to repeat the mistakes made by the international community in underestimating figures like Adolf Hitler half a century before. As Bush prepared to address the American people on August 8 regarding the crisis in the Persian Gulf, memories of Western retreat remained at the forefront of his mind. "I tightened up the language to strengthen the similarity I saw between the Persian Gulf and the situation in the Rhineland in the 1930s," Bush recorded in a memoir of his administration's foreign policy. His reference was to Hitler's March 1936 decision to send twenty-two thousand German troops into the industrial community on the Franco-German border, a direct violation of the Treaty of Versailles, imposed on Germany by the Allied powers after its defeat in World War I. "This time, I wanted no appeasement," Bush said.[12]

***

George Bush's deep understanding of history played a crucial role in his decision to launch a campaign to drive Saddam Hussein out of Kuwait. That experience also included his extensive knowledge of the Middle East and the strong relationships built with world leaders through decades of experience in the oil business and government. These assets enabled him to forge a broad thirty-five-nation coalition that resulted in a swift, decisive military campaign that restored the Emirate's sovereignty in just under five days. The victory testified to Bush's skill in personal diplomacy as well as contributing to the restoration of the nation's confidence in the American military, whose morale and stature had been deeply shaken by the United States' humiliating defeat in Vietnam fifteen years earlier. The victory over Saddam Hussein also affirmed Bush's belief that the success of any grand strategy required the active participation of the United Nations, the North Atlantic Treaty Organization (NATO), and other key governmental organizations that had historically supported the United States in its role as leader of the free world.[13]

The American success in the First Gulf War represented one of several key foreign policy accomplishments during President Bush's administration. Most significantly, Bush used his diplomatic skill and steady temperament to guide the nation through defining moments that marked the end of the Cold War, including the fall of the Berlin Wall in 1989 and Germany's reunification in 1990. He also fostered a strong working relationship with Soviet leader Mikhail Gorbachev, culminating in the 1993 Strategic Arms Reduction Treaty (START II), through which both countries agreed to reduce their nuclear stockpiles by more than one-third. Bush's achievements in global affairs highlighted his aptitude for personal relationships and his strong belief in supporting an international system developed by the United States and other members of the Western alliance following World War II.[14]

Bush believed the United States had a duty to serve as a beacon of freedom for the world. In this regard, he served as a direct link to Secretary of War Henry Stimson, a Republican who had served in the Democratic administration of Franklin D. Roosevelt, and to other statesmen who shaped American foreign policy throughout the twentieth century. During the era, an insular group of patrician financiers, who attended elite educational institutions like Harvard, Princeton, and Yale, held key government positions as they advised presidents from FDR to Ronald Reagan on navigating the complexities of the Cold War. These figures included Secretary of Defense Robert A. Lovett, Ambassador W. Averell Harriman, and diplomat John J. McCloy, who together had long-standing ties to what became known as the American Establishment.[15]

On March 21, 1989, Secretary of State James A. Baker III delivered a eulogy on behalf of President Bush at McCloy's funeral. A man of remarkable energy and achievement, McCloy served as both president of the World Bank and US high commissioner for Germany. As Baker addressed McCloy's family and a distinguished audience at New York's Brick Church—including Ambassador Vernon Walters, who worked with Presidents Truman and Eisenhower, and the widow of Secretary of State Dean Acheson—the words used to honor McCloy's legacy seemed equally reflective of George Bush himself. "He never flagged in pursuing the public good in the many private trusts he held. His energy and interests were boundless. So were his accomplishments." The expertise and dedication McCloy and his contemporaries exhibited in shaping US foreign policy reflected the very qualities Bush admired and embodied throughout his own distinguished career, culminating in four challenging years as president of the United States.[16]

Bush and his patrician class held a distinguished place in American society. Historian Geoffrey Kabaservice described the Protestant establishment "as society's guardians: modern leaders of the country's institutions, who had national responsibilities and tried to take a national perspective." Like earlier statesmen such as Lovett, Harriman, and Acheson, Bush and many of those who served in his administration shared similar pedigrees and traditions.[17]

Bush and Baker, as well as Treasury Secretary Nicholas Brady and Commerce Secretary Robert Mosbacher, came from privileged backgrounds rooted in communities like New York City; Greenwich, Connecticut; and Houston, Texas. Educated at prestigious Eastern preparatory schools such as Phillips Academy, St. Mark's School, Choate, and The Hill School, all were instilled with a strong sense of duty to uphold the principles of fairness, equality, and service to the common good. Through distinguished careers in oil, law, and banking, each man developed a deep appreciation for the importance of process and attention to detail. Their broad networks across business, philanthropy, politics, and sports also taught them the value of listening to diverse perspectives and engaging with differing points of view.

As they transitioned into public service, Bush and his closest advisors brought with them a shared commitment to advancing American economic prosperity and promoting global stability. Like many senior figures in the administration, Baker, Brady, and Mosbacher had long-standing personal ties with Bush, developed during his years at Phillips Academy, his post–World War II years at Yale, or his early business ventures in Texas during the 1950s. These enduring relationships reflected not only Bush's gift for friendship and loyalty but also his belief in surrounding himself with steadfast defenders of America's democratic ideals that promoted economic and political freedom, as well as the conviction that the United States had a duty to lead on the world stage.[18]

Descendant of a prominent WASP family that amassed its fortune through industry and banking, George Bush's upbringing blended deep-rooted familial values with the conviction that opportunities were not simply given but earned. As former speechwriter and *Wall Street Journal* columnist Peggy Noonan reflected after Bush's passing in 2018, "The lesson of that life was clear: He worked for it, he poured himself into it. He gave it everything he had. He made sacrifices to be who he was."[19]

With twenty-five years of experience across all branches of government, Bush developed the deep expertise necessary to lead the United States through the final stages of the Cold War. He restored the sovereignty of a nation threatened by an aggressive Arab dictator, and he championed domestic legislation that broadened access to the American Dream for immigrants, individuals with disabilities, and communities of color.

Rising through the ranks of politics and public service, Bush benefited from the connections established by his father, Prescott Bush, a liberal Republican who served two terms as a US senator from Connecticut. During his time in the Senate from 1952–1963, the elder Bush played a key role as a bridge between President Dwight D. Eisenhower and conservative Republican Senate Majority Leader Robert A. Taft. Known for his friendly demeanor and talent for bringing together differing perspectives, Prescott Bush supported many of Eisenhower's initiatives, such as the 1956 Federal Highway Act, which led to the creation of the interstate highway system. Eisenhower held Bush in such high esteem that when making a list of those he believed should succeed him in the presidency, the former World War II general placed an "A" beside Bush's name. The senator's friendships with those such as Eisenhower and Richard Nixon also provided his son, George, with the opportunity to build relationships with these prominent Republicans and other nationally recognized leaders. Launching his career in local Texas politics, the younger Bush strategically leveraged these connections into a series of high-profile public roles that ultimately led him to the White House.[20]

These positions included congressman, ambassador to the United Nations, chairman of the Republican National Committee, head of the US Liaison Office to the People's Republic of China, director of the Central Intelligence Agency, and vice president of the United States. From 1967 to 1989, the former oil executive and World War II veteran cultivated relationships with Richard Nixon, Gerald Ford, and Ronald

Reagan, experiences that honed his skills in diplomacy and leadership. As a result, George Bush emerged as the most prepared chief executive the nation ever produced.[21]

While Prescott Bush's professional network proved critical to his son's rise, he and his wife, Dorothy Walker, also schooled him in the values of fairness, humility, and a strong sense of duty to engage in charity and public service. They emphasized that success did not come by seeking attention or capitalizing on the family name, but rather through hard work and discipline. While George Bush remained steadfast in these principles, his political career occasionally forced him to reconcile his aversion to self-promotion with his ambition to win elected office. That tension was particularly evident in his 1988 campaign pledge not to raise taxes—a promise he later reversed, prioritizing what he saw as sound fiscal governance over what *The Washington Post*'s Bob Woodward described in 1992 as "his sacred word."[22]

Although Bush believed that effective governance required building consensus to address the nation's challenges, he entered Republican politics in the 1960s as the party began shifting away from moderation toward ideological rigidity. At the same time, national disillusionment with government deepened in the wake of President John F. Kennedy's assassination in 1963, followed by the decision in 1965 of his successor, Lyndon B. Johnson, to increase American involvement in the Vietnam War. The disaster that resulted from the nation's involvement in Southeast Asia led many Americans to conclude that allowing an insular, socially privileged group of men, united by their experience at Eastern prep schools and Ivy League universities, to shape national policy was both problematic and contrary to the meritocratic principles on which the nation was founded.[23]

In addition to losing credibility over their handling of the Vietnam War, those who preceded Bush as the leaders of the American establishment faced growing criticism for their lack of empathy toward the daily struggles of black Americans, Jews, and other ethnic minorities. However, as elite educational and professional institutions increasingly opened their doors to a more diverse population based on merit, the continued exclusivity and insularity of those among the Eastern elite created the impression that, despite holding positions at the highest levels of government, many remained disconnected from the lives and concerns of the ordinary voter.[24]

Although President Bush appointed more women and minorities to his cabinet than any previous Republican president, his establishment background, formal demeanor, and emotional reserve caused many Americans to see him as the embodiment of a ruling class that had held power for far too long. The perception became amplified during the 1992 presidential campaign when *The New York Times* reported that Bush seemed surprised by a supermarket checkout scanner: a technology widely in use since the early 1980s. Although it was later clarified that the president had been shown a more advanced model, the incident nonetheless reinforced the impression of Bush as a patrician figure, seemingly oblivious to the economic struggles of everyday Americans.[25]

Ironically, the decline of the WASP patrician class was driven by the very meritocratic ideals upon which the United States was founded. As Ross Douthat of *The New York Times* argued in 2018, the exclusive network of elite prep schools, Ivy League universities, top law firms, investment banks, and social clubs began to open to a broader range of talent. The same institutions that had once molded leaders like George Bush and his forebears became pathways allowing a more diverse and competitive generation to rise, ultimately reshaping the American elite.

President Bill Clinton, who came from an exceptionally modest background, benefited from that change by being accepted to Georgetown University as well as Yale Law School. Despite Clinton's impressive political and oratorical skills, as well as his substantial experience as a four-time governor of Arkansas, he lacked the extensive résumé and vast professional network of George Bush. Clinton's predecessor had participated in multiple White House transitions, gaining valuable insight into the types of expertise and knowledge required for success.

In contrast, Clinton's choice to surround himself with close associates from Arkansas—such as his first chief of staff, Thomas "Mac" McLarty, along with a group of young, intellectually talented progressives—showed little deference or interest in the advice of veterans from previous administrations. That refusal to learn and listen from members of the Eastern establishment created difficulties for Clinton in building strong relationships with members of Congress and other long-established Washington institutions. The limitations of equating achievement in the classroom with political effectiveness are aptly captured by *Wall Street Journal* essayist Joseph Epstein in 2013, who wrote, "having been a good student…is no indication of one's quality or promise as a leader."

Epstein is also right to highlight that a president like Harry S. Truman, despite little formal education other than high school, achieved a great deal of success. Truman's strength, like that of George Bush, lay in his humility and his understanding of the importance of surrounding himself with experienced advisors such as Acheson, Harriman, and Lovett. These men and others of similar pedigree and experience offered the Missouri-bred Truman valuable counsel—not only on the controversial decision to drop two atomic bombs on Japan but also in shaping key postwar initiatives, like the Marshall Plan in 1948 and the formation of NATO in 1949.

In addition, Bush entered the presidency with a reputation for a sterling character, shaped in part by his service as a combat pilot during World War II. Bush also had a stable personal life and a history of being devoted to his wife and children. In contrast, Bill Clinton, who emerged from a dysfunctional family, came of age during the deeply divisive Vietnam War. His decision to defer military service to attend Oxford University on a Rhodes scholarship became a point of controversy during the 1992 campaign and continued to polarize opinion throughout his presidency. Further complicating Clinton's public image were criticisms of his personal conduct, particularly an affair with a White House intern and a series of other alleged extramarital relationships. These scandals, as writer Peter Beinart described in *The Atlantic* in 2018, contributed to a "crisis of legitimacy" that plagued his tenure in office.

Like President Clinton, Barack Obama gained admission to prestigious institutions such as Columbia and Harvard. However, despite having one of the smoothest White House transitions in recent memory, Obama assumed the presidency with one of the thinnest résumés in modern history, having served in the Illinois State Senate and only briefly in the US Senate. Yet, the differences between the forty-first and forty-fourth presidents go beyond their political experience.

Whereas Bush was known for his ease in building relationships across the political aisle, Obama—despite holding Democratic majorities in both houses of Congress during his first two years in office, from 2009–2011—was viewed as distant and intellectually aloof, even by members of his own party. His limited political networking, combined with a progressive agenda and the persistent racial and cultural anxieties held by some on the right, including conspiracy theories about his birthplace, also contributed to a deeply adversarial relationship with the Republican Party.[26]

Obama's reluctance to engage with opposing viewpoints, particularly in his interactions with Republican members of Congress, highlighted how his limited political experience hindered his ability to build effective relationships on Capitol Hill. Despite his humble origins and early work in underserved communities, Obama's tendency to criticize and lecture others, including the United States itself for failing to meet the ideals he championed, led *Washington Post* columnist and former George W. Bush speechwriter Michael Gerson to describe the president in 2010 as an "intellectual snob." In contrast, despite George Bush's privileged background, his genuine respect for people from all walks of life reflected the familial values that helped shape him into both an admirable man and an effective president.

While those who served in the Clinton and Obama administrations were ethnically diverse—much more socially inclusive and often more professionally and intellectually accomplished than in the past—many also lacked the expertise, as well as the same sense of selflessness and reverence for institutional processes, that Bush and his circle saw as essential to effective governance. As commentator David Brooks observed in *The New York Times* during the Obama presidency in 2010, those administrations that followed George Bush after his defeat in 1993 were less concerned with pursuing a gradualist approach to policy, and more focused on the constant struggle to maintain public approval. In pursuit of that aim, Clinton, George W. Bush, and Obama pursued bold but controversial initiatives—like promoting members of the LGBTQ community to serve in the military, reforming the health-care system, or advocating a freedom agenda for the Middle East. While George Bush faced a Democratic Congress throughout his four years as president, his innate conservatism and lack of hubris caused him to prioritize legislation that limited national anxiety.[27]

Ironically, even as American institutions have become more meritocratic, resulting in the elevation of figures like the Clintons and the Obamas, their policies, coupled with a perceived social arrogance and detachment, have led the public to see them as equally responsible for political polarization and economic inequality as the elites they replaced. As Christopher Lasch argues in *The Revolt of the Elites*, "Thanks to the decline of old money and the old money ethic of civic responsibility, local and regional loyalties are sadly attenuated today." The current generation of those in power, unlike George Bush and his contemporaries, often place personal ambition above public service, distancing themselves from the communities and values that once earned figures like Senator Prescott Bush the public's respect. Although George Bush's career took him across the nation and around the world, he never lost sight of the values infused in him from an early age.[28]

Many Americans elected Donald Trump in 2016 and 2024 out of frustration with well-meaning, well-educated elites who had grown complacent and disconnected from the social and economic struggles facing the lower and middle classes. Trump successfully helped fuel that growing anger among many in the nation's Rust Belt and Midwest, where people believed that those who had attended Ivy League institutions, followed by lengthy periods in government not only ignored their concerns but had also caused their communities lasting harm. Following the war in Afghanistan in 2001, the Second Gulf War in 2003, and the financial crises in 2008, Americans became increasingly more cynical about government, as well as the value of the Washington leadership class responsible for producing those like George Bush and his contemporaries.

Despite serious concerns about Trump's character, voters saw in him a disruptive force: someone who could upend the status quo and push a national agenda that addressed issues the Washington establishment seemed unwilling or unable to confront. However, unlike 2016—when Trump initially surrounded himself with advisors who understood and valued those who had devoted their lives to public service, as well as the international system built by leaders like George Bush and his predecessors—his second term has marked a significant shift. With the coming of "Trump 2.0," loyalty has taken precedence over expertise, with appointments favoring media personalities more effective at critiquing policies than creating or implementing them.

President Trump frequently asserts that his administration is made up of some of the most successful individuals in America. While that claim remains debatable, what has become increasingly clear is the administration's deep distrust of government and institutions that represent a hallmark of education and expertise, coupled with a striking disregard for upholding the standards and practices that were once revered by Bush and other members of the patrician establishment.

As historian Jon Meacham wrote in *The New York Times* in 2016, throughout his long life Bush showed little interest in actively making himself the center of attention. Guided by his mother's advice not to be a "braggadocio," he consistently avoided behavior that might be seen as self-serving. From declining to "dance on the Berlin Wall" in 1989, to resisting calls for regime change in Iraq after expelling Saddam Hussein from Kuwait in 1991, Bush deliberately chose to dismiss opportunities to enhance his personal popularity, especially when it might have come at the expense of leaders like Mikhail Gorbachev. His restraint reflected a principled and dignified style of leadership, while it also underscored his discomfort with the media-driven nature of modern politics and contributed, in part, to his failure to win a second term.

Bush and other members of the WASP establishment are rightly criticized for their arrogance and for making compromises to accommodate the rising power of populist conservatism. However, they also upheld a strong commitment to sacrifice and service, qualities that were once fundamental to the nation's success. Though the WASP elite has seen its influence wane, the competence and steadiness that Bush and other political elites brought to national leadership in the final decades of the twentieth century offer valuable insights for today's leaders.

Bush's service across multiple branches of government provided him with both a deep understanding of the administrative state, appreciation for consensus-building and the inclusion of diverse perspectives in effective policymaking. Bush and the post–World War II establishment figures who shaped his rise were far from perfect. However, they demonstrated a generosity of spirit, driven by a commitment to serving "a cause greater than themselves." Their dedication to fundamental values such as honesty and integrity remains vital to the republic's leadership today. In an era where knowledge is often undervalued and those with experience go unappreciated, examining the experiences that defined George Bush and his era can offer a blueprint for restoring the caliber of public service the nation both needs and deserves.

PART I

APPRENTICESHIP

CHAPTER 1

Virtues and Values: Family

George Bush's parents, Prescott and Dorothy Walker Bush.

On June 13, 2014, President George Bush celebrated his ninetieth birthday not with a quiet family gathering but by parachuting from a helicopter six thousand feet above Kennebunkport, Maine. Though no longer able to walk, the forty-first president completed the jump with the assistance of retired Sergeant First Class Mike Elliott, a former member of the Army's elite Golden Knights parachute team. Dressed in a black jumpsuit with red and white trim and bright orange socks, the former

World War II naval aviator continued a tradition begun at age seventy-two and repeated every five years. The quinquennial leap represented one of many moments that exemplified Bush's lifelong spirit of adventure and his willingness to embrace the unknown.

As the red, white, and blue parachute touched down on the lawn of St. Anne's Episcopal Church, the former president couldn't hide his excitement. "He's smiling like a kid in kindergarten," Elliott told the Associated Press after the jump. Much like his hero, President Theodore Roosevelt, Bush's leap from the helicopter reflected his passion for action. Whether speeding across the waters of Maine in his cigarette boat, *Fidelity*; rapidly playing a round of golf; or visiting multiple European capitals in a single day during his one term as president, Bush never let age or physical limitation diminish his drive. Even in his later years, when most would have been content to reflect on their accomplishments, Bush remained committed to embodying what Roosevelt famously called "the strenuous life," a philosophy that pushed one to pursue challenges that were not only personally fulfilling but also contributed to the common good.

***

George Bush and other establishment figures who held influential roles in their nation's institutions often traced their ancestry back to the founding of the republic and, in some cases, even earlier. While many came from families that built significant wealth through industries like textiles, shipping, or finance, others descended from clergymen, academics, and respected professionals who were seen as pillars of their communities. As sociologist Howard Schneiderman observes, these men represented "a moral force within the putatively amoral world of politics and power elites."[29]

Within this close-knit circle, those who upheld the nation's cultural and political ideals embodied values essential to its continued prosperity. As historian Richard Brookhiser notes, these virtues included a strong sense of "conscience, civic duty, and industriousness." The point is further illustrated by authors Leonard Silk and Mark Silk, who argue that individuals who reflected these principles were widely respected for their professional integrity and unwavering moral compass, even in the face of external pressures. As influential figures within the establishment, they promoted a broad and inclusive worldview, encouraged open dialogue, and welcomed differing perspectives, believing that such engagement nurtured deeper consensus and contributed to a more unified, harmonious society.[30]

Prescott Bush, the father of George Bush, embodied the core values of the American establishment class. Descended from a family that first settled in New England in the seventeenth century, the Bushes took pride in their ancestor Dr. Samuel Prescott, who rode alongside Paul Revere on his iconic late-night ride of April 18, 1775, to warn fellow colonists of the approaching British invasion. Other descendants included Obadiah Bush, who fought in the War of 1812 only to die prematurely as he prepared to seek his fortune during the California Gold Rush in 1851.[31]

Obadiah's son, James Smith Bush, George Bush's great-grandfather, displayed personal qualities that came to define the future president. As Bush biographer Jon Meacham writes, of James Smith Bush "there was a restlessness, an eagerness to break away from the established order of life, but not so much that one could not return."[32]

Prescott Bush, a respected investment banker, shared a devotion to family as well as a deep sense of civic responsibility, notably serving as the moderator of the Representative Town Meeting in Greenwich, Connecticut, and as a United States senator. Known for his unwavering moral principles—including a commitment to civil rights, opposition to Senator Joseph McCarthy's tactics to limit intellectual freedom, as well as support for raising immigration quotas—Prescott held himself and his family to the highest standards.

He was born into privilege in Columbus, Ohio, in 1895, the son of railroad executive Samuel P. Bush and his wife, Flora. Raised in the disciplined environment of the Victorian era, he believed in balancing professional achievement with personal and spiritual fulfillment. Prescott stood at six feet four, and he had little tolerance for vanity or inappropriate language. As a husband and father, he stressed the importance of a strong moral foundation, emphasizing that wealth should serve a higher purpose rather than simply be accumulated for its own sake.[33]

Thrifty and reserved, Prescott Bush brought diligence and discipline to his role as a partner at the investment firm Brown Brothers Harriman. The firm's leadership epitomized what many considered to be the WASP elite. Like Bush, partners such as W. Averell Harriman and Robert A. Lovett attended prestigious Northeastern boarding schools before continuing their education at Yale University, where all three were inducted into the exclusive secret society, Skull and Bones. The shared experience of enduring the society's time-honored rituals forged lifelong bonds among them. Moreover, those who passed through these institutions often came from similar backgrounds, sharing commonalities in race, religion, and unified worldview.[34]

After leaving New Haven in 1917, Prescott Bush's strong sense of duty and service led him to join the United States Army. In 1918, during the final months of World War I, he deployed to France where he served as a captain in the 158th Field Artillery Brigade. From September 26–November 11, he took part in the Meuse-Argonne Offensive, a grueling five-week campaign of attrition against the forces of Kaiser Wilhelm II. The battle resulted in devastating losses, with American forces suffering more than 256,000 casualties either killed or wounded.[35]

In a letter to his parents, the young artilleryman expressed both enthusiasm and a touch of immaturity by embellishing his battlefield experiences. Impressed by what she saw as her son's bravery, Flora Bush submitted the letter to *The Ohio State Journal*, which subsequently published Prescott's exploits on its front page. There is no record of the incident in his oral history or the reaction of his parents. He either may have thought little of the incident or it may have caused him such embarrassment that he chose not to mention the matter.[36]

After relocating to St. Louis, Missouri, to work in sales for the Simmons Hardware Company, Prescott married into a family of greater financial stature than his own. Despite Dorothy Wear Walker's privileged upbringing, the spirited and athletic daughter of wealthy financier George H. "Bert" Walker was known more for her love of tennis courts and polo fields than for high fashion or elite social circles. The younger of two Walker sisters, she also shared Prescott's deep commitment to honor, integrity, and leading by example.[37]

Dorothy Walker came from a family with a lineage as distinguished as her husband's. After settling in Maine and later Maryland in the seventeenth century, the Walker family rose to prominence in St. Louis. George Bush's great-grandfather, David Davis "D. D." Walker, founded a successful dry goods business. He was named after the family's first cousin David Davis, a lawyer and key figure in Abraham Lincoln's 1860 presidential campaign. Dorothy Walker's paternal grandfather valued moderation, a trait that stood in stark contrast to the temperament of his son, George H. "Bert" Walker.[38]

A rebellious, tempestuous character, Bert Walker epitomized the wealth and extravagance of the Gilded Age. The family lived on a lavish estate in one of St. Louis's most affluent neighborhoods and maintained additional residences on Madison Avenue and Sutton Place in New York City—as well as on the North Shore of Long Island and in Santa Barbara, California, plus an antebellum plantation in Barnwell County, South Carolina. While Bert Walker embodied the era's opulence, his fierce and unyielding personality also reflected the period's brutal competitiveness. Known within his family as "a real son of a bitch," Walker had no compunction about using physical force to assert authority. He often boxed with his four sons, believing that toughening them through physical combat represented the best path to manhood.[39]

Despite being regarded as a difficult man in and out of the boardroom, Walker also possessed a certain code he passed down to his children, one remarkably like the values of Prescott's father, Samuel P. Bush. "Father counts on you to do your best and he knows you will...you are gentlemen and not muckers and that your word is your bond," Walker wrote to his four young sons in May 1920. While the grandfather of George Bush had a reputation as a wheeler-dealer, he encouraged his offspring to "play fair" and make positive contributions to society.[40]

Dorothy Walker deeply admired her father's determination and ambition. However, his reckless business dealings, ostentatious wealth, and unpredictable temperament prompted her to seek a partner whose values stood in contrast, qualities she found in the thrifty and conservative demeaner of Prescott Bush. Dorothy Walker mirrored her father's competitive drive, but she also embodied her mother Lucretia Wear's warmth, kindness, and strong commitment to family and community—qualities that defined George Herbert Walker Bush, born on June 12, 1924.[41]

While ambition and drive to succeed were valued, Prescott and Dorothy Bush also imbued in their children the importance of humility and gratitude for life's blessings, principles that strongly influenced the upbringing of George Bush and his four siblings. Prescott disapproved of gambling, drank only in moderation, and lived with deliberate simplicity. "Dad believed in the old Ben Franklin copybook maxims when it came to earning, saving, and spending. In other ways, too, he and my mother embodied the Puritan ethic," Bush reflected in his 1987 autobiography, *Looking Forward*.[42]

The qualities that the younger Bush so admired were frequently displayed in the family household. In one recollection, Bush's sister, Nancy Bush-Ellis, recalled her mother's outrage when the children left their bicycles out in the rain, resulting in a weeklong loss of bike privileges. The Bush parents also conveyed the value of gratitude through daily Bible readings. While they did not require interpretation of scripture, they hoped its themes of goodwill and the importance of helping others would resonate in their children, grounding within them a strong foundation of faith. However, Dorothy believed that while religion played an important role in life, it had to be combined with initiative. "Prayer is essential. So is taking action," she once told the woman who managed the family home in Greenwich.[43]

The belief that the whole remained more important than the individual was a guiding principle in the Bush family's code of conduct. During Bush's childhood, he and his older brother, Prescott Jr., shared a bedroom, not out of necessity, but as a reflection of this value. Despite having ample space for their five children, the Bushes prioritized shared experiences and a sense of togetherness. "We were taught that brotherhood was more important than winning an argument," William Bush said.[44]

Sharing a common space taught the two boys the importance of mutual respect and the necessity of compromise for harmonious living. The spirit of devotion fostered a deep bond among all the Bush children. The same principle applied when one of them misbehaved. Failing to meet their parents' standards did not simply represent a personal shortcoming but an embarrassment to the entire family, thus reinforcing their collective sense of responsibility. "Knowing that we disappointed our parents. That was the most painful punishment we could get," William Bush said. The point is underscored by an incident in which George and his older brother, Prescott Jr., played a prank on a neighbor's daughter, convincing her to run naked through her house. When their father found out, he insisted the boys walk to the girl's home and apologize to both her and her mother. "It wasn't a short walk either," Bush later recalled.[45]

That sense of obligation extended to achievement as well. Although the idea of finishing first was rarely spoken aloud, Bush and his siblings understood that excellence was simply expected. "To be a good son, then, meant *doing* as well as *being*," wrote author Jon Meacham. The Bush children knew they were deeply loved, but they also noticed that individual success seemed to brighten their parents' demeanor. That desire for parental approval helped shape Bush's relentless ambition. "You have goals, and you want to meet them. Without letting it show through in everyday life," he said in an interview. Throughout Bush's rise to political prominence, he relied on his grit and determination to achieve success, persevering through both emotional and physical challenges.[46]

For the Bush family, accomplishments were more than simply personal or professional. Prescott and Dorothy viewed themselves and their children as leaders within their community. Each member had an obligation to set an example for others to follow. As a result, any success or failure reflected both on the reputation of the individual and on the broader perception of the family. The Bush children learned early that one's reputation and family name mattered.[47]

That perception also applied to one's personal behavior. Despite occasional fights between George and his siblings, the fear of provoking their father's temper kept all five children in line. "We were scared of him when it came to discipline," Bush admitted. Despite Prescott's imposing presence, the future president saw his father as a role model, embodying qualities he aspired to emulate. "[My father] was an overwhelming, respected figure that had the respect of everybody he worked with in business and the respect of those with whom he served," Bush reflected in a 1996 interview with *Time*'s Hugh Sidey for a documentary on the American presidency.[48]

That commanding presence came into sharp focus each evening when Prescott returned from his daily commute to New York. As author J. Randy Taraborrelli describes in his book, *Grace and Steel*, the family's maid, Lucy Larkin, "would spring into action" the moment he neared the house. The library—considered a sanctuary for the Bush parents—had to be rapidly prepared. "All of you out of the room this minute!" she would shout at the children. Once George and his siblings had scrambled upstairs, Larkin would straighten the cushions and set out fresh ice for Prescott's evening cocktail.

The 1930s were marked by economic and political upheaval. Amid the uncertainty of the Great Depression, the elder Bush, a critic of the New Deal's expansion of government into private enterprise, would sit in the club car of the New Haven Railroad, traveling from Greenwich to New York City, closely studying *the New York Herald Tribune* and *The New York Times* in search of clarity about the nation's direction.[49]

While Prescott loved his children, he remained a deeply formal man, not always present in the everyday life of his family. "He didn't get down and play with you on the floor. He wasn't big on vacations and going sight-seeing. He was more formal than that…fathers simply didn't do that sort of thing back then," his son William Bush told authors Peter Schweizer and Rochelle Schweizer. That emotional reserve and commitment to social propriety were defining traits of the WASP elite, and they played a significant role in shaping George Bush's public persona.[50]

The stringent refusal to deviate from the rules that defined the Bush household was evident in Prescott Bush's personal life and in his professional conduct. These WASP values—ingrained in Prescott Bush, Harriman, and Lovett through prep school traditions and university societies like Skull and Bones—shaped their working relationships at Brown Brothers Harriman. This ethos was particularly apparent in the firm's weekly partners' meetings, held every Thursday at 9:45 a.m. at its Wall Street offices. A spirit of camaraderie among executives was central to the decision-making process. "This was an organization with no officers, and its smooth functioning depended on the ability of the managing partners to get along easily with each other, without jealousies or anything like that," Prescott reflected, emphasizing the firm's collaborative culture.[51]

Camaraderie and mutual respect among the firm's executives fostered an open exchange of ideas. While disagreements occasionally emerged, each of the partners offered diverse perspectives that ultimately enhanced decision-making. The mutual respect Prescott and his colleagues had for one another helped each develop the discipline to set aside personal interests and embrace differing viewpoints. Their shared commitment to prioritizing the long-term goals of the organization over individual ambition proved invaluable as Prescott Bush, Lovett, and Harriman each rose to prominence in public service during the administrations of Franklin D. Roosevelt, Harry S. Truman, and Dwight D. Eisenhower.[52]

Even as Prescott traveled for business or assumed greater responsibilities as moderator of the Greenwich Town Meeting, the household remained disciplined and orderly. "Dad was the commanding general, make no mistake about that, but Mother was the one out there day in and day out shaping the troops," George Bush recalled to Hugh Sidey. Though she could be firm, Dorothy represented a steady and nurturing presence. As her children grew, she remained a dedicated athlete and an unwavering cheerleader, leading by example and emphasizing in her family the importance of dedication and perseverance.[53]

Dorothy Bush's competitive spirit was legendary. A skilled tennis player who could defeat opponents twice her age, she approached every challenge with determination. President George W. Bush once recalled how his grandmother "swam a mile race in the water off Kennebunkport, Maine's Walker's Point." Given her relentless drive, those who knew Dorothy would not dispute Barbara Bush's description of her mother-in-law as "the most competitive woman I've ever known."[54]

Like Bert Walker, Dorothy Bush also believed that toughness and resilience were essential to success. Throughout Bush's boyhood, his mother consistently encouraged her children to put forth maximum effort in everything they did. These activities often included spirited competitions, such as seeing who could climb the highest tree. No matter how many mishaps her children endured, Bush remembered, "Mother never seemed afraid."[55]

The point was vividly illustrated one day when the Bush family matriarch took her three-year-old son, Prescott Jr., out for a sail. A sudden torrential storm struck, overwhelming their boat with water. In a panic, her husband quickly rented another boat and rushed out to rescue them. While most people would have been terrified, Dorothy remained calm, later saying the event would give their young son a memorable experience.[56]

The spirit of competition and camaraderie also defined the childhoods of Bush and his siblings at the family home on 15 Grove Lane in Greenwich, Connecticut. Prescott and Dorothy encouraged their children to welcome others, regardless of social or economic background. Their large Victorian home, built in 1903 and "surrounded by two and a half acres," became a lively hub of neighborhood activity, fondly remembered by many. Bush's mother ensured that the house was always filled with laughter and plenty of food for the constant stream of children engaging in a variety of sports and games. "Whatever your background, if you were a friend, that's all that mattered," recalled Fay Vincent, former commissioner of Major League Baseball.[57]

Those playdates throughout the year gave the Bush children a comforting sense of routine. "There was a seasonal quality to our lives," his sister Nancy recalled. Each year, the family spent Christmas at the Walkers' expansive ten-thousand-acre estate, Duncannon, in northwestern South Carolina. As in their home in Greenwich, the Bush children were surrounded by local friends and filled their days with horseback riding and quail hunting. Nancy's favorite memories included the daily fires lit by the domestics, which warmed the spacious rooms of the estate. Despite Bert Walker's intense nature, the family patriarch cherished his grandchildren and gave them complete freedom during these treasured annual visits.[58]

The Bushes' competitiveness, frequently displayed during their stays in South Carolina, continued during the summer at the secluded "Walker's Point" in Kennebunkport, Maine, which Bush described as "a world apart" from the crowded summer hamlets of the Northeast. Purchased by Dorothy's father and grandfather in 1902, the eleven-acre property resembled other exclusive coastal retreats, such as Northeast Harbor and Deer Island, which dotted the shoreline of the Pine Tree State.[59]

The summer months were marked by spirited competitions that, while intense, cultivated both enjoyment and camaraderie. "You didn't go to Kennebunkport to spend time alone or curl up for hours with a book," one biographer observed. The days were devoted to constant activity, from sailing to tennis as well as basketball and baseball. These regimens also gave Dorothy Bush the opportunity to show her athletic form. As historian Herbert Parmet writes, "None of the children, it was said, had really grown up until they had beaten their mother at tennis." Regardless of who won or lost, the retreat remained a unifying space, strengthening the family's bonds and reinforcing the values of mutual love and support. "Walker's Point has always been the anchor to windward. It was always here. Always stable. Long memories. Long on values. Happiness. It just repeats," Bush told Tom Fiedler of the *Miami Herald*.[60]

Though these competitions were intense, humility in victory and grace in defeat were expected. Throughout their upbringing, Bush's parents stressed that dignity was essential both on and off the field. "Don't be a braggadocio," "give credit to others," and "make a friend if you can" were guiding principles the future president carried with him throughout his life. "There was never any question about the absolute importance of those values," Bush wrote in 1985. When Dorothy Bush died eight years later in 1992, *The New York Times* noted that Barbara Bush believed her mother-in-law "had 10 times more" influence on her son than his father did.[61]

George Bush's character was shaped by his parents' guiding principles and by their unwavering love and support, inspiring him to excel in every endeavor. "I can't think what it would be like in life without the strength and the love you get from family," he reflected in the 2012 *HBO* documentary, *41*. This foundation of unconditional acceptance, coupled with a deep-seated confidence, became the driving forces that propelled him to embrace leadership and helped him navigate the disappointments he faced along the way.[62]

CHAPTER 2

Friends and Mentors: Phillips Academy

George Bush, Phillips Academy, Andover, MA. Circa 1940.

On June 12, 1940, as Germany invaded France and the Low Countries of northwestern Europe, a fifteen-year-old George Bush sat in the audience of Cochran Chapel watching his elder brother, Prescott Jr., graduate from Phillips Academy in Andover, Massachusetts. That morning, Henry L. Stimson, a member of the class of 1883, delivered the annual commencement address.

A prominent representative of the WASP establishment, the former corporate attorney had extensive experience in government, having previously served as secretary of war and secretary of state in the cabinets of

Republican presidents William Howard Taft and Herbert Hoover. A regal figure with iron-gray hair and a manicured mustache, Stimson's devotion to principles of leadership and public service—a legacy dating back to his association with President Theodore Roosevelt and Secretary of State Elihu Root—defined the values that Phillips Academy represented.[63]

In his remarks, Stimson argued that the escalating global crisis had occurred due to the result of "a reign of international law flouted and denied by a group of powerful governments." He contended that the failure to confront the actions of Adolf Hitler and other dictators had led to "the sovereignty of small, peaceful nations invaded and destroyed without justification or excuse." For Stimson, the United States had a moral obligation to help lead a unified international response, believing that only through collective action could the forces of freedom prevail against the advance of tyranny. Days after delivering his speech, Stimson demonstrated his own commitment to that cause by crossing party lines to join President Franklin D. Roosevelt's administration as secretary of war.

Bush shared Stimson's conviction, understanding even at a young age that weakness had no place in the face of global peril.[64]

***

The values George Bush inherited from his parents and extended family were reinforced during his years at Phillips Academy. From 1937 to 1942, Bush's time on "Andover Hill" played a crucial role in broadening his perspective. Meditating on his experience during a 2015 visit, Bush remarked, "The lessons learned and the relationships forged here have meant so much throughout my full and adventurous life." At Andover, Bush cultivated focus and discipline, excelling both academically and athletically. Away from home for the first time, he adapted by forming meaningful relationships with classmates and faculty, whose guidance helped hone the qualities that contributed to his lifelong success.[65]

Eastern boarding schools played a pivotal role in shaping the American establishment. Prestigious institutions such as the Groton School, the Hotchkiss School, the St. Paul's School, and Bush's alma mater, Phillips Academy, drew students from the nation's most influential families. Renowned for their excellence, these schools embraced a philosophy of "intellectual rigor and social responsibility," fostering discipline, leadership, and civic duty, qualities that deeply resonated with Prescott and Dorothy Bush.[66]

In a 1988 article on the history of Eastern preparatory schools, academic Edward Saveth contended these schools rose to prominence in the mid-to-late nineteenth century as the nation's patrician upper class sought educational institutions that could shield their children from the sweeping economic and cultural changes of the era. These developments included vast accumulations of wealth, but also the moral decay and corruption often associated with such prosperity. At the same time, many members of the WASP elite grew increasingly uneasy about the surge of immigrants pouring into American cities in search of stability and opportunity.

The vision behind these elite institutions, Saveth writes, traced its roots to the founding of the nation, when figures like John Adams and Thomas Jefferson championed the idea of a "natural aristocracy": a class of leaders defined not by birth, but by innate talent and moral character. Guided by these ideals, prep schools aimed to attract children from the nation's most distinguished families with the objective of "serving as stepping stones between the homes of the American gentry and the universities." These schools, which blended their curriculum of rigorous academics with demanding athletic programs, were designed to cultivate a new generation of leaders, whose intellect and integrity would draw them toward public service and also serve as an example for the broader citizenry, in the hope of curtailing the greed and avarice of the Gilded Age.

The emphasis on character development at these schools had the strong support of President Theodore Roosevelt, who, according to Saveth, sent all his sons to Groton, believing that such institutions existed to transform the children of the idle rich into individuals who were "cleaner, sturdier, and more high-minded." At the heart of this mission were educators like Groton's Endicott Peabody, who insisted that a young man's character was forged through a rigorous regimen of hard work and athletic discipline. "The best thing for a boy is to work hard and then, after a short interval, to play hard and then to work hard again," Peabody wrote, convinced that only through constant exertion could one avoid a life of "idleness and passivity." The blend of mental and physical challenge, combined with a strong emphasis on moral development, was precisely what drew families like the Bushes to Phillips Academy.

Founded on April 30, 1778, the school embodied the Bush family's ethos in merit-based achievement. The Bushes favored Phillips Academy over other prep schools because of its commitment to providing scholarships for students from underserved communities. While prominent figures like Averell Harriman and Robert Lovett attended Groton and The Hill School, respectively, Prescott Bush was impressed with Phillips Academy's goal of "developing the whole man" and believed it was equally important for his children to interact with peers from diverse social and economic backgrounds. His preference for a more inclusive environment reflected his own upbringing in the Columbus public school system. The experience left a lasting impression and reinforced his lifelong values of gratitude and humility.[67]

The elder Bush valued the school's commitment to drawing "citizens of various types and ideals," and also supported Phillips Academy's mission to provide an educational experience that offered students a broader, more realistic perspective of the world. Many who arrived at the school in the 1930s had grown up in insular environments that did little to challenge bigotry or provincialism. By filling its picturesque campus with "youth from every quarter" and instilling in students the importance of selflessness and service, the school's leaders sought to foster a spirit of enlightenment that could serve as a model for others. Phillips Academy also embodied other admirable qualities. Its guiding principle, "not for self," where "each boy is made to recognize that he is a unit in a highly developed social entity," resonated deeply with Dorothy Bush, who had little patience for the "la di das"—those who exhibited pretension or self-importance.[68]

The school's philosophy was embodied in the stern demeanor of Andover's headmaster, Claude M. Fuess. A stoic and puritanical academic,

Fuess began teaching English at Phillips Academy in 1908 before being appointed head of school in 1933. A 1918 image from the school publication *Pot Pourri* captures him as an unsmiling figure with a cleft chin, high forehead, and dark, thinning hair. Dressed in a tailored suit, a stiff high-collared shirt, and a dark colored tie, he exuded an air of formality and discipline. His pale, unlined face and narrow eyes were framed by small, silver-rimmed spectacles. As the years passed and his hair grew even thinner, students gave their stern headmaster the nickname "Bald Doctor," or simply "B.D."[69]

Fuess firmly upheld the patrician virtues, believing that the only true path to success was rooted in "honesty, industry, and self-reliance." Phillips Academy provided students with the finest resources available, but Fuess maintained that the goal for any young man who attended was to ensure "that he will ultimately…stand on his own feet." That included the headmaster's belief that, to ease each boy's transition into university life, he should be granted a certain degree of "personal liberty," enough to allow him to learn not only from his wise decisions but also from his mistakes. However, in the aftermath of the excesses of the "Roaring Twenties," Fuess also believed that a "relaxation of the old Puritan principles" had led to stagnation within the institution. His commitment to reviving values of "piety and virtue" made it no surprise that his philosophy resonated with Bush's parents.[70]

One of Andover's enduring traditions was the daily 7:45 a.m. church service, a routine that Bush and his classmates often found tedious. However, the constant exposure to Judeo-Christian values deepened Bush's understanding of faith and its significance, providing him with a source of comfort in the years to come. Recalling that morning regimen during a speech at the school in 1989, Bush remarked, "but somehow, what I got out of it all here was a sharpening of my own faith."[71]

Beyond the elegance of Cochran Chapel, the school's architecture reflected the classic design of many New England boarding schools. Its church steeple towered over a meticulously maintained sixty-five-acre campus, while the wood-paneled library—adorned with chandeliers and high ceilings, named for 1825 alumnus Oliver Wendell Holmes

Sr.—provided an atmosphere of academic grandeur. Amid the economic turmoil of the Great Depression, the school offered students a secluded oasis of stability and refinement. In addition to expansive athletic fields, students could explore an art gallery featuring works by Winslow Homer and photographs by Civil War–era photographer Mathew Brady, enriching their cultural and historical awareness.[72]

Following chapel, the school structured the student's day around academics and athletics. Physical activities included tennis, lacrosse, cross-country running, and soccer, moving to indoor gymnasium training during the winter months. Beyond sports and academics, students were encouraged to engage in a variety of extracurricular pursuits. These included two debating societies—the Forum and the Philomathean—a literary publication known as *The Phillipian*, as well as musical and theater clubs, language societies, and student government organizations. Headmaster Fuess believed such activities were essential for providing students with a well-rounded and enriching experience. The school also maintained a strict code of discipline. Students were not permitted to be absent or idle "except when given a signed excuse by their house officer for good and sufficient reasons," Fuess wrote in an article on the school in 1914.

Under Fuess's leadership, the curriculum became more rigorous and comprehensive. Students were required to study the sciences alongside both European and United States history. Believing that the young men under his care should develop a strong understanding of the foundations of the American republic, Fuess introduced a mandatory US history survey for all seniors, ensuring they graduated with a deeper appreciation of the nation's past.

"Andover meant more to me than Yale," Bush remembered years later. "You had to read *War and Peace*, do your languages. You were made to study, made to think.... The minute I walked into that place I took a giant leap ahead of many others out there in the educational system.... I was blessed."[73]

Determined to elevate academic standards, Fuess recruited the esteemed Yale history professor Arthur B. Darling. A no-nonsense educator,

Darling became notorious for the high number of students who failed his class. Despite his demanding grading and mercurial temperament, he was among the select teachers whom Bush regarded as a mentor.[74]

Darling's rigorous and uncompromising teaching style mirrored the broader experience of students at Phillips Academy. The belief that "life is hard and winning is essential for survival" aligned with the philosophy of "muscular Christianity," a doctrine embraced by many preparatory schools of the era. It was also a mindset that George Bush had absorbed from his parents. Remembering his time at the school, Bush remarked, "I loved those years. They did indeed teach the great end and real business of living. And even now its lessons of honesty and selflessness, faith in God—well they enrich every day of our lives," Bush said, echoing Fuess's language from an article written about the school in 1914.[75]

Over time, Bush came to personify the Andover experience, which emphasized leading by example. He embodied this creed through his role on the student council, where he served as an extra set of eyes to deter cheating during exams. Though he admitted to being "no scholar" academically, Bush earned the admiration of his peers, not only for his warm and outgoing personality but also for his achievements on the baseball and soccer fields.[76]

In addition to Darling, Bush found a mentor in the school's basketball coach, Frank "Deke" DiClemente "From the first day I saw him [Bush], I knew he was something special. He came from a family with the right priorities, always hustling," recalled the longtime coach. The two quickly formed a strong bond, one that Bush would carry with him throughout his life. During the challenging 1992 presidential campaign, Bush wrote to DiClemente, saying, "Don't worry about me; for you see I learned about life's ups and downs from you—years ago!"[77]

However, Bush's admiration for his old coach went beyond mere words. In 1947 and 1952, Bush worked to convince the school's administration that DiClemente was the perfect candidate to serve as athletic director. "I would like to urge that Mr. DiClementi [sp] be given every consideration for the job," Bush wrote to school headmaster John Kemper. "I know Deke well, but it is not out of mere friendship that

I write this letter. I maintain that he is well qualified in every respect and he will bring nothing but credit to Andover." Even after receiving Kemper's response, which indicated he did not believe the coach suitable for the role, Bush persisted in his support. "I should like very much to sit down with you and discuss the thing in some detail because, being a friend of Deke's, I believe I can recognize his weaknesses as well as his strong points," Bush wrote in November 1952.[78]

The support from Darling and DiClemente gave Bush the confidence that made him a role model on campus. On one occasion, when an older and larger student bullied a smaller Jewish boy named Bruce Gelb, Bush's firm command, "Leave the kid alone," stopped the bully in his tracks. It was a moment Gelb never forgot. "This guy dropped me like a hot potato," recalled Gelb, who would later become president of the cosmetics company, Clairol. Bush simply saw it as his duty to protect someone smaller and younger than himself.[79]

By his sophomore year, Bush had adjusted to the school's demanding program. However, Bush's industriousness and competitiveness drove him to push himself to the limit, leading to frequent visits to the infirmary. Ignoring advice to adopt a more balanced schedule, he instead intensified his efforts. In the spring of 1940, his relentless drive to catch up took a toll, resulting in a severe staph infection that ultimately required admittance to Boston's Massachusetts General Hospital.[80]

As one biographer notes, during the ordeal Bush exhibited "an air of indifference about life's worries." The attitude in the Bush household was emblematic of perseverance. Expressions such as "keep at it," "don't give up," and "you can do it" were frequent reminders not to let any obstacle stand in the way of success. Determined to meet his parents' expectations, Bush maintained a relentless pace. However, his determination to succeed at all costs sometimes led to decisions that were both physically taxing and also at odds with the very values he had been raised to uphold.[81]

Determined to make up for the time lost to illness, Bush repeated his junior year at Phillips Academy. As he regained his strength, his confidence and optimism flourished. He went on to become captain of the baseball team, class president, and, as Bruce Gelb would later learn, one of the most popular students on campus.

A key reason for Bush's popularity was his ability to make everyone feel included, regardless of age or ability. For example, when the school baseball coach asked team captain Bush to get ready to play, the young man proposed that one of the reserve players take his spot instead. Bush, in that moment, understood that the game was about the team and that everyone should have the chance to contribute.[82]

While Bush experienced much joy, the 1930s were also a time of turmoil. Prescott Bush grew more alarmed by the rise of Adolf Hitler in Germany and Benito Mussolini in Italy, and his son could not help but notice the growing tension and instability spreading across Europe. As the rise of totalitarianism in Italy, Germany, and Japan became more alarming, Henry Stimson grew increasingly critical of those who ignored the geopolitical turmoil unfolding in Asia and Europe. In an October 1937 op-ed in *The New York Times*, Stimson wrote, "There has been no excuse except faulty reasoning for the wave of ostrich-like isolationism which has swept over us."[83]

Long-time associates of Phillips Academy, who saw the school as embodying all that was good and virtuous, viewed Stimson as its ideal representative. As one biographer noted, "Stimson held honor, duty, service, honesty, obedience to authority, and physical challenge as the highest values." These qualities, deeply aligned with the school's philosophy, made it unsurprising that Claude Fuess described Stimson as "the ablest man I ever met."[84]

As Stimson, FDR's soon-to-be secretary of war, prepared to deliver his address to the 1940 graduating class, he joined Fuess for a "hike through the [Andover] countryside." During their walk, Stimson spoke candidly about his growing concerns over the aggressive actions of Hitler, Mussolini, and the Japanese Empire. With global events becoming increasingly dire, the statesman feared that the public would be slow to rally to the cause of freedom. "We could have stopped all this in Manchuria if we had been willing to take the decisive step, but our country will support a war only when we are attacked," Fuess recalled Stimson telling the board of trustees in 1935.[85]

Stimson informed Fuess of his determination "to speak out." Ready to serve his third president, and trusted by numerous public officials, Stimson's decision to voice his opinion reflected the character fostered during his time at Phillips Academy. The statesman understood that his views might not be popular, but he had learned from history that certain moments demanded doing what was morally right, rather than what was politically expedient.[86] The New Yorker shared a conviction with contemporaries like Massachusetts Senator Henry Cabot Lodge that the United States had a duty to play a significant role on the world stage.

These principles were evident when Stimson spoke at the school's Cochran Chapel that June day. As Bush and his family listened, Stimson told the graduating seniors they were "leaving Andover in what is certainly a very dark hour for the civilized world." He was not exaggerating. At that very moment, the German army was advancing through France and the Low Countries—Belgium, Luxembourg, and the Netherlands. Though Stimson remained frustrated with the complacency of many Americans in the face of the growing global crisis, he believed the time had come for a national response.[87]

Stimson urged the students not to retreat into indifference, emphasizing that they stood at the threshold of a pivotal moment in history. As they prepared to embark on their journeys to college or the wider world, he maintained that he saw ahead of them not a burden but a unique challenge. "I am filled, not with pity for you," he declared, "but with a desire to congratulate you on your great opportunity. I would to God that I were young enough to face it with you."[88]

In a tone reminiscent of Theodore Roosevelt's evangelical style, Stimson urged the boys to emulate the previous generation by stepping forward to help their nation in its moment of need. "Today our world is confronted by the clearest issue between right and wrong which has ever been presented to it," Stimson said. In his view, those trained in what Fuess called "the Andover Way" were perfectly suited to meet the moment. The students had received the finest instruction and were inculcated with a deep sense of duty to make a meaningful impact on the world.[89]

Throughout his address, the man who had graduated from Phillips Academy more than fifty years earlier highlighted many of the principles the school stood for. These included "the respect for justice and fair play between individual men; the sovereignty of reason rather than force; and above all the Christian principle of the equal value of all human personalities." With those words, Stimson encouraged the young men departing Andover Hill to stand with those who chose freedom over tyranny.[90]

When FDR called upon Stimson to assist the nation in its time of crisis, the New Yorker didn't hesitate to prioritize patriotism over partisanship. His words and example resonated with George Bush, whose parents had encouraged service to others and a deep commitment to community and country. These principles shaped Bush and others, helping them understand that while personal success mattered, there was also a duty to a higher purpose.[91]

In the months that followed, Stimson's words lingered in the minds of Bush and his classmates, reinforced by CBS correspondent Edward R. Murrow's reports on the resilience of the British people during the German bombing of London. Throughout the summer and fall of 1940, many young Americans postponed their college plans to join the British Royal Air Force or the Royal Canadian Air Force. As Bush entered his final year at Phillips Academy, Stimson's message remained with him, strengthening his resolve to answer the call when his country needed him.[92]

Claude Fuess shared Stimson's commitment to the Andover philosophy of supporting those in need. As the Battle of Britain intensified, the headmaster and members of the school's alumni worked to admit several English boys whose families had sent them overseas. Continuing a tradition established during the First World War, the school also created a fund to provide an ambulance to aid the victims of the London Blitz.[93]

Additionally, Fuess mandated that students make their own beds and serve one another at meals. The headmaster believed that war was a shared responsibility, one that could only succeed if everyone contributed their fair share. While Fuess prioritized preparing the school for war, he, like many Americans, held the view that Hitler and Mussolini were too absorbed in European affairs to pose a direct threat to the United States.[94]

The outbreak of war on December 7, 1941, came as much of a shock to the headmaster as it did to George Bush. While walking near the school chapel with his friend George "Red Dog" Warren, the high school senior was stunned to hear about the Japanese attack on Pearl Harbor. Reflecting on that moment fifty years later, Bush stated: "that walk across the campus marked an end of innocence for me."[95]

Bush felt an immediate and unwavering resolve to join the fight for democracy. "It was a red, white, and blue thing," he told biographer Jon Meacham. "Your country's attacked, you'd better get in there and try to help." With his father having served in the First World War, Bush wanted to emulate his example. "I knew right then that I wanted to go into the service," Bush wrote in a 1989 essay for *Life* magazine.[96]

Claude Fuess recognized that the outbreak of war would prompt many students to leave their studies and enlist in the military. Eager to give his boys the best possible preparation for the future, Fuess believed that every student should earn their diploma and secure admission to college. At the same time, Fuess was a realist. He understood the harsh realities of war, yet he could not deny his young men the chance to fight for those under siege by totalitarianism.[97]

On December 8, 1941, the entire school assembled in George Washington Hall to hear Fuess address the student body. The headmaster echoed the themes Stimson had shared six months earlier. The global situation appeared grim and uncertain, but Fuess believed that the defining traits of Phillips Academy students, courage and perseverance, were more essential than ever before.[98]

Bush, present on that memorable day, was ready to follow "the bald doctor's" advice and answer his nation's call. After the playing of "The Star-Spangled Banner," Fuess instructed everyone to rise whenever the anthem was played. "You will stand at attention, hands at your sides, and you will show respect," Fuess commanded. "From that day on, without fail, I have stood at attention when 'The Star-Spangled Banner' was played," Bush recalled.[99]

The patriotism that deeply moved George Bush mirrored much of the nation's sentiment. After years of division, from September 1939 to the first week of December 1941, over the issue of military intervention in Europe, the attack on Pearl Harbor united the country. For the boys of Phillips Academy, the mission was clear: "Good vs. evil, tyranny against freedom." When Bush and his classmates left for the Christmas break, they had little doubt about which side they stood on, or which side would prevail.[100]

In January 1942, Bush and his graduating class returned to Andover facing an uncertain future. During the holiday break, he had attended a party at Greenwich's Round Hill Club, where he met a striking sixteen-year-old from the affluent hamlet of Rye, New York, named Barbara Pierce. She was captivated by his good looks, quick wit, and charm. "It was one of those love at first sight situations, the kind you don't know for sure really happens in life, until it happens to you," George Bush reflected more than fifty years later.[101]

The future first couple, like many of their generation, shared not only similar values and personalities but also comparable upbringings. Raised within the exclusive world of the Eastern elite, the Pierces came from distinguished lineage, including a distant connection to Franklin Pierce, the fourteenth president of the United States. Barbara was the daughter of a *McCall's* publishing executive and his wife. At the time she met George Bush, Barbara was attending Ashley Hall, an all-girls boarding school in Charleston, South Carolina.[102]

Bush focused on completing his studies before graduation, while the Andover campus continued its preparations for war. Despite his best efforts to concentrate, his thoughts often drifted to the raven-haired beauty he had met just weeks earlier. The two exchanged letters throughout the winter and spring of 1942, and Bush invited her to Phillips Academy's formal. Even during those special moments with the woman he eventually married, Bush remained aware that more pressing matters demanded his attention.[103]

On June 12, 1942, the day Bush turned eighteen, Secretary of War Stimson returned to address Phillips Academy's graduating class, arriving in a bulletproof car. Stimson had closely followed Claude Fuess's efforts to prepare the school for wartime service, and he admired the patriotic fervor that filled the student body. But believing the conflict would continue for an indefinite period, he emphasized that neglecting one's education was not a wise course of action.[104]

Stimson also attempted to dissuade Bush's classmates from enlisting by highlighting the harsh realities of war, revealing that four recent graduates of the school had been killed while serving with the Royal Air Force. Though Stimson spoke with power and conviction, Bush remained undeterred. "I remember…my own gut feeling was the same as that of many young Americans—we wanted to fight for our country." Bush considered Stimson "a towering world figure," but he couldn't help questioning the advice to hold back. "I wondered about this call of his," he later recalled. [105]

Prescott Bush shared the secretary's perspective. Having experienced combat firsthand, the elder Bush understood the pull of patriotism. But as a determined man himself, he recognized he could do little other than support and respect his son's desire to serve.[106]

Despite the anxiety and uncertainty surrounding their son's decision, the Bush family, like so many others, focused their efforts on supporting the war effort. Prescott Bush took on the role of national chairman of the USO war fund, which aimed to assist the families of soldiers serving abroad. With the help of John D. Rockefeller Jr., the organization raised over $30 million to support the cause.[107]

On August 6, 1942, George Bush prepared to board a train from New York City to begin flight training in Chapel Hill, North Carolina. Standing on the platform at Grand Central Station with his father, neither man said much. Prescott Bush, a man not known for showing emotion, found it difficult to hold back tears as his son set off into the unknown. "I knew then how proud Dad was of me," Bush later recalled.[108]

Assessing Bush's time at Phillips Academy, alumnus and historian Michael Beschloss believes that the Andover experience played a pivotal role in shaping Bush's life and ultimately set him on the path to the presidency. "There's a good chance that if he hadn't gone to Andover, he never would have become president," Beschloss said. Not only did it shape his values, but it was at PA that he decided to enlist in the navy, which led to his World War II heroism and helped pave the way for his success as a political candidate," the historian recalled from a conversation with Bush.[109]

George Bush never lost his deep appreciation for the years he spent at Phillips Academy, or for the morals and values promulgated by the faculty. In 1971, during a series of board meetings at the school, Bush found himself visibly moved when Headmaster John Kemper calmly documented his recent diagnosis of lung cancer. "He was unemotional but firm and direct, and I thought to myself what terrific courage it took to do this," Bush recalled. Later that year, at the commencement ceremonies, Bush was further impressed by Kemper's ability to uphold Andover's most important tradition. "No mention of self, no mention of his own fate, his own illness, what he felt, etc.," Bush described, speculating that Kemper didn't have long to live. Bush's instincts proved correct, as Kemper passed away that December at the age of fifty-nine.[110]

That same sense of self-discipline and focus strengthened Bush's resolve to take part in the defining event of his generation. As the train prepared to depart New York on that summer day in 1942, the future naval aviator later admitted he was "a scared little guy," uncertain of what lay ahead. Yet, he never wavered on his decision to go to war. The distinction between right and wrong was clear, and Bush knew that duty, character, and courage were the values that mattered most.

CHAPTER 3

Courage Under Fire: World War II

Downed pilot Lieutenant Junior Grade George Bush is rescued by the Navy submarine, USS Finback. September 2, 1944.

On June 12, 1944, twenty-year-old Lieutenant (Junior Grade) George Bush sat alongside fellow naval aviators in the ready room aboard the aircraft carrier USS *San Jacinto*, awaiting their orders. At the front of the room, Lieutenant Martin E. Kilpatrick stood before a blackboard, briefing the pilots. He explained that a Japanese-controlled naval air station had become a problematic deterrent for American forces trying to conquer the Ogasawara Islands. Unless that installation was destroyed, the island would remain a serious obstacle to the United States war effort in the Pacific theater.[111]

Bush served as part of a seven-man squadron assigned to eliminate the Japanese target. Flying Avenger bombers, rugged torpedo aircraft first deployed during the Battle of Midway two years earlier, the group launched into action. As Bush climbed to a cruising altitude of ten thousand feet and prepared to release his payload on the enemy air base, he spotted antiaircraft fire erupting from below. Struggling to stay composed while zeroing in on his target, he suddenly caught sight of an F6F Hellcat escort fighter, engulfed in flames.[112]

As the burning plane plummeted toward the earth, Bush realized with horror that his friend, Ensign Robert McIlwaine, was aboard. Though Bush managed to release his bombs, they only partially disabled the target. Shaken and heartbroken, he returned to the USS *San Jacinto*, longing to share the experience with his family. "I wish I could give you details—tell you incidents, but I can't," he wrote to his parents in frustration on June 15.[113]

***

In 1942, Bush was among the millions of Americans who put their lives on hold to serve their country in war. World War II represented a pivotal moment in American history, uniting people of all backgrounds in the shared mission of defeating totalitarianism. As a naval aviator, the Phillips Academy graduate joined a distinguished group of airmen, including future senators John Glenn, Barry Goldwater, and George McGovern, who, after their combat experiences in the Atlantic and Pacific, dedicated themselves to public service. "When I look back at my life, I put my experience as a combat Navy flier right up at the top of the list of experiences that truly shaped my life," Bush wrote to NBC broadcaster Tom Brokaw.[114]

Bush's determination to succeed once again drove him to push his physical limits. As he and his fellow enlistees endured grueling hikes under the oppressive North Carolina heat, he feared he might not complete his training. "My desire to win my wings and become an officer is tremendous. I'm afraid if I fail for any reason, my disappointment will be very deep," he confided in a note to his sister, Nancy.[115]

The anxiety surrounding the unknown extended beyond the physical dangers of flight, to include a world Bush had never encountered. He genuinely enjoyed meeting men from a wide range of regional and ethnic backgrounds. "I thought when I was away at school I understood it all, but being away in the Navy for this long and with so many different types of fellows has made me see more clearly still how much I do have to be thankful for," he wrote to his parents. He also met young women who were more comfortable with their sexuality than those he had known before. While many of his fellow servicemen embraced these new experiences, Bush chose restraint over indulgence. "The difference is entirely in what we have been taught; not only in 'what' but in 'how well' we have been taught it," he wrote.[116]

He also struggled to master the complexities of flight, a challenge that left him frustrated. "You cannot imagine the unnatural state that flying can get you in. I have experienced it on several occasions already.... It's an utterly depressing and demoralizing feeling—much worse than getting beat at tennis. You get mentally confused, and it's really terrible," he wrote to his mother, describing the difficulties of aviation. Bush told her that during his first flight experience at a naval station near Minneapolis in October 1942, he was "so nervous that in the beginning my legs were shivering around. Once in the air I was completely cool much to my surprise."[117]

While Bush faced difficult challenges, he believed that nothing remained more important than getting into the fight. "I will never feel right until I have actually fought. Being physically able and young enough I belong out at the front and the sooner there, the better." That unwavering confidence in his mission was essential, strengthening his resolve for the hardships ahead. "I wanted to fly in combat. All my classmates wanted to fly in combat. Our country was at war—united," he later summarized that defining moment. Six months later, on June 9, 1943, after completing training in North Carolina and Minnesota, Bush earned his wings at the Naval Air Station in Corpus Christi, Texas. The excitement of the moment, combined with his outgoing nature, helped him forge lasting bonds with many of those he met during his military service. Recollecting that time, Bush later remarked, "It was the first time I'd been anyplace but the playing fields of Greenwich Country Day or Andover."[118]

In the spring of 1944, Bush's squadron was assigned to the aircraft carrier USS *San Jacinto.* Joining the ship at Pearl Harbor, Hawaii, he became part of the VT-51 squadron, tasked with flying missions against Japanese-occupied Marcus and Wake Islands. As Bush spent time with his fellow airmen, he recognized that while they took pride in their diverse backgrounds, they had all united in a shared commitment to the cause of freedom. "The enemy mistook our diversity, our Nation's diversity for weakness. But Pearl Harbor became a rallying cry for men and women from all walks of life, all colors, and all creeds. In the end, this unity of purpose made us invincible in war and now makes us secure in peace," he reflected later.[119]

In Bush's early correspondence, one also sees the emergence of the future president's deepening sense of duty and responsibility. As one of the youngest men aboard the warship, Bush received the assignment of reviewing letters written by crew members to their families and friends, ensuring they didn't reveal any details about the ship's mission or location. In carrying out this duty, he gained a unique window into the lives of his fellow sailors. "As I did my duty…I learned about life—about true love, about heartbreak, about fear and courage, about the diversity of our great country." Reading these deeply personal letters gave Bush a profound appreciation for the human condition and the shared hopes and struggles that bound him and his comrades together at sea. Bush also received the difficult task of writing letters to the families of fallen servicemen. These moments exposed him to the brutal realities of war and the profound toll it took on those who served. [120]

In June 1944, Bush felt the deep sorrow of personal loss when his close friend and roommate, Jim Wykes, went missing during a combat mission. Despite the sadness of the moment, Bush sought to offer Wykes's family a sense of reassurance and comfort. "I realize that the news of his being missing has undoubtedly brought into your home a good deal of grief and sorrow—but however difficult it may be, you must never give up hope," he wrote his friend's mother.[121]

Bush's gesture symbolized the advice he had received about supporting those in pain, whether through a comforting word or a simple act of kindness. Despite the profound sadness, he displayed remarkable self-control, knowing he would "just have to learn to take it." Even in the face of personal loss, whether the death of a relative or a fallen comrade, Bush's resolve to help defeat the Axis powers never wavered. "I feel so strongly that the Nazis, fascists, or whatever moniker they use should all be dealt with severely. The leaders—those responsible for murder, famine, treachery, etc.—must be killed," he wrote to his parents, expressing the depth of his conviction. The young aviator understood that his mission was clear: to defeat the enemy and nothing else. Even at the age of nineteen, Bush had the clarity of mind to recognize the gravity of the situation, knowing that no additional motivation was needed. [122]

The pivotal moment came on the morning of September 2, 1944, when Bush received orders to fly his Avenger aircraft over the Japanese-occupied island of Chichi Jima. The enemy had established a radio facility, and Bush's mission was to destroy it. That day, Bush's crew included gunnery officer Ted White and communications officer Jack Delaney. While Bush and Delaney frequently flew together, White had not flown with Bush and Delaney before. Determined to succeed, Bush knew that previous attempts to destroy the communications tower had failed. The mission was critical, as it was the last opportunity for the men of the USS *San Jacinto* to complete their objective before the ship set sail for its next destination.[123]

Much is written about Bush's heroics that day, detailing how his torpedo bomber was shot down at an altitude of six thousand feet. Despite his plane being engulfed in flames, Bush remained focused enough to drop the plane's explosives as close to the target as possible. He then ejected into a hurricane-force wind blowing at a staggering one hundred and twenty miles per hour. As he struggled to open his parachute, Bush's head struck the plane's tail, causing brutal pain. The anxiety intensified as he plunged into the Pacific Ocean, only to face the overwhelming struggle of his lungs filling with seawater.[124]

During the ninety minutes in the ocean, Bush could do little as he waited for help. Without a paddle, his yellow raft shifted with the currents. As the airman drifted ever closer to an island inhabited by cannibals, he could do nothing but wait. Using his arms in the pointless effort to steer the raft away from the shore, Bush learned later that the Japanese had dispatched a patrol boat to capture him. "For a while there I thought I was done," Bush recalled.[125]

Adrift alone on a raft in the vast ocean, Bush found himself haunted by the deaths of White and Delaney. "Did I do enough to save them?" he wondered. Even after being rescued four hours later by the G-class submarine USS *Finback*, Bush could not escape the weight of his crew's loss. Flying had brought him great joy, not just from the thrill of aviation, but from the camaraderie of being part of a crew. The crash, however, left Bush consumed by the memories of his fallen comrades, memories that would stay with him for the rest of his life. "When a friend or comrade in arms falls in battle, war grabs a part of your soul," he reflected decades later. In a letter to his fiancée, Barbara Pierce, Bush shared the deep emotional toll of his experience.

"I hope my own children never have to fight a war. Friends disappearing. Lives being extinguished. It's just not right," he wrote to his future bride.[126]

One of the principal values imparted in Bush by his family centered on the unwavering commitment to always do his best. When he felt he had fallen short of those standards, he became harshly self-critical. The loss of his crewmates, Delaney and White, weighed heavily on him. "My mother and dad had drilled into us the lesson that we were never to let anyone down, and here I was alive while they were gone," he said, his eyes welling with tears during a conversation with a biographer.[127]

While recuperating on the submarine, Bush couldn't shake the deep sense of turmoil over the loss of his crew. "I cannot get the thought of those two boys out of my mind," he confided to his parents. Despite the immense courage Bush had shown during the battle, he had more than earned the right to stay home for the remainder of the war. However, returning to the States held no appeal for him. "I wanted to finish my mission. It never occurred to me not to rejoin the unit, get back in the fight, back in the air," he later recalled.[128]

Time on the USS *Finback* gave Bush a moment to reflect on the consequences of war as he realized many of his fellow servicemen would never return home. When the submarine surfaced, Bush often chose to stand watch. Alone on deck, he considered questions of his own mortality. "There was peace, calm beauty—God's therapy." While on the submarine Bush also took time to contemplate the significance of gratitude. "Having faced death and been given another chance to live, I could see just how important those values and principles were that my parents had instilled in me," Bush said. After spending a month aboard the *Finback*, Bush returned to the *San Jacinto*. By the time the war ended in August 1945, more than sixty-two thousand members of the United States Navy had lost their lives.[129]

The loss of Delaney and White stayed with Bush, but his animosity toward the Japanese did not. When he returned to Chichi Jima in 2003, Bush held no ill will toward the country that had become a strong ally of the United States after the conflict. "Japan did their part in going for democracy as opposed to totalitarianism," the president told CNN's Paula Zahn.

In 1989, Bush demonstrated his empathy toward the Japanese when, as president, he attended the funeral of Emperor Hirohito, Japan's World War II ruler. While other heads of state chose not to attend, Bush believed that one should focus on the present and prepare for the future, not dwell on the past. This perspective echoed the lessons Henry Stimson offered Bush's senior class at Andover about how to conduct oneself in military service: "Brave without being brutal, self-confident without boasting, part of an irresistible might without losing faith in individual liberty." Stimson's guidance also influenced Bush during his presidency, particularly when he deployed American troops to Iraq, Panama, and Somalia.

In 1991, during an address commemorating the fiftieth anniversary of the bombing of Pearl Harbor, Bush acknowledged how deeply that moment on December 7, 1941, had stayed with him. "Over the years, Pearl Harbor still defines a part of who I am," he remarked at the ceremony in Honolulu. The memory, he explained, allowed him to honor and pay his respects to those the nation had lost.

Returning to the United States in November 1944, the young war veteran eagerly anticipated marrying his fiancée and beginning their life together. With his war service behind him, Bush received the Distinguished Flying Cross for bravery. However, he considered the recognition unnecessary. "They wrote it up as heroism, but it wasn't," Bush recalled. "It was just part of my duty. People say "war hero." How come a guy who gets his airplane shot down is a hero, and a guy who's good enough that he doesn't get shot down is not?" In Bush's view, his inability to complete the mission and the loss of his two comrades did not merit celebration.[130]

The award also conflicted with Bush's mother's rule about drawing attention to oneself. "Nobody likes the Big I Am," Bush remembered Dorothy Bush saying. Despite the deep trauma of combat, a transformed George Bush emerged. The fearful young man who left Grand Central Station in 1942 returned mature, resolute, and focused. "I had grown up. I had flown with the best off a great carrier that flew the Texas flag into battle. I was part of a team. We cared about each other.... We understood each other's fears and loves. We played together, sang together, flew together...twenty years old and we knew exactly what had to be done. We knew we were right and that we would win," Bush recalled of those days.[131]

The experience of war taught Bush how to make decisions under immense pressure. In those critical moments when a choice had to be made in an instant, he understood the weight of responsibility that came with leading men into battle. Bush reflected in how his experiences influenced his approach to decisions about deploying American troops during his time in office. "I am sure that my own, little personal confrontation with death made me more sensitive, and perhaps more concerned as president in having to send these people off to fight."[132]

Time abroad also exposed Bush to a different side of life. Connecting with men from diverse backgrounds gave him a profound appreciation for the nation's ability to unite in times of hardship. The war also helped him step beyond the insular world of his boyhood. This newfound sense of independence, cultivated through perseverance, arrived at the perfect moment as he and Barbara prepared to begin their life together.[133]

CHAPTER 4

Young Man in a Hurry: Yale

George Bush at bat (ball, high, inside) at the Yale vs. Navy baseball game. April 19, 1947.

In 1946, after returning from service in World War II, George Bush enrolled in Yale University, where he played first base for the Yale Bulldogs baseball team. A talented athlete, Bush deeply admired New York Yankees first baseman Lou Gehrig for his "standard of quiet excellence both on and off the field." The Hall of Famer displayed that character in his unwavering determination, by playing a then Major League Baseball record of 2,130 consecutive games, and in his profound courage, manifested during his battle with the terminal neurological disorder ALS.[134]

Bush reflected his idol's influence through his leadership and defensive skill on the field. "The key thing about Poppy, as everyone called him, was that he was so sure-gloved. All the infielders knew that if they threw the ball anywhere near him, he was going to pull it in," recalled teammate Frank "Junie" O'Brien. However, the same did not apply to Bush's performance at the plate. By the end of that season, he was batting just .212, a statistic he found deeply disappointing. "I was happy…to be called a classy first baseman, but was strictly in the lower half of the batting order when it came to hitting," Bush remembered.[135]

During that year, as Bush worked to improve his hitting, he received an unexpected note from Morris Greenberg, the university's head groundskeeper. "Dear Sir," Greenberg wrote, "after watching you play since the season started, I am convinced the reason you are not getting more hits is because you do not take a real cut at the ball. I am confident that if you would put more power behind your swing, you would improve your batting average 100%…" [136]

Bush appreciated the groundskeeper's thoughtful encouragement and honest critique. Recalling the moment decades later, Bush realized that the only way to follow Greenberg's advice was "to put more practice time into attacking the ball." The impact showed surprising results. Over the next two seasons, Bush—now team captain—led Yale to the 1947 and 1948 College World Series, raising his batting average to .280, a significant improvement. Like many people who offered Bush guidance throughout his life, Morris Greenberg left a lasting impression as someone who encouraged Bush's enduring pursuit of excellence.[137]

***

Bush and his contemporaries returned from their service in the Atlantic and Pacific theaters to enter a postwar world that *Time-Life* publisher and Yale alumnus Henry Luce proclaimed "the American Century." Luce had written the essay in February 1941, less than a year before the Japanese attack on Pearl Harbor, aiming to inspire the nation to embrace global leadership in the fight against totalitarianism. However, with the war's conclusion came a period of unprecedented economic prosperity, and

Luce's article carried a broader message: one that called on the United States to use its economic strength and intellectual resources to advance the ideals of democracy worldwide.[138]

As historian James T. Patterson notes, despite ongoing racial and class divisions, many Americans believed the war had sparked a renewed sense of freedom. People from all walks of life had united in the effort to achieve victory, fostering a powerful spirit of optimism. This collective triumph entrenched a belief that no objective was beyond the nation's grasp.[139]

The spirit also shaped the outlook of Yale University's incoming freshman class of 1946. That fall, Bush joined eight thousand new students on the New Haven campus, including five thousand returning veterans. Having married Barbara Pierce on January 6, 1945, Bush, like many of his classmates, was more mature and reflective after the experiences abroad.[140]

The university itself remained in a wartime state, as Judith Schiff chronicled in a 2016 article for the *Yale Alumni Magazine.* During the war, the grounds were used to train Air Force officers, with over three thousand cadets living in various university buildings. After the war, many public buildings continued to serve as housing for members of the armed forces who still resided on campus, though rare books and valuable paintings that had once adorned the university's libraries were returned to their rightful places. With residence halls filled, many new students were forced to sleep on cots in the university gym, while an old West Haven hospital was converted into a dormitory.

The Bush family, along with their newborn son, George W., settled into a home at 37 Hillhouse Avenue, right next door to university president Charles Seymour. "There were a dozen other veterans' families sharing the house with us—each with one child.... That made 40 in all," Bush recalled.

Bush's drive to complete his education as quickly as possible reflected the determination of many of his classmates. These men were shaped by a war that would define the second half of the twentieth century. They had returned home, hardened by the loss of comrades, yet motivated by a deep resolve to build meaningful lives. Future Yale President

Kingman Brewster articulated the incoming class's spirit during a speech in November 1945. "This generation does not inherit the world of its fathers, it inherits a world made by its own fighting and building.... The responsibility for the future is ours.... Wanted or not, for this generation of Americans a coincidence of time and circumstances makes their best years fall in the zenith of American power and potential." Brewster's words echoed Henry Luce's optimism about the immense opportunities awaiting Bush and his peers as they set out to shape the postwar world.[141]

Like Bush's fellow veterans, the men of Yale's class of 1946 came from diverse backgrounds. Many were able to pursue a college education thanks to the 1944 Servicemen's Readjustment Act, known as the GI Bill of Rights, which allowed veterans to leverage their military service for academic opportunities. The legislation embodied the American ideal of advancement based on ability and talent. However, many of those who led elite educational institutions at the time did not fully embrace this egalitarian vision. President James Conant of Harvard questioned the expansion of university education, expressing doubts about whether all students would truly benefit from the experience.[142]

Having not served in combat during either of the world wars, Conant's observation revealed his lack of awareness of the accomplishments of these veterans and of the ambition they carried with them. Bush, like many of his contemporaries, exemplified the desire to focus on their studies rather than engage in the extracurricular activities typically associated with college life. The shift was highlighted in the *Yale Class Book* of 1948, which noted that "an interesting change [on campus] was the size of the Dean's Lists, which increased in much greater proportion than the size of the student body."[143]

Bush embodied his class's determination and ingenuity. "I came back to civilian life feeling that I needed to get my degree and go into the business world as soon as possible. I had a family to support," he recalled of his time on the Yale campus. Graduating Phi Beta Kappa in economics in just two years, Bush received the Francis Gordon Brown Prize, an honor given to a junior who demonstrated exceptional "scholarship and character." A standout athlete as well, his leadership in guiding the Yale baseball team to postseason success further contributed to his selection for the award.[144]

Bush's role as captain of the Yale baseball team echoed Prescott Bush's own collegiate achievements decades earlier. Bush also followed in his father's footsteps by being tapped for Skull and Bones, Yale's most prestigious society. Founded in 1832, and famed for its secrecy and its network of powerful members, its founding principles were based on a commitment to leading honorable lives and advancing the cause of "social good." Many of its initiates came from the nation's most prominent families, including the Tafts and Rockefellers, reflecting the society's deep ties to both finance and government.[145]

Those who selected Bush for membership in 1947 saw him as an ideal candidate. He came from a well-connected, affluent background, possessed a distinguished war record, as well as a belief in achieving more in life than simply making money. Like Averell Harriman and Henry Stimson, Bush's commitment to serving others, a trait he inherited from his father, aligned with one of the core principles of Skull and Bones.[146]

Bush took his admission to the collegiate fraternity seriously. During the moment when members are asked to present their "Life History," he delivered a moving account of how the loss of Delaney and White impacted him during that fateful day in 1944 over Chichi Jima. Seated in the windowless building on High Street in New Haven, Connecticut, Bush recounted the experience in vivid detail. Even as he acknowledged that he had done all he could, the memory continued to haunt him. "It tore him up, real anguish," one Bonesman recalled in a conversation with Bob Woodward and Walter Pincus of *The Washington Post* in 1988.

Bush's parents had raised him on the principle of not dwelling on misfortunes or negative circumstances. However, the sense of camaraderie within the select community of Skull and Bones allowed him to disclose the most traumatic moment of his young life. The men around him that evening were veterans themselves, individuals who both respected his courage and understood his pain. The bonds formed between Bush and those he met during his time at Yale became relationships he cherished for more than fifty years. "I made a lot of friends—friends I learned to count on, both on and off the field. And we trusted each other to come through no matter how tough it got.... I learned that the kind of people you make your friends can either give you strength or take it away," Bush reflected in a speech in the fall of 1989.[147]

Like many men of his generation, Bush remained deeply affected by the loss of his comrades during the war. The realization that fate had spared his life left him conflicted about what the next chapter would hold. Many of his classmates wrestled with similar emotions. "The war was in a way a sort of *Wanderjahr*. It was an opportunity to collect your thoughts, to figure out what you really thought and felt and believed," recalled Bush's classmate Yale Chaplin William Sloane Coffin Jr. "Many people changed their ways, and a lot of people decided that they didn't want to do what they had been expected to do before the war."[148]

While the war inspired many of Bush's contemporaries to pursue public service, the responsibilities of supporting a young family led him to prioritize financial stability. At the same time, his wartime experiences reinforced his belief that personal achievement was more fulfilling than relying on family relationships. "I am not sure I want to capitalize completely on the benefits I received at birth.... Such qualities as industriousness, integrity, etc., which I have or at least hope I have had inculcated into me by my parents...I do want to use, but doing well merely because I have had the opportunity to attend the same debut parties as some of my customers, does not appeal to me," Bush wrote to friend Gerry Bemiss.[149]

Bush's wartime experience taught him the fulfillment that came from achieving independent success. While a traditional career in finance appealed to many of his classmates, with some pursuing jobs on Wall Street and settling into suburban life, Bush felt little interest in following that path. In that regard, Bush echoed the ambitions of his father and both grandfathers, demonstrating a strong desire to carve out his own path based on ability and talent. The drive for independence symbolized a defining trait of the Bush-Walker family legacy, and his wartime experience played a pivotal role in shaping that decision. "I think it gave me a kind of confidence," Bush told *The Washington Post*'s Walt Harrington in

1986, weighing how the war influenced his determination to build a life and career on his own terms.

The opportunity that captured Bush's imagination, a career in the oil and gas industry, occurred with the help of his father's old Yale friend Henry Neil Mallon. In 1928, the elder Bush had persuaded his colleagues at Brown Brothers Harriman to appoint Mallon as president of Dresser, a small Pennsylvania-based manufacturing company with two hundred employees. By 1950, Mallon had relocated the company to Dallas, Texas, shifting its focus to manufacturing equipment for the oil industry. A longtime bachelor, Mallon played a significant role in Bush's life. Describing the dynamic businessman as "a friend and a mentor second only to my father," Bush credited Mallon as one of the key figures who helped him achieve the professional independence he so deeply sought.[150]

Bush and his siblings adored Mallon, who possessed an upbeat attitude and a good sense of humor. "He taught me everything I knew in life including how to throw a baseball," Bush wrote to Mallon's family following his death. Mallon believed that fundamentals were the keys to success. He understood that Bush wanted to chart his own future, and out of loyalty to Prescott Bush, Mallon decided to help the younger Bush reach his objective.[151]

Mallon viewed Texas as the cornerstone of the nation's economic future. As the economy expanded and global markets grew, the demand for oil and gas surged. Under Mallon's leadership, Dresser developed specialized divisions focused on designing advanced drilling equipment. Recognizing Bush's potential, Mallon encouraged him to begin his business education at a Dresser subsidiary, the International Derrick and Equipment Company (IDECO) in Odessa, Texas. "There's not much salary, but if you want to learn the oil business, it's a start," he told Bush.[152]

The prospect of moving to an unfamiliar region was daunting for Bush and his family, yet the opportunity ahead filled him with excitement. "I would be seeing new people, learning something of basic importance," he wrote to Gerry Bemiss just days before his Yale graduation.

That phrase—"learning something of basic importance"—resonated deeply with Bush.[153]

At twenty-three, Bush believed he needed to cultivate a skill, an expertise that would set him apart from those solely interested in making money. As he explained to his wife, the oil industry attracted him because it offered the chance to create something tangible. It also provided an opportunity to prove his worth by succeeding on his own terms. "I didn't want to live in the suburbs and be Pres Bush's boy," he wrote Bemiss.[154]

A career in the oil industry carried significant uncertainty. While Bush knew he had a strong support system, the desire to achieve financial independence inspired him to rely on his own abilities to reach that success. "The world I'd known before the war didn't interest me. I was looking for a different kind of life, something challenging, outside the established mold," he reflected in his 1988 autobiography.[155]

Bush's near-death experience in World War II, like that of many fellow veterans, engendered a deep sense of confidence and independence. Embracing marriage and family, he turned away from the stability of a comfortable life in East Coast finance to venture into a promising yet uncertain future in the Texas oil fields. In moving west, Bush embodied the independent spirit, discipline, and ambition of his fellow veterans, virtues that characterized "the Greatest Generation."

CHAPTER 5

Triumph and Tragedy: Businessman

George Bush holds his daughter, Robin. 1953.

One day in the fall of 1948, as George Bush was working as a sales associate with the International Derrick and Equipment Company in Odessa, Texas, his superiors asked him to familiarize a Yugoslavian engineer with the organization's drilling equipment. As the Cold War grew in intensity, none of Bush's colleagues had an interest in driving "a damn communist" around the Texas oil fields. Wanting to give their guest an authentic taste of local culture, the Bushes invited the engineer to join them at a high school football game. That evening, the visitor from Eastern Europe witnessed the full force of the community's spirit as twelve thousand passionate fans displayed their excitement and pride.[156]

The young oilman's decision to introduce his Eastern European client to American football was a notable one. Amid rising tensions between the United States and the Soviet Union, Bush offered his guest a perspective of the American people that contrasted sharply with the hostile and corrupt image often portrayed by communist-controlled media. Recognizing that sports transcend language and ideology, Bush used the game as a powerful symbol of how competition can unite people across cultural and political boundaries, a form of personal diplomacy that became a hallmark of his political career.

***

George Bush's decision to move his family to West Texas in pursuit of success in the growing oil industry reflected the ambition of many postwar Ivy League graduates. As Bush biographer Herbert Parmet notes, "George landed on the same soil with others who were mirror images of himself: well-educated, from upper-class homes, off to duplicate on their own the success of their fathers, all mid-twentieth-century prospectors." Although Bush's family had no background in the oil business, his father and both grandfathers forged successful careers outside their families' traditional professions.[157]

The oil boom began with a massive well explosion near Beaumont, Texas, in 1901, resulting in the expansion of oil production rising from 836,039 barrels in 1900 to 4,393,658 the following year. That growth attracted Eastern financiers to the Permian Basin, eager to capitalize on the region's economic potential. As a result, communities like Odessa and Midland emerged as key hubs of Texas's oil industry.[158]

In 1948, Odessa, a town of thirty thousand, became one of many destinations for ambitious individuals like the recent Yale graduate who sought success in the rapidly growing petroleum industry. Bush's work selling drilling equipment with IDECO was lonely and tedious. However, he recognized that working with Mallon's firm in a junior capacity allowed him to gain an education in the intricacies of the oil business.[159]

George Bush's upbringing prepared him with a strong ability to adapt, but transitioning from the manicured lawns of Greenwich to the dusty, desolate landscape of Odessa, Texas, in 1948 was no easy feat. Upon arriving in the small oil town, Bush found himself in an environment that bore little resemblance to the comfort and familiarity of his East Coast roots. "As far as my mother was concerned, we could have been living in Russia," Barbara Bush later recalled.[160]

Bush's new position with the Dresser subsidiary paid $375 a month and involved a range of routine tasks, from organizing drilling equipment to cleaning the warehouse floor. Though monotonous, Bush understood that gaining firsthand experience was essential to long-term success. The role also gave him time to reflect on whether building a life in rural Texas, far from the comforts of home and the familiarity of friends and family, was truly the right path.[161]

Though later critics often painted Bush as a privileged patrician who coasted through life based on his familial network, his challenging early years in Texas told a different story. "There's no doubt that my father got the position because of his family's connections.... While they can open doors, they cannot guarantee success," George W. Bush later wrote, underscoring the reality that his father's achievements were earned through determination and hard work, not entitlement.[162]

In April 1949, Neil Mallon assigned Bush to a Dresser subsidiary in California, another important step in Bush's hands-on education. The move gave him the opportunity to deepen his understanding of various types of oil equipment. Although the location had changed, the nature of the work remained much the same. Over the course of the year, as the family relocated from one part of the Golden State to another, Bush lived the life of an itinerant salesman, gaining both industry experience and a deeper appreciation for the challenges of starting from the ground up.[163]

As Bush focused on his career, he began to envision his future as an independent oil executive. Determined to pursue this goal, in 1950 Bush asked Mallon to transfer him and his family twenty-one miles, from Odessa to Midland. By the late 1940s, the latter community, once defined by ranching and its ties to the railroad, had begun to exhibit a new cultural identity, proudly supporting several bookstores and a symphony orchestra.[164]

It was not just the city that aspired to a more cosmopolitan identity. Bush's arrival mirrored a broader influx of the "adventurous Ivy League managerial investment classes" into a community being transformed by the oil boom. Most newcomers were married couples in their late twenties from affluent backgrounds, all eager to build their fortunes. Many of Bush's new acquaintances worked for established business interests backed by powerful families like the Gettys, Mellons, and Rockefellers.

In Midland, the postwar years were marked by the influence of an Ivy League culture. Many of the city's wealthiest residents lived on streets named Harvard, Princeton, and Yale, and socialized in exclusive alumni clubs affiliated with those institutions. Bush appreciated the sense of camaraderie the community fostered. It reminded him of his time in the navy, where people from different backgrounds came together, united by a common goal. "We were all…young people with a considerable amount of ambition," he later reflected.[165]

Even with the Walker estate in Kennebunkport, Maine, as a summer retreat from the Texas heat, the Bushes remained deeply engaged in the bustling West Texas community. Whether socializing at the Petroleum Club or teaching Sunday school at the First Presbyterian Church, the family played a prominent role in Midland's growth. Bush also actively supported the local business community, helping to establish Midland's Commercial Bank and Trust Company and working to enhance the city's commercial reputation as chairman of the local Chamber of Commerce.[166]

In the spring of 1950, as Bush and his family were settling into life in West Texas, he received a job offer from Brown Brothers Harriman. "This suggestion did not originate with your father and, in fact, he has had nothing to do with it," wrote Tom McCance, a general partner at the firm, underscoring that the offer was made on Bush's own merit. The opportunity was tempting; it would allow the family to return to a more comfortable and familiar life. But as George W. Bush later noted, his father wasn't looking for "an escape hatch." After thoughtful discussion with Barbara, the couple chose to stay in Midland. Bush's decision reflected a core principle of his character: Once he set a course, he was determined to see it through.[167]

Beyond his determination to finish what he started, Bush also felt a deep sense of devotion to Neil Mallon. "I have a great feeling of loyalty to Dresser and to Mr. Mallon; and I am convinced that there is a real opportunity here," he wrote McCance. The loyalty Bush displayed was a defining trait throughout his life. In moments of both triumph and hardship, he remained a steady, supportive presence for family and friends alike.[168]

After moving between Texas and California, the Bushes felt that Midland was the ideal place for their family. The warmth and determination of Bush's peers embodied a spirit that, according to George W. Bush, enabled his parents to thrive. "The mixture of competition and community reflected my father's upbringing. He had taken the values that he had learned at home and plopped them down in the middle of the Texas desert," wrote the forty-third president.[169]

With Bush frequently traveling, his wife took on the responsibility of managing the home and raising the children. A woman of great energy, Barbara Bush shared many qualities with her mother-in-law, Dorothy Bush. As George W. Bush recalled, his mother always seemed to be everywhere at once. Whether driving the children to French lessons or serving as the Midland Cub Scouts' "den mother," one biographer noted, Barbara Bush became "the commander in chief of her brood."[170]

Despite Bush's efforts to remain involved in his children's lives, work often interfered. As he continued to travel across the Texas Plains selling Dresser oil equipment, he grew increasingly frustrated by his lack of professional progress. Taking time to reflect, Bush again considered the possibility of starting his own oil company. The path would allow him to tap into his entrepreneurial spirit and potentially earn a substantial income.

The idea began to take shape during conversations at barbecues with his neighbor and fellow veteran, John Overbey. Bush admired the University of Texas graduate's expertise in oil leases and his skill in interpreting geological data to identify potential drilling sites. While the former Marine did not share Bush's level of affluence, both men possessed a competitive spirit, ambition, and a relentless drive to succeed in their industry. Together, they decided to start a company they named Bush-Overbey.[171]

As Bush prepared for his new venture, he struggled with how to break the news to Neil Mallon. When he visited Mallon in Dallas, Bush presented his case for striking out on his own. Bush never forgot Mallon's response. After listening quietly, Mallon "went into the next office, returning with a legal-sized yellow pad. 'I really hate to see you go, George,' he said, working his way down the pad, 'but if I were your age, I'd be doing the same thing—and here's how I'd go about it." For the rest of their conversation, Mallon offered Bush a lesson on how to build "an independent oil company," a gesture that left a lasting impression. In April 1951, Bush wrote to Mallon, "I shall always be grateful to you, not only for the wonderful training which I had with Dresser, but also for everything which you personally have done for me and for the family."[172]

The meeting with Mallon proved pivotal in helping Bush understand the complexities of starting his own business. It also taught a crucial lesson in leadership that Bush carried with him throughout his life. "Whenever anyone working for you wants to move on, don't stand in the way. Lend a hand," Bush said. There is no doubt Mallon had invested time and resources in preparing Bush for a bigger role within the company. Yet, Mallon also wanted his former protégé to find personal happiness and success. The lesson had a profound impact on Bush, one he later passed down to his children as an example of selflessness and gratitude. "Rather than harbor resentments…he chose to encourage and mentor," George W. Bush wrote, recalling Mallon's thoughtful gesture.[173]

In addition to offering valuable business advice, Neil Mallon sowed in Bush a lasting belief in the importance of preparation and experience as the foundation for success. Under Mallon's guidance, Bush had received a range of opportunities that helped shape him into a well-rounded and capable executive. Mallon's emphasis on learning the fundamentals of how every part of an organization functioned remained with Bush throughout his career. As he moved from business into politics and public service, Bush repeatedly drew upon that wide-ranging foundation of experience. In many respects, his entire professional path could be viewed as a long apprenticeship for the presidency—a point his son Neil, named in honor of Mallon, emphasized in a conversation with the author.[174]

Bush valued Mallon's advice, and he applied it when faced with a situation involving his younger brother. In the 1950s, while Jonathan Bush worked for his brother and John Overbey, he expressed a desire to pursue an acting career. Although concerned about the risks involved, Bush realized that Jonathan's decision to follow his passion was no different from his own choice to leave Dresser. "Please have no feeling of embarrassment.... You are doing just exactly the right thing, and I am very happy for you.... However, our main concern is that you be happy in life, and if your new career will give you this happiness, then all of us all will rejoice with you," Bush wrote in July 1955.[175]

As George Bush embraced both the joys of family life and the challenges of building his own business, he carried with him a deep awareness, shaped by his wartime experience, that tragedy could strike at any moment. That reality became heartbreakingly clear in the spring of 1953. One day, Bush received an urgent call from his wife. Concerned about the ongoing fatigue experienced by their three-year-old daughter, Robin, Barbara Bush took her to the local pediatrician. After a series of tests, the Bushes received devastating news: Robin had developed an aggressive form of leukemia.[176]

Even in the face of a terminal diagnosis, the Bushes were determined to do everything possible to prolong their daughter's life. Bush's uncle, Dr. John Walker, recommended treatment at New York's Memorial Sloan Kettering, and family and friends rallied around them with unwavering support. During Bush's short returns to Midland, his Yale classmate Thomas "Lud" Ashley stayed by Robin's side at the hospital, providing comfort and companionship to the family. Bush would never forgot Ashley's kindness. "We will have many wonderful memories of people who helped us and tried to help us," he wrote to Ashley in May 1953, "but none will exceed in my mind your many gestures of true friendship."[177]

On October 11, 1953, despite the best efforts of her doctors, Robin Bush died. In a decision marked by both grief and generosity, George and Barbara Bush chose not to bury their daughter in the family plot purchased by Prescott Bush but instead donated her body to Memorial Sloan Kettering for medical research. "To this day, like every parent who has ever lost a child, we wonder why," Bush reflected on the tragedy in his early campaign memoir.[178]

The death of his daughter was a stark reminder to Bush "that life is unpredictable and fragile." Despite the crushing grief, Bush drew strength from the loss and found a lesson in perseverance. "Keep going, charging ahead," he said. That inner resolve grounded in his faith and an unwavering sense of duty enabled both him and Barbara to carry on, personally and professionally.[179]

Determined to help his family heal, Bush rallied friends and loved ones to support Barbara during the severe depression she experienced following Robin's passing. Throughout this painful time, the Bushes chose not to speak publicly about their daughter. "There is a real emphasis on being and staying positive—almost to a fault. You are not to complain. And you are not to draw attention to yourself," recalled Bush's cousin Elsie Walker, highlighting one of the family's core principles.[180]

Seeking solace from their loss, the Bush family channeled their energy and resources into supporting others facing similar struggles. Leveraging their name and financial means, they became actively involved in fundraising efforts to advance research aimed at curing the disease that claimed their daughter's life. "My mother says that Robin's death instilled in both her and Dad a compassion that has stayed ever since," Bush's daughter, Dorothy Bush-Koch, reflects in her memoir about her father.[181]

In late 1953, Bush-Overbey joined forces with Hugh and Bill Liedtke to establish Zapata Petroleum Corporation. Natives of Oklahoma, both brothers attended Amherst College before pursuing advanced degrees. Hugh earned a business management degree from Harvard and a law degree from the University of Texas, while Bill also obtained a law degree from UT. Like Bush, both served in the Pacific theater during World War II before channeling their ambition into the oil industry. The company quickly achieved success, drilling 127 oil wells in the 8,100-acre West Jameson Field.[182]

The success of Zapata reflected the tremendous growth that the post–World War II generation had brought to the Midland economy. By 1953, total deposits in Midland banks had increased by $3,271,617.45 ($36,471,547.67 in 2025 dollars), the highest annual growth recorded at that time. Continued investment in the community spurred infrastructure modernization, including the construction of a new public safety building and the installation of a new radio tower for the local television station.[183]

The steady production from the wells provided Zapata with a solid financial foundation. While Bush never amassed the wealth of legendary oil barons like H. L. Hunt or Sid Richardson, the company's strong performance by 1956 enabled him and his partners to shift their focus to offshore oil exploration. This expansion included ventures in the Middle East, Mexico, and other regions around the world.[184]

The decision to expand the company's drilling operation illustrated another example of Bush and his fellow veterans' willingness to take risks in pursuit of long-term rewards. One such gamble involved signing a contract with R. G. LeTourneau, an innovative designer and inventor credited with developing the first offshore drilling platform. Confident that the technology represented the future of the industry, Zapata invested $3.5 million in LeTourneau's device. The risk proved highly beneficial. In addition to Zapata's own offshore success, the company boosted its profits by leasing the equipment to other drilling operations. By 1959, after going public on the American Stock Exchange, Bush's investment had grown to an estimated $600,000 ($7.1 million in 2025).[185]

That same year, the Zapata partners decided to split the company into two separate entities. Drawn to the potential of offshore drilling, Bush retained control of those operations, while the Liedtkes took ownership of the other half of Zapata's interests. Understanding the importance of greater access to capital and the benefits of being at the center of the offshore industry, Bush moved his family from Midland to Houston.[186]

As a CEO, Bush applied the lessons he had learned from Neil Mallon, prioritizing the hiring of employees who were both ambitious and passionate about their work. Bush recognized that he didn't always have the answers and valued listening to and relying on those with greater expertise. "When things went right, he shared the credit. When things went wrong, he took the heat. This experience helped him develop a leadership style that he would employ for decades to come," George W. Bush later wrote.[187]

Bush also continued to grow from his interactions with people whose life experiences differed from his own. His enjoyment in developing personal relationships proved invaluable as he became increasingly involved in Midland's civic affairs. With no established Republican Party presence in Texas, Bush's entry into local politics in the late 1950s and early 1960s mirrored the same sense of risk and unpredictability that had drawn him to the Lone Star State in search of independence eight years earlier.[188]

CHAPTER 6

The Pragmatic Conservative: Politics

The Bush family poses on an elephant during the 1964 Senate campaign, (left to right) Barbara, Doro, Marvin, Neil, Jeb, George (George W. away at school). 1964.

On November 10, 1964, George Bush wrote a thoughtful letter to former Vice President Richard M. Nixon. In addition to his expression of gratitude for Nixon's support at a Houston campaign rally, Bush provided a frank assessment of his Senate loss to incumbent Democrat Ralph Yarborough. During the race, Bush had aligned himself with the conservative positions of Republican presidential nominee Barry Goldwater, opposing both the 1964 Civil Rights Act and the 1963 Limited Test

Ban Treaty. Although Bush's embrace of populist conservatism resonated with many Texans, earning him 1,134,337 votes, a record for a Republican candidate in the state at the time, it was not enough to defeat Yarborough.[189]

In his letter to Nixon, the forty-one-year-old Bush observed that while Republican strength had shifted from the Northeast to the Western Sunbelt, the party's narrow ideological stance limited its broader appeal. "The immediate job would be to get rid of some of the people in the Party…who through their overly dedicated conservatism are going to always keep the Party small," he wrote the GOP's 1960 presidential nominee. Bush expressed respect for Barry Goldwater but criticized aspects of his campaign in Texas, saying it had been taken over by "a bunch of 'nuts' whose very presence at a rally would shake up a plain fellow coming in to make up his mind." That insight proved prophetic, as Bush spent much of his political career reconciling his pragmatic, mainstream conservatism with the demands of the GOP's more ideologically driven base.[190]

***

During the 1950s, as George Bush advanced his career in the oil industry, the Republican Party encompassed a wide range of ideological perspectives, with liberals, moderates, and conservatives each advocating distinct views on economics and foreign policy. In 1952, after two decades out of power, the GOP reclaimed the White House with the election of the hero of the Second World War, Dwight D. Eisenhower and his forty-year-old vice president, Richard Nixon. An internationalist, Eisenhower governed as a pragmatic centrist, believing that most Americans supported his balanced approach.[191]

Eisenhower's vision of moderate Republicanism represented more than just pragmatic centrism. As Geoffrey Kabaservice writes, the philosophy embodied Eisenhower's temperament of "balance, reasonableness, prudence, and common sense." His moderate stance and respect for expertise were well received by many within the Eastern establishment, including the St. Paul's- and Harvard-educated foreign policy analyst Charles E. Bohlen, whom Eisenhower appointed as ambassador to the

Soviet Union. The new president also retained Prescott Bush's colleague, Robert Lovett, who, following his service as Harry Truman's secretary of defense, became a key advisor to the State Department on nuclear arms and intelligence matters.[192]

While prioritizing fiscal responsibility by balancing the federal budget three times, Eisenhower also upheld key aspects of the New Deal, including Social Security and other government welfare programs. Though not a New Deal liberal, the Kansas native recognized these policies as a stabilizing force in Americans' lives. "I should like to put ourselves clearly on the record as being forward-looking and concerned with the welfare of all our people," he wrote to his budget director. Rather than dismantling Roosevelt's social safety net, his administration sought to reform and strengthen it.[193]

In addition to maintaining key New Deal programs, Eisenhower expanded the federal government's role in national infrastructure through projects like the Interstate Highway System and increased funding for science and education. While these initiatives contributed to his consistently high 64 percent approval rating, they also fueled skepticism within the GOP's growing conservative wing. Many on the right had expected Eisenhower to scale back what they saw as an expanding liberal welfare state. His reluctance to do so prompted *National Review* founder William F. Buckley Jr. to criticize his presidency as an "easy and wholehearted acceptance of the great statist legacy of the New Deal."[194]

Prescott Bush admired Eisenhower's moderate political approach. In 1951, Bush was one of many prominent GOP liberals who traveled to Brussels, where Eisenhower served as NATO commander, to persuade him to run for president. Bush also pursued his own political ambitions, running for the US Senate from Connecticut in 1950. Despite being fiscally conservative, his support for birth control proved politically costly in a state with a predominantly Catholic electorate. His stance on contraception ultimately cost him the election, which he lost by a narrow margin of one thousand votes.[195]

In the summer of 1952, the investment banker found another opportunity to run for the Senate, following the sudden passing of Senator

Brien McMahon. During a campaign event in Bridgeport, Connecticut, Bush witnessed the growing popularity of conservative firebrand Senator Joseph McCarthy. The Wisconsin legislator had come to prominence two years earlier with a speech in Wheeling, West Virginia, where he claimed to have a list of 205 State Department officials sympathetic to communism.[196]

McCarthy's accusations were part of a broader effort to discredit patrician elites, whom the right blamed for allowing the Soviet Union to tighten its grip on Eastern Europe after World War II and for the 1949 communist victory of Mao Tse-tung over the Nationalists in the Chinese Civil War. While anti-communism served as the unifying force within the GOP, McCarthy's embrace of conspiracy theories and exploitation of political grievances foreshadowed the party's shifting trajectory in the years ahead.[197]

Prescott Bush disliked McCarthy, feeling that the senator's attempts to smear figures like General George C. Marshall and Truman's secretary of state, Dean Acheson, as communists were excessive. At a dinner following the event, Bush made his distaste for McCarthy clear by turning down the senator's offer to help fund his campaign. McCarthy held significant influence among the state's Catholics, and Bush's decision to reject his support risked making the election more challenging.[198]

Fortunately, when voters went to the polls in November 1952, Prescott Bush, benefiting from Dwight Eisenhower's widespread popularity, achieved victory by a thirty-seven-thousand-vote margin over Democratic challenger Abraham Ribicoff. With limited time to focus on his father's campaign, George Bush concentrated his efforts on building support for Eisenhower in the deeply Democratic bastion of Harris County, Texas. As he campaigned for the Eisenhower-Nixon ticket, Bush was encouraged to see parts of the county showing growing support for the GOP. On election night, when Eisenhower secured Texas with 53 percent of the vote, it marked a pivotal moment. Four years later, Eisenhower won the state again with 55 percent. The 1956 election was the first time in Texas history a Republican had carried the state in two consecutive presidential elections, signaling the beginning of the Lone Star State's eventual shift into the Republican camp.[199]

Arriving in Washington in January 1953, Prescott Bush used the consensus-building skills developed at Brown Brothers Harriman to forge relationships with a wide range of politicians and administration figures. Settling into a large home in Georgetown, he and his wife leveraged their connections from Wall Street with figures such as Secretary of State John Foster Dulles; his brother Allen, who headed the CIA; and other influential officials. Through these efforts, Bush embodied the establishment ethos, building alliances not just with members of the new administration but also with Democratic senators.[200]

Bush's arrival in the Senate provided him with the opportunity to strengthen his relationship with Senate Majority Leader Robert A. Taft. Seven years his senior, Taft, a fellow Yale alumnus, had come to know Bush through their shared involvement in Republican politics. Taft helped secure prestigious appointments for Bush on the Committees for Atomic Energy and Public Works. Additionally, Bush worked to build relationships with prominent Democrats, including J. William Fulbright, Senate Minority Leader Lyndon B. Johnson, and a young John F. Kennedy. By engaging with figures across the political spectrum, Bush demonstrated his commitment to Eisenhower's nonideological approach, showing a deep respect for differing viewpoints.[201]

During the Eisenhower years, Prescott Bush became a key intermediary between the White House and Senate Republicans. Bush believed in leveraging government to improve the lives of the American people. His policy priorities included advocating for less restrictive immigration laws, weakening the Taft-Hartley Act to give unions more bargaining power, and using the judiciary to advance civil rights for African Americans.[202]

Bush also developed a close relationship with President Eisenhower. Both Midwesterners with a shared love for golf, Eisenhower valued Bush's discretion. "I never talked to the press about what the president said on the golf course. Nor did I share his thoughts or comments with anyone else, unless I had reason to believe he wished me to do so," Bush recalled of their relationship. Yet perhaps Bush's most significant contribution during his public life came when he chose to stand up against one of the most prominent figures in his own party.[203]

On December 1, 1954, Prescott Bush rose and formally condemned Senator McCarthy for a politically motivated crusade against those in the country and within the government he believed possessed communist sympathies. Standing behind his desk, the senior senator from Connecticut delivered a statement against McCarthy for actions he considered detrimental to the dignity of the institution and unbecoming of one who held the office. During comments filled with indignation, Bush accused McCarthy of causing "dangerous divisions among the American people." The senator also criticized his fellow Republican for behaving like a dictator. "Either you must follow Senator McCarthy blindly…or in his eyes you must be a communist…or a fool who has been duped by the communist line," Bush declared.[204]

While Prescott Bush liked McCarthy personally, he believed the senator lacked the character essential for serving in the Senate. However, McCarthy's widespread popularity made Bush wary of the political consequences of a public rebuke, particularly as he faced reelection in 1956. The prospect of supporting McCarthy's censure triggered a flood of hostile letters from constituents, with many threatening to withdraw their support if Bush took a stand against the Wisconsin senator.[205]

Raised in a household where honesty and integrity were paramount, Bush believed that his duty as a senator required him to take the right stand, not just the popular one. He understood that the people had elected him to exercise sound judgment in the best interests of both his state and the nation. His decision to condemn McCarthy was ultimately validated by his reelection in 1956, and many constituents later commended him for his act of political courage.

During the McCarthy crisis in 1954, Bush served on a bipartisan committee tasked with evaluating whether to formally censure McCarthy for his actions. The committee's chairman, Utah Republican Senator Arthur Watkins, became a prime target of McCarthy's wrath. The Wisconsin senator denounced Watkins as "cowardly and stupid."

Despite these attacks, Watkins remained steadfast, determined to guide the Senate through the crisis with integrity and resolve.[206]

After the committee's unanimous 6–0 vote to censure McCarthy, Bush felt that Watkins deserved recognition from the White House. "I think it would be appropriate if the president sent for [Watkins] and gave him a good pat on the back for doing an unpleasant job well and with courage," Bush recalled telling Eisenhower's chief of staff, Sherman Adams, on December 3. According to *The New York Times*, hours after Bush's call, the press assembled in the Oval Office as Eisenhower publicly commended Watkins for his leadership, praising him for doing "a splendid job" as chairman of the select committee.

The White House made no mention of Bush's role in arranging Watkins's commendation. In fact, Bush himself had no knowledge the event had taken place until hours later, when he and his wife heard the announcement on their car radio. Bush neither publicized his access to the president nor sought media attention for facilitating the meeting. In these moments, he adhered to a principle that his son later embraced: "When things go well, always give credit to others."[207]

In April 1957, after years of heavy drinking, McCarthy's deteriorating health resulted in the senator being admitted to Bethesda Naval Hospital. On May 1, while at the same hospital for a routine physical exam, Bush inquired about visiting McCarthy. When a nurse informed him that the senator's illness had become too severe to receive visitors, Bush quickly wrote a note and asked her to deliver it when appropriate. Later that day, upon returning to the Senate, Bush's staff relayed that McCarthy had deeply appreciated the gesture. McCarthy died the following day. Bush's act of kindness demonstrated his belief that, while a senator's duty required him to exercise sound judgment in service of the public good, political disagreements should never become personal.[208]

As George Bush diligently built his oil business, he closely followed his father's Senate career and his friendship with President Eisenhower. To the younger Bush, Eisenhower embodied the optimism of the 1950s, exemplifying bipartisanship, strong character, and a deep faith in American institutions. Discussing Eisenhower's influence in a later interview with Hugh Sidey, Bush described the profound impact the president had on his worldview. "I was inspired by him. It was a steady, principled leadership," he recalled of a visit to Eisenhower's home in Gettysburg, Pennsylvania. "I learned a lot from him.... One of the things is you don't have to be glamorous, on the cutting edge all the time," Bush said.[209]

Prescott Bush's son saw himself as a Republican in the Eisenhower tradition of free markets and deregulation. As a businessman, he believed these principles enhanced economic growth by encouraging competition and lowering prices. However, as his business thrived, a political issue arose that put him at odds with his father, highlighting their contrasting views on the role of government.[210]

In 1956, Senator Bush opposed a bill that aimed to deregulate the oil and gas industry. After the legislation passed the House of Representatives in 1955, lobbyists began pressuring the younger Bush to sway his father's opinion in favor of the bill. Despite the oil executive disagreeing with his father on the issue, the pressure intensified, with some even threatening to boycott Bush's oil business and ruin his career.[211]

During a visit with his father, Bush shared his concerns about the threats he had received. Senator Bush reassured him, saying, "This [bill] will not affect you at all. I'm going to vote against the bill because on the whole I think that's in the best interests of my state, as well as the United States. But don't you worry about it, and if there's any after-effects from it, just tell me about them, and we'll take care of that." Ultimately, the lack of civility surrounding the legislation upset Eisenhower so much that he described it as "the sort of thing that can make American politics a dreary and frustrating experience for anyone who has any regard for moral and ethical standards." This concern over the growing intensity of partisanship became an issue that George Bush would often confront as he navigated his way to the top of the Republican Party.[212]

Watching his father in the Senate taught Bush a great deal. He admired his father's nonideological approach to issues and his attempts to develop a bipartisan consensus on legislation. The younger Bush also appreciated his father being a man of his word, cultivating those who disagreed with him and the general joy of being in the political arena. "[My father] gave me advice about life that I hope helped me in politics—tell the truth, be honest, work hard, try to see the other guy's point of view while sticking to your own principles. I mean these were truisms you might say that we had inculcated into us growing up," Bush told an interviewer.

The dignity and leadership Prescott Bush demonstrated throughout his political career left a lasting impression on his son as he began contemplating a future in elected office. "Philosophically I was a Republican," Bush wrote, recognizing that Texas in the late 1950s "was solidly Democratic." However, signs of change were beginning to appear. Eisenhower carried the state in both 1952 and 1956, and without Lyndon Johnson on the Democratic ticket, John F. Kennedy might have lost Texas to Richard Nixon in 1960. Then on May 27, 1961, John Tower, a political science professor from Midwestern State University in Wichita Falls, Texas, won a special election to fill the Senate seat vacated by the new vice president. Tower's victory made him the first Republican senator from Texas since 1870, signaling to Bush that the state's political landscape had begun to shift, creating new opportunities for the GOP.[213]

Tower's support, rooted in Republican principles of individual liberty and limited government, had not developed overnight. Rather, it reflected the growing frustration of Democratic liberal voters who had long endured the dominance of conservative factions within the Texas Democratic Party. In 1961, many liberal Democrats backed Tower, hoping that a Republican win would legitimize the GOP and prompt conservative Democrats to shift their political loyalties. Tower's success represented a significant triumph for the small but determined group of Texas Republicans after years of political disappointment.[214]

Another key driver of Republican enthusiasm in Texas concerned the rise of a new wave of populist conservatism, led by outspoken Arizona Senator Barry Goldwater. His campaign, backed by influential conservative intellectuals, including those associated with *National Review*, energized a growing base of young, college-educated Texans. They were drawn to Goldwater's antiestablishment rhetoric, which denounced the expanding power of the federal government, criticized the Eisenhower administration for its perceived weakness against communism, and opposed elite Eastern figures like United Nations Ambassador Henry Cabot Lodge Jr. and New York Governor Nelson Aldrich Rockefeller, whom they believed wielded excessive control over the administrative state.[215]

In 1963, after actively supporting Eisenhower's campaign in his local community, George Bush successfully ran for chairman of the Harris County Republican Party. Much like his experience working for Neil Mallon, Bush understood that to truly master any profession, one had to start at the bottom. "This was the challenge I'd been waiting for an opening into politics at the ground level, where it all starts," he reflected years later.[216]

Bush learned from his father's Senate career that success depended on building consensus. Elected in February 1963 as the new chairman, he believed the Texas GOP should prioritize unifying issues rather than those that fueled division. Bush also understood that to remain a viable candidate for higher office, he needed to engage the state's growing base of ideological conservatives without alienating other factions.[217]

That included confronting the influential John Birch Society, a far-right organization founded in 1958 by candy magnate Robert Welch. According to a profile on the organization by *Politico* in 2017, the group promoted controversial beliefs, including claims that communists had infiltrated the government, that the United Nations served as "an instrument of communist global conquest," and that the civil rights movement aimed to "establish an independent Negro-Soviet Republic." Welch's views had a popular following in Texas. They included those like oil magnate H. L. Hunt and the chairman of the House Un-American Activities Committee, Texas Congressman Martin Dies.

George Bush prioritized pragmatism over ideology in his efforts to build a broad, inclusive Republican coalition. While he initially sought to engage the Birchers by appointing some as local party officials, he quickly grew weary of their conspiracy theories and rigid thinking. Accusing the organization of relying on "smear and slander and guilt by association,"

Bush echoed the same language his father, Prescott Bush, had used to denounce Joseph McCarthy years earlier. Despite his frustration with the far-right group, Bush remained focused on tempering ideological conflicts and strengthening his branch of the GOP to compete in Texas elections. "The Republican Party in the past, and sometimes with justification, has been connected in the mind of the public with extremism. We're not, or at least most of us are not, extremists. We're just responsible people," Bush stated.[218]

As he traveled across Texas raising funds and connecting with voters, Bush began considering a challenge to incumbent Democrat Ralph Yarborough for a US Senate seat in 1964. Confident in his grasp of the state's political climate, he believed that many of Texas's inherently conservative Democratic voters would favor his traditional conservatism over Yarborough's liberal populism.[219]

After defeating four opponents in the GOP primary, Bush launched a campaign that sought to capitalize on the momentum of Republican presidential nominee Barry Goldwater. Though Bush's Republicanism represented a more conservative bent than his father, many of Bush's positions conflicted with the values that had shaped his character. A longtime supporter of the United Negro College Fund since his days at Yale, Bush nonetheless attempted to capitalize on Goldwater's populist appeal by opposing the recently passed Civil Rights Act, criticizing American involvement in the United Nations, and advocating for another invasion of Cuba despite the recent failure of the Bay of Pigs invasion in 1961.[220]

Determined to shed his patrician image, Bush attempted to position himself as independent from the old Republican elite. Concerned that his father might make critical remarks about Goldwater, Bush asked the senator to sit out the 1964 campaign. However, as the race progressed, Bush grew uneasy with many of the positions he had taken and the deep divisions Goldwater had created within the GOP. "I want to win, but not at the expense of justice, not at the expense of the dignity of any man… nor teaching my children a prejudice which I do not feel," Bush wrote to a supporter during the campaign.[221]

Despite Bush's determined efforts, the Republican Party struggled to generate enough support to pose a serious challenge to Yarborough's campaign. Additionally, Goldwater's far-right positions and combative rhetoric contributed to Lyndon Johnson's landslide election victory, winning the presidency in his own right with 61 percent of the vote, the largest margin since the start of popular elections in 1824. Though Bush could have blamed the lack of political support or divisions within the state party, he believed the candidate had the responsibility to accept the outcome. "Believe me, your endorsement helped me a great deal in the campaign. I just wish I could have done better for you at the polls," he wrote to Eisenhower in the first week of January 1965.[222]

Bush also began closely observing and listening to Richard Nixon. Admiring Nixon's political instincts, he shared the Californian's view that the party needed to move beyond rigid ideological divisions and promote policies that could unite conservatives of different perspectives. Eager to remain active in politics and demonstrate his loyalty, Bush did not hesitate to offer Nixon his support as the former vice president sought to revive his political career. "If there is ever any way in which I can be helpful...let me know. I am anxious to see the Party grow, and I believe the ideas that you spelled out in the papers...make a hell of a lot of sense," he wrote to Nixon in the second week of November 1964.[223]

Both Bush and Nixon understood that for the GOP to regain national influence, it needed candidates who not only exuded optimism but also addressed issues that resonated with a broad base of Republican voters. In future campaigns, Bush adopted this pragmatic approach, aiming to balance his establishment background with the party's evolving ideological shift.

"I hope this defeat, far from discouraging you, will only whet your appetite for making another race the next time the proper opportunity is presented," Nixon wrote to Bush in mid-November 1964.[224]

Although he started with uncertainty, Bush had developed the skill to deliver a pragmatic political message. With guidance from his father, he built key relationships with influential figures such as Eisenhower, Nixon, and other prominent establishment politicians who could offer advice and create opportunities for the future. While the Senate defeat remained difficult, Bush saw it as a crucial learning experience, one that would prepare him for greater political success in the years to come.

CHAPTER 7

Listening and Learning: Congressman

Congressman Bush with President Dwight Eisenhower. Circa 1960s.

On January 20, 1969, as George Bush prepared to attend Richard Nixon's inauguration, his office manager, Rose Zamaria, suggested Bush do something different. "What you ought to do is go out to Andrews [Air Force Base] to say good-bye to President Johnson, to wish him well." When Bush arrived to offer his best wishes to the Johnsons, he was surprised to find there were no other Republicans present.[225]

Despite their political differences, Bush held a deep admiration for Lyndon Johnson's service to the nation. "He has been a fine President and invariably courteous and fair to me and my people, and I thought that I belonged here to show in a small way how much I have appreciated him," Bush told Johnson's friend Joe B. Frantz. The outgoing president appreciated Bush's gesture, writing, "Please know that I value your friendship, as I do your father's, and that I am glad you are one of us down here in Texas. When you are home sometime, come to see us."[226]

Frustrated by his limited influence in the House of Representatives, where power is determined by seniority, the two-term congressman began contemplating a 1970 campaign for the Senate against his old rival, Ralph Yarborough. As Bush weighed the possibility, he saw an opportunity to capitalize on the growing local rift between conservative Democrats and the more populist Yarborough, and he believed that cultivating a relationship with President Johnson might help him navigate and exploit those divisions.[227]

On April 9, 1970, Bush visited the former president at his expansive ranch on the Pedernales River, just outside Austin, Texas. The Bushes had previously visited Johnson shortly after his return from Washington. During that earlier visit, Bush and his wife received what he described as "the legendary ranch tour LBJ gave all visitors. That meant moving over dirt roads in a white Lincoln Continental at seventy-five to eighty miles an hour."[228]

In April, Bush, accompanied by his friend Jack Steel, had a more substantive visit with Johnson. As always, the former president continued to be engaged in all aspects of politics. Aware Bush had considered a run against Yarborough, Johnson reaffirmed his long-standing position of supporting the Democrat in any campaign. However, LBJ said that decision did not preclude his friends from supporting another candidate.

While Bush expressed little surprise about Johnson's loyalty to his party, he decided to concentrate on seeking the former president's counsel. "Mr. President, I've still got a decision to make, and I'd like your advice," Bush said, outlining his dilemma. Even as Bush considered a Senate run, he remained hesitant, wary of risking a secure seat in the House of Representatives. Johnson paused thoughtfully before offering his response. The former Senate majority leader acknowledged that both houses of Congress offered strong opportunities for political advancement. Then, with his characteristically blunt insight, Johnson shared a piece of advice that Bush would carry with him for the rest of his career. "[T]he difference between being a member of the Senate and a member of the House is the difference between chicken salad and chicken shit. Do I make my point?" Bush wrote in recalling Johnson's earthy piece of wisdom.[229]

***

Following the Republican defeat in the 1964 election, *National Review* published an issue in which it analyzed Goldwater's overwhelming loss and attempted to offer a solution for what the GOP needed to do to regain political power. As part of that analysis, the magazine invited several prominent Republicans, including George Bush, to offer their opinions on the party's political future. The recently defeated Senate candidate contended that the party needed to broaden its approach and "welcome all who want to be Republicans." Those who favored that inclusive message included Republican moderate John Davis Lodge, who had served as President Eisenhower's ambassador to Spain.[230]

In a clear reflection of the GOP's internal divide, Bush's remarks drew criticism from Goldwater supporters, who argued that the Eastern-educated oil executive did not represent true conservatism. One critic observed that Bush's failure to mention Goldwater's name during the campaign highlighted his lack of authenticity. However, William F. Buckley Jr. came to Bush's defense, recognizing him as "an attractive, articulate campaigner and a man of personal integrity." Like Bush, Buckley, a believer in political pragmatism, contended that ideological rigidity was not the path to victory. "Emphasize the positive, eliminate the negative, warn of the dangers from the left but do so without always questioning the patriotism of those who hold those liberal views. Conservatism can and will survive—it needs to be practical and positive," Buckley wrote in *NR*'s December 1964 issue.[231]

While Bush did not disagree with the criticism he had received about his lack of enthusiasm for Goldwater's policies, the forty-one-year-old found himself more disappointed with the views he had adopted than the campaign he had run. As biographer Herbert Parmet writes, Bush's upbringing and education had taught him to compete hard and live life with integrity. The fact that Bush wrote little about the 1964 campaign in his 1988 memoir suggests he had allowed himself to support positions that clashed with his personal values. "I took some of the far-right positions to get elected. I hope I never do it again. I regret it," Bush told his Episcopalian minister.[232]

Despite his frustration over the campaign's outcome, Bush stood by the strategy he believed offered the best chance of winning. Driven by a deep conviction that second place was not an option, he was willing to adopt positions that didn't fully align with his personal views if it meant securing victory. The approach, rooted in his competitive nature, remained a consistent part of his political career. As one of his presidential speechwriters observed in 1989, "in Bush's mind, the nitty-gritty boorishness of campaigning for office was wholly distinct from the lofty business of actually governing the nation. What you had to *say* to get elected had no real bearing on or relationship to what you subsequently *did* once elected."[233]

The 1964 election allowed the Democrats to capitalize on Goldwater's defeat by strengthening their control over both houses of Congress. The victory enabled President Lyndon Johnson to focus on advancing his "Great Society" agenda, which involved significant government spending on programs aimed at addressing poverty in the United States. The administration launched initiatives that included medical care for the elderly and low-income families, and a Job Corps, reminiscent of the Civilian Conservation Corps initiated as part of the New Deal by Johnson's political hero, President Franklin D. Roosevelt.[234]

However, Johnson's efforts to expand FDR's social welfare agenda were complicated in 1965 by his decision to send thousands of additional troops to Vietnam to address the escalating Southeast Asian conflict. At the same time, frustration among African Americans over limited economic opportunities contributed to the rise of the Black Power movement, which marked a shift toward more militant tactics, departing from the nonviolent approach in the struggle for civil rights. The tensions within the African American community exploded that August when a series of riots occurred in the Watts neighborhood of Los Angeles, prompting LBJ to deploy the National Guard to restore order.[235]

The unrest in Watts and other urban areas, including Baltimore, Cleveland, and San Francisco, raised questions about the Democrats' commitment to law and order. It also fueled the belief among many white Americans that the administration had become overwhelmed by "the resentment and demands of the black underclass." Bush shared the concerns of many Republicans regarding the growing radicalization of the civil rights movement. Despite his reservations about the nation's increasing racial tensions, Bush supported the principles behind LBJ's Great Society. While he described the administration's program as offering "a better life for all," he believed the policies could achieve greater effectiveness if they were implemented at the local level rather than from Washington.[236]

In 1966, Bush received another chance at political office when he received the opportunity to run for the newly created Seventh Congressional District in Houston. Ironically, although Bush had lost the Senate race by three hundred thousand votes, he had won a majority in the areas that encompassed the new district. Musing upon his father's decision to persist in pursuing elected office, George W. Bush wrote, "[T]he loss [in the Senate race] stung, but…it didn't dampen my father's enthusiasm for politics or his desire to serve."[237]

The new district reflected the character-driven campaign Bush decided to run. Composed of affluent, well-educated residents, many shared Bush's moderate to conservative attitudes in their politics. For Bush, the campaign offered an opportunity to highlight what came naturally. The nonideological demographic allowed him to focus the campaign on his personal qualities—to present himself as a vibrant and energetic "man of action," as an optimistic and pragmatic conservative—in stark contrast to the rigid and stern persona that Barry Goldwater had exhibited in the previous presidential race.[238]

In 1966, Bush embodied what *The Wall Street Journal* described as "part of the large number of new and appealing Republican personalities across the nation." The strategy, crafted by Republican Party Chairman Ray Bliss, contended that by focusing on the politics of optimism and inclusion, the party could succeed in that year's midterm elections. While Bush also advocated a more aggressive policy in Vietnam, reduced government spending, and a right-to-work law, he followed Bliss's strategy in extending his hand to African Americans by calling for "civil rights and domestic tranquility on all fronts."[239]

As violence continued to plague the inner cities, concerns about safety grew among Houston's white voters. Despite these worries, Bush showed his commitment to racial equality by funding an integrated girls' softball team. Bush also made efforts to engage black support, aiming to leverage the increased voter turnout following the passage of the Voting Rights Act of 1965. His campaign deposited its funds in a black-owned bank and opened an office near one of the state's historically black colleges. The approach mirrored the strategies of other moderate Republicans running for national office, such as Senate candidates Howard H. Baker Jr. of Tennessee and Charles Percy of Illinois.[240]

Bush also took advantage of his father's contacts to assemble a series of glittering endorsements. These included President Eisenhower, who happily and publicly praised Bush's candidacy while privately giving him encouragement. "I can't tell you how much I am hoping for your overwhelming victory in November," the former president wrote in the fall of 1966.[241]

Bush received strong support from other influential figures in the Republican Party, once again including Richard Nixon. Nixon, planning to run for president in 1968, offered his campaign services that year to all Republican candidates, regardless of their ideological leanings. "To say that one cannot support a party that entertains men of varying views in this country is tantamount to saying that one cannot remain within a party that has a chance of national success," Nixon remarked as he campaigned across the country. Alongside Nixon's support, Bush also gained endorsements from rising Michigan Congressman Gerald

R. Ford, a former golfing companion of Prescott Bush, as well as from Senate Minority Leader Everett Dirksen of Illinois.[242]

Bush's pragmatic approach to the issues stood in stark contrast to his conservative Democratic opponent. The demographics of the district, along with Bush's approachable demeanor and compelling message, contributed to his first political victory. He won with 57.6 percent of the vote, capturing 35 percent of African American and Hispanic voters—a dramatic increase from the 3 percent he had received just two years earlier.

Even as he celebrated the win, Bush began looking beyond his current success. Many viewed the Senate as the next logical step in a political career; however, Bush had more ambitious goals. "I don't want to move just up to the Senate," he confided to his friend Ross Baker in 1966. "I'd like to be President."[243]

Bush's victory mirrored the Republican Party's strong nationwide performance. Despite the Democrats remaining in the majority in both houses of Congress, the GOP gained seats in the House of Representatives and in the Senate, and captured several governorships across the country. The most notable victory of 1966 came from former actor and General Electric spokesperson Ronald Reagan, who defeated incumbent Edmund G. Brown to become California's new governor. Like Bush, Reagan ran a disciplined yet personable campaign, a stark contrast to the more rigid positions of Barry Goldwater, whose views Reagan had praised in a well-regarded speech just two years earlier. The Republicans were also able to take advantage of President Johnson's and the Democratic Party's failure to control racial unrest, rising crime, and growing public unhappiness over the Vietnam War.[244]

In January 1967, shortly after the newly elected congressman and his family arrived in Washington, Bush's parents hosted a black-tie event to welcome the young couple to the city. Those who attended the exclusive F Street club that evening constituted a bipartisan representation of the American political establishment. The guest list included Kentucky Senator John Sherman Cooper, influential syndicated columnists Rowland Evans and Joseph Alsop, as well as Alsop's socially prominent wife, Susan Mary. Other notable media figures present included Katherine Graham, publisher of *The Washington Post*, whose father, Eugene Meyer, served as an early investor in the Bush-Overbey Development Company.[245]

Even when Bush's parents were not in Washington, the elder Bush used his influence to help his son navigate the corridors of power. Living in Hobe Sound on Florida's Gold Coast, Prescott Bush enlisted the support of old colleagues like Averell Harriman, Robert Lovett, and former Secretary of the Treasury Douglas Dillon. These men, who frequently traveled between Florida and Washington, were advising President Johnson on the escalating war in Vietnam. Despite retiring from the Senate at the end of 1962, Bush's father remained active in the nation's capital, maintaining his membership in the "Monday Morning Club," a weekly gathering attended by numerous Republican senators.[246]

After speaking with House Minority Leader Gerald Ford, Congressman Bush formally requested an assignment to the Appropriations Committee. "I know you are swamped with all kinds of grandiose requests...but whatever you all decide will be fine with me...I will heed your advice and see that any words on my behalf are put in without any "pressure." I am anxious not to get off on the wrong foot in the House," Bush wrote on November 25, 1966.[247]

Bush also contacted GOP conference chairman and Ford confidant Melvin Laird, whom he would later get to know while they both served in the Nixon administration. In his letter to the Wisconsin Republican, Bush stated that he did not want "to offend any of the wiser and older hands around the House." The new congressman recognized that Ford and Laird were both rising stars, and building positive relationships with them was crucial to his future. He also understood that both men were seasoned political veterans who could offer valuable insights into the intricacies of the legislative process.[248]

While Bush honored his word by refraining from pressing either man for a committee position, his father, on the other hand, did not hold back. Determined to secure a prestigious committee assignment for his son, the elder Bush contacted his former colleague, Arkansas Senator J. William Fulbright. The legislator happily introduced his friend to Wilbur Mills, a Harvard Law School graduate and veteran congressman, in office since 1939. Mills held the powerful chairmanship of the Ways and Means Committee. However, when Mills received a call from former Senator Bush, he informed the Connecticut Republican that he could not assist him in his objective. "I said I'm a Democrat, and I don't think I can do anything," Mills told the *Washington Post*'s Walt Harrington nearly twenty years later. "He said could I call Jerry Ford? And so I did."[249]

After a discussion with Ford, Mills decided to give the new congressman a chance. Bush understood that despite his father's influence, preparation and hard work and the willingness to learn from others were the only ways to truly prove his worth. "Wilbur Mills appears to be fair-minded and will give everybody a chance, though I must say, when it came my time to take a shot at the Secretary of the Treasury, I decided to listen rather than talk," Bush wrote to constituent Paul Dorsey in February 1967.[250]

Excited about the opportunity to serve in Congress, Bush also recognized his position as "a freshman member of the House…one of 435 lawmakers.…at the absolute bottom of the totem pole." With little seniority, Bush understood that the best way to learn the intricacies of the legislative process required him to observe and seek guidance from his more experienced colleagues. In that regard, Chairman Mills proved an ideal mentor.[251]

Bush found in Wilbur Mills both an exceptional legislator and also an advisor who taught him valuable lessons about navigating a group with diverse political views. During his time on the committee, Bush dedicated himself to studying and reading diligently. His strong work ethic impressed Chairman Mills, and in turn Bush came to admire Mills's scholarly approach and meticulous attention to detail. "Wilbur was a worker.… He figured we had a job to do right where we were, in Washington.… when he talked, his colleagues listened and learned. Best of all, however, Wilbur was unfailingly courteous, a leader who got his way not through bullying but by patiently working out a consensus," Bush wrote of his experience working with the Arkansas congressman.[252]

Mills held Bush in high regard, as well. He appreciated the new congressman's humility, his preference for staying out of the spotlight, and his eagerness to learn from the experience of his more seasoned associates. During his time in business, Bush had surrounded himself with smart colleagues who also offered diverse perspectives. He applied that same approach in Washington, seeking out varied viewpoints and valuing the wisdom of others.[253]

Remaining attentive to Mills's management of complex issues, Bush also looked to Gerald Ford and Melvin Laird as models for achieving success in Congress. These leaders demonstrated qualities such as courtesy, preparation, and the ability to collaborate with others across party lines. Bush wrote that no one "had a better grasp of the details of pending legislation than Jerry Ford when he was House Republican leader."[254]

As Bush began his tenure in the House of Representatives, the Vietnam War emerged as a dominant issue in American politics. By early 1967, US troop deployments in South Vietnam had surged to 490,000, and that year alone more than 11,000 American soldiers were killed in action. As the death toll rose, so did public anxiety. Anti-war sentiment, especially on college and university campuses, became increasingly forceful and widespread. In October, opposition culminated in a major protest, when 20,000 demonstrators gathered at the Pentagon, leading to a violent confrontation.[255]

President Lyndon Johnson, who had hoped to leave a legacy as a champion of liberal policies addressing poverty in America, became increasingly fixated on the conflict. In 1967, he had three large televisions and electronic newswires installed in the Oval Office to stay informed about the progress of the war. Even after receiving a memo from Defense Secretary Robert McNamara in November warning that "continuation of our present action in Southeast Asia would be dangerous, costly in lives, and unsatisfactory to the American people," Johnson remained resolute in his decision to press on. He feared that a defeat in Vietnam would severely damage America's credibility with its allies and embolden its Cold War adversaries. "I am not going to be the President who saw Southeast Asia go the way China went," LBJ told his ambassador to South Vietnam, Henry Cabot Lodge Jr.[256]

On November 2, Lodge joined ten other prominent figures, collectively known as "the wise men," in the White House Cabinet Room to offer their insights on the Vietnam War. Among them were Averell Harriman, Prescott Bush's former business associate, and Dean Acheson, a fellow Yale Corporation board member. Acheson, the former secretary of state, aligned with President Johnson's firm stance that the war should persist until the United States achieved a clear victory. "We must understand that we are not going to have negotiations. When these fellows decide they can't defeat the South, then they will give up. This is the way it was in Korea, this is the way the Communists operate," Acheson asserted.[257]

LBJ was a deeply insecure man who believed members of the Ivy-educated Eastern elite viewed him, a graduate of Southwest Texas State Teachers College, as unsophisticated and ignorant. For that reason, he constantly cultivated experienced and erudite statesmen like Acheson as well as John J. McCloy, and he may have appreciated the validation his decision to stay the course received from such leading figures of the establishment. However, William Bundy, Acheson's son-in-law and Johnson's assistant secretary of state, contended that these elder statesmen's age, as well as their belief that the United States had a duty to stop the communist wave, clouded their once-thoughtful judgment. "Quickie consultations deprived [Acheson] of the facts he needed to fully engage his lawyerly acuity," Bundy said.[258]

George Bush, whose background at Phillips Academy and Yale aligned with the pedigree of Acheson and his contemporaries, had also become increasingly concerned about the direction of the war. In December 1967, Bush decided to visit the Southeast Asian nation. Over fourteen days, and at his own expense, the congressman traveled to eleven of South Vietnam's forty-four provinces. During his visit, Bush met with the newly appointed American ambassador to South Vietnam, Ellsworth Bunker, who had replaced Henry Cabot Lodge Jr., as well as other prominent diplomats. He also visited American troops, gaining firsthand insight into the progress of the conflict. "I wish you could have seen our young pilots in the carrier briefing room as they discussed their hazardous mission over the flak-ridden skies of Hanoi," Bush wrote after his trip.[259]

The empathy Bush showed for the Marines and infantrymen he met during his visit reflected his own military experience from two decades earlier. While Bush supported the Johnson administration's war policy, he confided to his Yale friend Richard G. Mack, "I think in retrospect that we should have learned from the history books. . . ." Drawing a contrast with the clarity of the mission and the national unity experienced during World War II, Bush acknowledged that the turmoil on the home front and the heavy loss of life in Vietnam were undermining public support for the war. However, one could not overlook "the terror of the VC and the past slaughters by Ho," Bush explained in response to his friend, who had grown disillusioned with President Johnson's handling of the conflict.[260]

Even after his extensive visit to the region, Bush remained aligned with Acheson and others in believing the United States could still win the war, a sentiment that resonated with his Houston constituency. However, Bush put his political future at risk when he announced he would support the 1968 Open Housing Act. A cornerstone of Johnson's Great Society, the legislation prohibited housing discrimination based on race, color, or creed. Bush shared these views with other Republican moderates, like Michigan Governor George Romney, who believed that all Americans, especially those serving their country in war, were entitled to the same rights, regardless of skin color.[261]

In supporting the legislation, which impacted 80 percent of the nation's housing, Bush followed his father's pragmatic approach to politics, placing good judgment above rigid political ideology. He believed the voters of the district had elected him to make decisions based on reason and fairness. Bush empathized with African American men and women who suffered under the violent attacks of white supremacists, particularly those led by Birmingham, Alabama, Sheriff Eugene "Bull" Connor. Representing a district that was 90 percent white, and where opposition to the bill ran high, Bush faced considerable backlash. He received a deluge of hate-filled letters, and his staff endured verbal abuse.

Nevertheless, Bush stood firm. "Were we supposed to tell these black soldiers when they came home that they couldn't buy houses in our neighborhood?" he later wrote.[262]

On April 11, 1968, after casting his vote in favor of the legislation, Bush returned to Houston to face his constituents. He addressed them at a meeting on April 17, just two weeks after riots had erupted across the country following the assassination of civil rights leader Martin Luther King Jr. As Bush entered the venue, he felt enormous tension. "The place was jammed…and it was also seething," Bush recalled. Many of the letters he had received criticizing his vote labeled him a "sellout" and a "nigger-lover."[263]

When the congressman took the stage to speak, the audience responded with boos and catcalls. Undeterred, Bush emphasized that his vote did not simply represent a piece of legislation, but a larger theme, one that concerned the support of the American ideal of equal opportunity for all, regardless of background. In delivering his remarks Bush spoke for those African Americans fighting in Vietnam who he believed deserved as much opportunity as anyone else. "Somehow it seems fundamental that this guy should have a hope," Bush remarked. "A hope that if he saves some money, and if he wants to break out of a ghetto, and he is a good character…the door will not be slammed solely because he is a Negro, or because he speaks with a Mexican accent." Following Bush's statement, his remarks were met with a large ovation from the audience, signaling that many in the crowd shared his belief in the nation's founding principles, that everyone should have access to liberty based on their abilities and talents.[264]

Bush strongly believed that government intervention should not hinder individual success, advocating for "private enterprise" as the most effective means to achieve national objectives. He also emulated his father's approach by maintaining a strong connection with his constituents and promoting inclusivity, including hiring a woman as his senior aide. Mary Matthews Raether, who served in this capacity, recalled that after a meeting with other members of Congress, Bush asked her to stop taking notes during conferences. "He didn't want the others to think I was a secretary," she said, highlighting his respect for her position and his commitment to challenging gender stereotypes.[265]

Bush also adopted his father's use of athletics to build strong relationships with prominent Republicans. Believing that "sports is the great equalizer," the congressman often exercised in the House gymnasium, where these activities helped him foster friendships with colleagues from both sides of the political spectrum, like Mississippi Democrat Gillespie "Sonny" Montgomery. Beyond Bush's controversial stance on open housing, he also supported a May 1968 Ways and Means proposal to raise taxes. The legislation, which focused on reducing spending and shrinking the deficit, displayed Bush's concern for the nation's long-term financial stability.[266]

That summer, with no opponent vying for his congressional seat, Bush shifted his focus to the upcoming 1968 Republican presidential race. Richard Nixon, recovering from his crushing loss eight years earlier, seemed poised to reclaim the nomination. A poll from the previous year indicated that 57 percent of state GOP chairmen supported Nixon's presidential aspirations. Meanwhile, President Johnson remained the front-runner for reelection. However, the president's approval ratings plummeted when, on January 30, 1968, the North Vietnamese launched coordinated attacks on US targets across southern Vietnam. Although the "Tet Offensive" signified a military failure for Ho Chi Minh's forces, the highly negative media coverage it received marked a significant turning point and played a key role in Johnson's decision to announce on March 31 that he would not seek another term in office.[267]

Throughout the 1968 presidential campaign, Richard Nixon solidified his position as the leading Republican contender, drawing on the experience and visibility gained from his eight years as vice president. His candidacy was further strengthened by the backing of Republican politicians he had supported during the 1966 midterm elections—among them, George Bush, who remained a loyal ally. Nixon, poised to appear on his fourth presidential ticket in sixteen years, hoped to continue to secure their support as he mounted his political comeback. Positioning himself as a moderate conservative, Nixon criticized the excesses of the

Great Society, pledged to implement a policy of "law and order" in the nation's cities, and promised a "secret plan" to win the war in Vietnam. He also sought to capitalize on the nation's racial unrest, appealing to Southern whites and a "silent majority" of working-class Americans who felt alienated by Johnson's policies, particularly those designed to benefit African Americans and other minority groups.[268]

Nixon also profited from the turmoil within the Democratic Party, which, after Johnson's withdrawal, saw the assassination of New York Senator Robert F. Kennedy and a chaotic, divided convention in Chicago. While Nixon benefited from the disarray, it weakened the Democrat's nominee, Vice President Hubert Humphrey. Nixon's chances were further bolstered by third-party candidate Governor George Wallace of Alabama, who ran on a platform that tapped into working-class white resentment toward both the Democratic and Republican establishments, setting the stage for future insurgent presidential campaigns.[269]

Bush remained a strong supporter of Nixon, appreciating the support Nixon gave him during his runs for Congress in 1966 and the Senate in 1964. He admired Nixon's tenacity, work ethic, and devotion to family. Recognizing Bush's growing reputation in the Republican Party, Nixon included him in a small circle of trusted advisors during the campaign. "I am writing this letter to you and a few other close friends and political leaders to get the benefit of your advice [on the selection of my running mate]," Nixon wrote Bush in July 1968.[270]

During the campaign, senior members of the GOP establishment sought to persuade Nixon to consider Bush as his running mate. The effort gained momentum when Eisenhower personally recommended Bush to his former vice president during a lengthy meeting in 1967 at Ike's farm in Gettysburg, Pennsylvania. Following Johnson's 1968 State of the Union address, Bush's ties to Eisenhower were further solidified when the two appeared on television on behalf of the GOP, to deliver responses to the president's remarks. Historian Derek Chollet notes that their joint appearance framed the two men as "generational bookends," symbolizing a measured, experienced approach to Republican leadership.[271]

As the Republican National Convention drew near, Bush secured endorsements from family friends Thomas E. Dewey, the Republican presidential nominee in 1944 and 1948, and the Reverend Billy Graham, a leading Southern evangelical and a close advisor to Nixon. Many believed that Bush had little chance of being selected, but the Nixon campaign received a flood of letters praising Bush's abilities and character. "Please take a long hard look at George Bush.... He is a young man of terrific charm, great intelligence, superb tact, and a fine war record.... Billy Graham is reported to have said that George Bush is the best on TV he has ever seen...I say without hesitation there is no one in the country who would so charm the younger segment...than George Bush," Neil Mallon wrote to the Nixon fundraiser, George Champion, in April 1968.[272]

Despite Bush's strong efforts, Nixon ultimately chose the outspoken conservative governor of Maryland, Spiro T. Agnew. Although disappointed, Bush understood that Nixon needed someone with more executive experience. "When I saw Nixon in San Diego last week he confirmed that he gave it very serious consideration but decided against it because of my short service in the House," Bush wrote to a constituent. Tom Dewey confirmed Nixon's reasoning in a note to Bush's father: "George made such a fine impression in Washington...my expressed views about him for Vice President came from conviction and admiration.... I think there was simply a feeling that he had not been in public office long enough," the GOP kingmaker explained.[273]

Always thinking ahead, Bush believed that if Nixon won the election in November, a position within the new administration might become available. With that in mind, he traveled the country, making appearances to support the Nixon-Agnew ticket. As biographer Herbert Parmet notes, the congressman's dedication to the Republican nominee "cemented the Nixon-Bush alliance."[274]

Nixon's slim victory over Vice President Humphrey provided the Republicans with a set of new strategies that they leveraged in future elections. Most notably, the GOP successfully articulated domestic policies that resonated with Americans disillusioned by the Democratic

Party's liberal agenda. By tapping into white resentment against minority groups, the Republicans gained a foothold in the South, a shift that would prove advantageous for Texas candidates like George Bush as his political career progressed.[275]

Following the election, Bush aimed to strengthen his growing relationship with Nixon and to seek his guidance on a potential 1970 Senate campaign against Ralph Yarborough. "Dear Mr. President, in June or early July, I would like a 15-minute appointment with you to discuss briefly the forthcoming Senate race.... I am reluctant to give up my seat on Ways and Means to gamble excessively, but a key to the whole ball game could be, depending on events, the Administration's role. More than all of this, I have always valued your advice," Bush wrote on May 8, 1969.[276]

On May 22, at 5:00 p.m., Bush met with the new president at the White House. During their forty-five-minute conversation, Nixon encouraged Bush to pursue another run for the Senate. As Barbara Bush noted in her diary, Nixon assured her husband that he would have full support from the administration. While excited by the chance to erase the defeat he had suffered five years earlier, George W. Bush believed the opportunity resonated with his father for a much deeper reason. "I've always suspected that part of the reason was that he wanted to serve in the same body in which his father, Senator Prescott Bush, had served."[277]

As Bush launched his campaign, concerns about Yarborough's populist platform potentially alienating moderate Democrats across the state led Texas Governor John Connally and political strategist Robert Strauss to conclude that the party needed a more moderate candidate to prevent the Senate seat from falling into Republican hands. To address the issue, the two men recruited Lloyd Bentsen, a business executive and former congressman, to challenge Yarborough in the Democratic primary. Bentsen's victory over the populist Yarborough set the stage for a contest between two politicians with similar positions and backgrounds.[278]

Political observers viewed the race as the most significant off-year contest of 1970. However, despite Bush's best effort, Bentsen defeated him with 53.4 percent of the vote. For Bush, the loss was even more painful than the one he had suffered eight years earlier. "God, it hurts to lose to Bentsen after all our hard work and trying and caring," Bush lamented after the election. Despite the setback, Bush remained hopeful. "Whatever we do, I'm sure it will be challenging," he wrote to a friend.[279]

One of the few bright spots of the campaign was the bond Bush developed with James A. Baker III, a prominent Texas lawyer and Princeton graduate. The two had known each other since 1958 and shared many similarities. Both were ambitious, driven individuals from affluent families, highly intelligent, and fiercely competitive. Baker also had political ambitions. Tired of practicing law, he considered running for Bush's congressional seat. However, his plans were derailed when in February 1970 his beloved wife, Mary Stuart Baker, passed away from breast cancer. Overwhelmed by grief and left to care for four young boys, Baker struggled with his emotions, turning to alcohol, which began to take a toll on him.[280]

With Bush's encouragement, Baker took charge of the Senate campaign in Harris County. The experience helped the attorney explore his own political interests while providing a welcome distraction from the difficult situation at home. The campaign marked the start of a more than two-decades-long relationship, during which Baker became Bush's closest advisor, ultimately serving as secretary of state during Bush's presidency.[281]

Between 1966 and 1970, George Bush's appealing persona and pragmatic approach to the issues of the day helped him develop a strong relationship with Richard Nixon, one that grew even closer after Nixon's victory in the 1968 presidential election. Despite being disappointed by another senatorial defeat in 1970, Bush had learned over the years not to give up hope. As he and his family prepared to return to Houston, the defeated candidate had no idea of the opportunity that awaited him.

CHAPTER 8

An Exercise in Diplomacy: Ambassador to the United Nations

George Bush is appointed US Ambassador to the United Nations by President Richard Nixon. January 12, 1970.

In January 1971, less than a month after being sworn in as US ambassador to the United Nations, George Bush attended his first Nixon administration cabinet meeting. As discussions with government department heads progressed, Bush appreciated President Nixon's thoughtful demeanor and deliberate effort to help him feel welcomed as part of the team. "The President graciously worked me into the conversation a time or two," Bush wrote in his UN journal. Known for his own instinct to put others at ease, Bush deeply appreciated the gesture. "He seemed to be including me in the official family which is a very helpful thing." The experience left a lasting impression and shaped Bush's own inclusive leadership style as president.[282]

Eighteen years later, in 1989, Condoleezza Rice, a young Soviet specialist, had a similar experience with President Bush. During a summit on the island of Malta with Soviet leader Mikhail Gorbachev, Bush personally introduced the thirty-four-year-old PhD to the Russian leader. Rice later recalled the encounter in an email to Bush's post-presidential chief of staff, Jean Becker. "This is my Soviet advisor, Condoleezza Rice," Bush said. "She tells me everything I know about the Soviet Union."[283]

Rice understood that the gesture held a deeper meaning than just impressing Gorbachev. "It was meant for all of those people standing around—including US and Soviet government officials who were twice my age," she said. Like Nixon before him, Bush made the young African American academic feel at ease among a group of experienced professionals and boosted her confidence. She recognized that the president had placed immense trust in her at a critical moment in history. That moment also fostered a deep sense of loyalty in Rice, motivating her to work tirelessly for the administration.[284]

***

After Bush's second failed Senate campaign, Charles Bartlett, a Washington-based columnist for the *Chicago Sun-Times* and close friend of President John F. Kennedy, had suggested that the former congressman approach President Nixon about an appointment as United States ambassador to the United Nations. "You'd be amazed what this campaign did for your image up here. A lot of people are thinking of you in national terms," Bush recalled the Pulitzer Prize–winning journalist telling him. While Bush had little diplomatic experience, the idea did not appear far-fetched. Nixon had also previously hinted that if Bush didn't win the 1970 Senate campaign, he would find a position for him in his administration. A skilled networker with a wide range of connections in New York City, Bush didn't have to wait long to find out what his next role would be.[285]

On December 9, 1971, Bush met with President Nixon and his chief of staff, H. R. "Bob" Haldeman, in the Oval Office. During the meeting, Bush presented a compelling case for his appointment to the United Nations. He emphasized his familiarity with the Eastern establishment and his ability to effectively communicate Nixon's policies, positioning himself as an ideal candidate to represent the United States at the international organization. "I felt I could really put forward an image there that would be very helpful to the administration," Bush wrote two days later.[286]

The idea intrigued Nixon. Fifteen minutes after Bush returned to his office on Capitol Hill, Haldeman called to inform him that the president had decided to appoint him to the UN position. The move proved significant. Throughout his career, Nixon, the ambitious politician from the small Southern California farming community of Yorba Linda, often felt sidelined by the Eastern establishment. Figures like Ike's chief of staff, Sherman Adams, and Senator Henry Cabot Lodge Jr., along with others from his time in the Eisenhower administration, had contributed to his sense of being an outsider. Upon arriving at the White House, Nixon made it a point to instruct his cabinet officers to "resist the Washington habit of recruiting their staffs solely from Eastern schools....and instead to branch out and get new blood from the South, the West, and the Midwest."[287]

Considering Nixon's long-standing distrust of men from Bush's social background, one can consider it ironic that he appointed him to the United Nations. Throughout his political career, Nixon had expressed open hostility toward the elite class, whom he saw as symbols of the nation's moral decline. He often accused them of harboring "misplaced idealism" and failing to effectively confront international communism, a failure he believed played a key role in America's difficulties in Vietnam. However—as authors Leonard Silk and Mark Silk point out—despite Nixon's resentment toward the establishment, his political sensibilities often leaned more toward a moderate internationalist stance, supporting policies like the Marshall Plan and institutions such as the United

Nations, rather than aligning with the views of ideological conservatives like Barry Goldwater.[288]

But even with those moderate positions, Nixon had a low opinion of the United Nations. In October 1971, writes historian Edward C. Keefer, the president expressed his frustration to Walter McConaughy, United States ambassador to the then Republic of China. "I'd just say to hell with the UN. What is it anyway? It's a damned debating society. What good does it do? Very little." In the years following World War II, as decolonization spread worldwide, the UN emerged as a forum where newly independent African and Asian nations voiced sharp criticism of Western imperialism. Tensions between the US and the international body continued to grow over issues like the American involvement in Vietnam. Many of these emerging nations used the General Assembly to voice their grievances, giving the UN an increasingly anti-Western tone. Firm believers that global politics were driven by motivations of self-interest, Nixon and his Harvard-educated national security advisor, Henry Kissinger, found little value in the organization and were determined to maintain tight control over American foreign policy.

By appointing Bush to the United Nations, Nixon likely saw an opportunity to have an establishment figure who could effectively advocate for his administration on the international stage. Yet, Nixon also seemed to have a personal affinity for George Bush. In a 1992 letter to one of Bush's biographers, Nixon explained that the appointment was not solely based on Bush's diplomatic skills but also because he believed that gaining significant foreign policy experience would be beneficial for Bush's future.[289]

Soon after receiving the news, Bush reached out for advice to former UN ambassadors and individuals with significant diplomatic experience. One of those he consulted, former Ambassador Averell Harriman, expressed "reservations" about Bush's ability to succeed in the role. While Bush's journal does not provide specifics about Harriman's concerns, Bush's respectful approach and willingness to defer to the older generation may have helped ease the diplomat's reservations.[290]

Bush's deference to Harriman's opinions resulted in a positive response. When Bush received a call from his parents saying that Harriman was "ecstatic" about his new role, Bush took it in stride, attributing the change of heart to the older diplomat's "eccentricities." "He is a gentleman, and he is like anybody else—he likes to be consulted." Bush understood that Harriman, involved in public affairs since the early 1930s, remained eager to stay engaged with the events of his time and to shape the future by advising those who would lead the country in the years ahead. Congratulations to the Bush family also came from former Kennedy CIA Director John McCone. "This, I believe, is a most important position, and one in which George, with his ability and his experience, can serve the President and our country admirably," McCone wrote in late December 1970.[291]

Bush also received congratulations from the former governor of Connecticut, John Davis Lodge, who drew comparisons between Bush's career and that of his sibling, Henry Cabot Lodge Jr. "When my brother was defeated by Jack Kennedy in 1952, President Eisenhower appointed him Ambassador to the United Nations...after 13 years in the United States Senate, I think that his appointment...was really the start of the most brilliant part of his career." Bush continued to seek advice from individuals with experience in foreign policy, including Lodge Jr. and Dean Rusk, who had served as secretary of state under President Kennedy. "It is amazingly simple to get in touch with these people, and so far, each one has seemed very cooperative," Bush wrote on December 15, 1970.[292]

As Bush prepared for his new role, he dedicated himself to extensive reading and study. He soon realized that those who excelled in the position often had a strong rapport with the White House. Within weeks of accepting the appointment, Bush demonstrated his diplomatic skill by thoughtfully responding to requests from administration members on issues related to his new role. While eager to assist, Bush made it clear to Nixon's team that, until his confirmation had occurred, he would do nothing to hinder the incumbent ambassador, Charles Yost, from completing his tenure.[293]

41

In early January 1971, Bush lunched with Ambassador Arthur Goldberg, a former associate justice of the Supreme Court and UN ambassador under Presidents Kennedy and Johnson. A vocal liberal, Goldberg believed that for Bush to make the most significant impact, he needed to fully embrace the prestigious aspects of the position. That included frequent use of the government limousine and chauffeur, as well as taking full advantage of the ambassador's large offices in both New York and Washington.[294]

The jurist also warned Bush about the hostile media landscape in New York, represented by *The New York Times*'s lukewarm response to Bush's appointment in December 1970. While the editors described the new UN designate as "an attractive, intelligent Republican," they noted, "there seems to be nothing in his record that qualifies him for this highly important position." Goldberg suggested that the White House should organize a grand signing ceremony to elevate the position in the eyes of the public. Although Bush found Goldberg to be "talkative" and "vain," he appreciated his predecessor's willingness to do everything possible to help him succeed. However, Bush expressed his determination to not allow the position to change his relaxed demeanor. "I'll bet it's going to be hard to be oneself…I am determined that we shall not change in the sense of getting formalized by this new job," he wrote in his UN journal at the end of December 1970.[295]

In the first week of January 1971, Bush met with veteran Republican statesman Henry Cabot Lodge Jr. A graduate of the Middlesex School and Harvard, Lodge was the grandson of Massachusetts Senator Henry Cabot Lodge and had served as a US senator from Massachusetts and ambassador to the United Nations. He had also been Nixon's running mate in the 1960 presidential election. In the years that followed, Lodge held several prominent diplomatic posts, including ambassador to both South Vietnam and West Germany in the Johnson administration.

Formal and dignified, Lodge embodied the principles of the Eastern establishment, with a focus on service and virtue. A contemporary of Prescott Bush, Lodge supported civil rights for African Americans and health care for the poor. His political outlook mirrored George Bush's moderate Republicanism and patrician approach to serving the nation in the political arena. During a visit to Lodge's mansion in Beverly, Massachusetts, Bush gained an appreciation for the former senator's political savvy, as well as his unexpected compassion "for the people." Bush also liked Lodge's "enthusiasm and spark" and his belief in the importance of entertaining, noting how making people "feel at home" could ease the diplomatic process.[296]

Lodge reinforced Bush's belief that building a strong relationship with the president would play a critical role in impacting policy. A pragmatic and sociable legislator, he emphasized that political talent would ultimately prove more valuable than "diplomatic language." He also offered a prescient warning, predicting that the UN would soon become a center of controversy, particularly after the admission of Communist China, an event that unfolded just ten months later.[297]

It is no surprise that Lodge's advice struck a chord with Bush. Both men were self-assured and thrived in the hands-on style of retail politics. Like Lodge, Bush understood that creating an informal atmosphere proved more impactful in building relationships than relying on stiff, ceremonial encounters. As Bush put it in a 1971 interview with *The New York Times*, "You can't do this job if you don't like people."[298]

The following week, Bush met with former President Lyndon Johnson to seek advice about his new UN role. However, the conversation added little to Bush's understanding, as LBJ expressed doubt about the institution's ability to effectively address global issues. However, Johnson did agree with Lodge and Goldberg on the importance of having a strong relationship with the president. "You can put in the potatoes and know all about the proteins buy you won't know all the rest of it. You have to rely on the president," LBJ remarked. Johnson also echoed Lodge's advice about the value of entertaining. "Be good to them, show them the best in America," he advised. The former president suggested that Bush invite visitors to see iconic places like the New York Stock Exchange, the Wilson School at Princeton University, the LBJ Library, and even take them on a cruise aboard the presidential yacht, Bush recalled in his account of the conversation.[299]

Reading Bush's United Nations journal, one is struck by his keen ability to capture vivid images of the people he encountered, as well as the temperaments and personal attitudes they displayed in their public roles. He had little fondness for Ambassador Goldberg's sense of self-importance. The notion of a grand office or a lavish automobile ran counter to Bush's values of humility. Despite receiving only a modest stipend, Bush's cabinet membership provided him the opportunity to upgrade his travel to first class. However, the idea conflicted with his natural inclination toward frugality and distaste for ostentation. "I don't think I should make special requests at all," Bush wrote, rejecting the idea.[300]

Immersing himself in his new role, Bush took the time to reflect on the dynamics between the government bureaucracy and the executive branch. Preparing for his confirmation hearing, Bush read Dean Acheson's 1969 memoir *Present at the Creation*, detailing the former secretary of state's years under President Truman. As Bush processed Acheson's experiences, he concluded that he needed to find a balance. "I am determined that do this job right we have got to have the right relationships. I told Henry [Kissinger] this," Bush confidently wrote in his diary. Despite his strong relationships with Kissinger and Nixon, Bush understood that to be effective in his new role, he needed to take initiative. "I think the best policy around here is to go to others, to ask advice, to be grateful, to get here earlier and leave later than the rest of the people. This will be the way I plan to do it at the Mission," he wrote on January 19, 1971.[301]

After a successful confirmation process, Ambassador Bush continued to draw on the wisdom of experienced diplomats from previous administrations. During a visit to Paris, he became reacquainted with Ambassador David K. E. Bruce, a seasoned diplomat who had represented the US in France, Germany, and Britain during the Eisenhower, Kennedy, and Johnson years. During their conversation, Bruce briefed Bush on the slow progress of negotiations to end the Vietnam War. "I was reimpressed with Bruce—his courtly manner, his pedigree, his Virginia gentleman credentials, and yet he had a certain steel about him that I liked," Bush reflected after their meeting.[302]

Bush also met with Ambassador T. Keith Glennan who had served as director of NASA under President Eisenhower. During their conversation, Glennan shared a story about Eisenhower's remarkable sensitivity to people. While discussing space matters, Eisenhower noticed the combative White House correspondent Sarah McClendon sitting nearby. Pausing the meeting, he said, "I have got to invite that woman over here." The remark followed a recent press conference where Eisenhower had sharply "put down" McClendon's question. The anecdote struck a chord with Bush, who recognized the significance of kindness and understanding in a leader.[303]

Bush may have recalled Eisenhower's gesture during his own contentious moment with the press in 1990, as he prepared for a potential war against Saddam Hussein. During a press conference, the president responded to a question from veteran ABC News White House correspondent Ann Compton in "a curt, uncharacteristically gruff way." The following morning, Compton received an envelope from Bush containing an apology, with the initials "GB" and a frown drawn at the bottom.

Recognizing that many of his old friends in Congress were skeptical about the UN's relevance, Bush took the initiative to invite members for a personal briefing on the issues he planned to address. "I know from my own experience in the House that I never really took a good look at the operation here in New York, and I want to be sure you realize that I would like to have you stop in at any time," Bush wrote to his colleagues in the legislative branch. Congresswoman Margaret Heckler, who later become Ronald Reagan's ambassador to Ireland, called Bush's idea "marvelous." She believed his congressional experience would be instrumental in "establishing a broader based understanding of international problems as they exist in the world today."[304]

On the morning of February 26, 1971, Bush officially took his place as the new United States ambassador to the United Nations, receiving the oath of office administered by his friend, Associate Justice of the Supreme Court Potter Stewart. President Nixon referenced Bush's previous Senate defeat, highlighting his new ambassador's ability to turn defeats into opportunities. "The fact that one door has been closed for him opens another door, a door of service for him and also for the United States of America," Nixon said. Grateful for the president's trust, Bush expressed his eagerness for the challenge ahead, acknowledging that "I don't suppose that anything worthwhile is not difficult, and I don't suppose anything worthwhile will not have its frustrations."[305]

In the weeks following his confirmation, Bush made a concerted effort to follow Lodge's advice on engaging with diplomats from all corners of the world. On one such occasion, Bush hosted a small dinner for African ambassadors. Although Third World nations frequently sided with the Soviet Union in the General Assembly, Bush believed that building relationships with these countries was a worthwhile endeavor. "I am convinced that the personal touch can go with these guys.... I know I am going to get clobbered on the votes, but it is worth a try to make them feel at home, and I am now convinced from this limited experience that we can do it," Bush noted after the event. Nixon, closely monitoring his ambassador's progress, expressed his approval at Bush's ability to engage with the diplomatic community. "At the dinner for the Turkish Prime Minister the Foreign Minister spoke glowingly of your work at the UN. He said that of all the American Ambassadors to the UN he had known, you were by far the best because you combined technical competence with great, as he put it, 'heart in heart,'" Nixon wrote on March 22, 1972.[306]

Bush also recognized that an organization can only thrive if its members are genuinely invested in their work. To build a unified team in New York, he believed it was crucial to "be seen and try to express an interest in what everybody in the Mission is doing. If they all feel their work is important, they are bound to produce more," Bush wrote, emphasizing the value of fostering engagement and morale among his colleagues.[307]

Bush aimed to demonstrate that he had the ability to engage with both US allies and opponents. To achieve that objective, he sought to meet with as many members of the UN General Assembly as possible. One example of Bush's personal diplomacy occurred during a surprise visit to the ambassador from Burundi. "I thought the woman [in the office] was going to have a heart attack.... But I knew that word would get all around the United Nations that we recognized and respected the sovereignty and the vote of every country there," Bush recalled to historian Jeffrey Engel.[308]

A key factor behind Bush's successful presidency, especially in the realm of international diplomacy, involved his ability to leverage the extensive relationships he had built during his tenure at the United Nations. "When we really needed something, he'd go to them, and they were inclined to support us because they knew who he was, where he came from, and it just made a world of difference in our diplomacy," recalled National Security Advisor Brent Scowcroft.[309]

As Bush became more comfortable in his role, he immersed himself in what he called "the social whirl." But as demonstrated throughout his political career, he consistently favored substance over ceremony. "The cocktails, the wine, the heavy meal, the whole thing...[is] a total waste of time. It is going to be difficult drawing the line between being polite and courteous and yet not wasting time." However, Bush also took to heart Lodge's advice on improving his guest's interaction during large social events. "The Lodge formula on entertaining seems to be a good one—mix the crowd...don't separate the men and women after dinner," Bush wrote, commenting on the success of one evening.[310]

Bush also utilized other personal qualities during his tenure. Living close to his parents' home in Greenwich, he hosted diplomats for Sunday brunches. He also extended invitations to international colleagues to unwind in the informal atmosphere of Kennebunkport and even took advantage of his uncle Herby Walker's partial ownership of the New York Mets by inviting foreign dignitaries to experience America's favorite pastime. "The United Nations is like a parliamentary body; you're working for votes. I learned that you can't always do it your way," Bush reflected in a 1999 interview with C-SPAN on the lessons he gained from his time in the role. For Bush, cultivating relationships with foreign diplomats became key in building trust that would prove invaluable when he needed their help in navigating a crisis.[311]

Bush enjoyed the role, but it did not come without frustration. While he maintained a good relationship with Secretary of State William Rogers and National Security Advisor Henry Kissinger, the tensions between Nixon's two main foreign policy advisors made effective communication difficult. Bush found the lack of unity disheartening, as neither man allowed him to have any meaningful influence on policymaking.

On several occasions, Bush turned to Kissinger's deputy, Brigadier General Alexander M. Haig Jr., to gather the information necessary to make his position in New York more effective. "The subject of Vietnam, Cambodia, Laos is not in front of the U.N., but it permeates the corridors and is all around us.... [I]t would be useful for me to study any information like this which you might have and then be sure that our own top people, that are dealing with ambassadors across the street, are fully versed in all of this," Bush wrote to the former NATO commander in May 1971.[312]

Bush also began to form views on the most effective ways to achieve policy goals in Washington. While recognizing that cabinet meetings provided access to high-ranking officials, he felt they often lacked meaningful results. Ultimately, Bush concluded that to have a significant impact on foreign policy, one needed a direct relationship with either Kissinger, Rogers, Nixon, or all three. The insight proved invaluable, particularly as Bush started to consider how his own administration would navigate foreign policy, especially in the context of the Cold War.[313]

As Lodge had predicted, one of the major issues that dominated much of Bush's time concerned the admission of the People's Republic of China (PRC) to the United Nations. The Bushes were not unfamiliar with the China issue. During Prescott Bush's 1950 Senate campaign, he criticized President Truman for the loss of China to Mao Tse Tung's communist forces. Similarly, during Bush's unsuccessful Senate bid in 1964, he had pledged support for the United States' withdrawal from the United Nations if Mao's People's Republic of China were admitted.[314]

In July 1971, the situation grew more complicated following Henry Kissinger's secret trip to China, followed by and the announcement that President Nixon had received an invitation to visit Peking (modern-day Beijing). That same year, a growing movement, driven by Third World nations and Soviet-aligned states, gathered momentum in support of admitting the PRC to the United Nations. A committed advocate for Taiwan, Bush worked diligently to counter the efforts of Mao's allies. As the vote approached, he promoted a compromise policy that would grant dual representation: allowing the PRC to assume China's seat on the Security Council while enabling Taiwan to retain its place in the General Assembly. Ever the pragmatic diplomat, Bush aligned himself with Nixon's strategic vision. "Bringing PRC in, in my view, is a move towards reality and I support it, but we must not let a big reality 'muscle out' a smaller reality," he wrote to Congressman William Brock, reaffirming his steadfast support for Taiwan.[315]

Pondering these developments, Bush could only conclude, "I don't know what our China policy in the U.N. will turn out to be, but all the U.N. people feel that the ball game is over. Peking is in and Taiwan is out." In the days after the announcement, Bush observed that many of his colleagues viewed Nixon's move as a brilliant diplomatic maneuver. He recalled the French ambassador's reaction, noting that "the Russians would be climbing the walls, and that it would make for a much more realistic world," Bush wrote in his account of the conversation.[316]

After Nixon agreed to visit China, Bush attended a cabinet meeting where the president chose not to disclose any details on how the initiative developed. Bush, who valued discretion, respected Nixon's decision, writing, "In a matter like this it's better not to know so that you don't inadvertently fowl up these very difficult negotiations." With the United States' decision to embrace Mao's China seeming inevitable, the coalition of nations that Bush had gathered to oppose Chinese admission to the UN collapsed.[317]

Despite the challenging circumstances, Bush remained committed to keeping Taiwan in the General Assembly. As the vote approached, he continued to hope for a favorable outcome. He and Secretary of State William Rogers did everything possible to rally the support of countries that had previously pledged to back the US position. Nevertheless, when the vote finally occurred, the United Nations expelled Taiwan by a narrow margin of 59 to 55.[318]

Following the vote Bush expressed his outrage at the results. "The villains are documented...ones who simply did not do what they said they would do," he wrote in his journal. While Bush acknowledged that Kissinger did not "deliberately sabotage the U.N. vote," he believed the national security advisor saw establishing a relationship with Peking as a higher priority than Taiwan's continued presence in the United Nations.[319]

Bush also believed that Kissinger's ego and his tendency to perceive enemies within the administration hindered the two men's ability to have a more transparent relationship. Bush grew frustrated with Kissinger's difficult temperament and his lack of appreciation for the efforts Bush and his team had made to protect Taiwan's standing in the international community. Although Bush believed Kissinger was "charming and bright...he can be totally dictatorial and rude." Bush had attempted to reassure the mercurial Kissinger he had no other priority than serving the president. "He ought to get that through his head," Bush wrote in his diary.[320]

Even in a disagreeable climate, Bush learned from the experience. In his frustration to try to walk a tightrope between Kissinger and Rogers, Bush realized he could not serve two masters. "Except in the rare circumstances when the president personally intervenes, the UN Ambassador must answer to the Secretary of State," Bush wrote in a collection of letters and writings entitled *All the Best, George Bush*. The tensions Bush faced during his time in New York influenced his decision as president regarding the ambassadorial role and its cabinet-level status. When assembling his foreign policy team, Bush appointed the highly skilled foreign service officer Thomas Pickering to represent the administration at the UN. However, in drawing from his own experiences nearly two decades earlier, Bush decided not to make the UN ambassador a cabinet position.[321]

In the fall of 1972, Bush received the news that his father had been diagnosed with lung cancer. As the former senator's health deteriorated, Bush informed President Nixon of the gravity of the situation. In a handwritten, undated account of their conversation, Bush recalled Nixon's response as being "warm, concerned, decent reaction." The president also tried to contact Senator Bush at New York's Memorial Sloan Kettering but could not reach him. As Bush prepared to leave the Oval Office following their conversation, Nixon stopped him, saying, "George, about the future—you must be an important part of the next administration. I've told our people that."[322]

Prescott Bush died on October 8, 1972. The loss devastated his son, who could only express his sorrow by writing, "my father, my mentor, my hero died. . . ." In a eulogy written by Dorothy Bush and delivered by Reverend Bradford Hastings at Greenwich's Christ Episcopal Church, the elder Bush was recalled as a thoughtful and loving father who saw each of his children as individuals, always ready to support any decision they made and willing to offer advice when asked. These words not only captured the essence of Prescott Bush but reflected the type of father his second son had become.[323]

Over one thousand people attended the service, including prominent figures such as Averell Harriman, New York Mayor John Lindsay, and Yale University President Kingman Brewster. In Washington, President Nixon and senators from both parties offered heartfelt tributes to a man widely regarded as a gentleman who embodied the very best qualities of the Senate. Bush also received a deeply warm condolence letter from Lyndon Johnson. "Your father was one of the finest men to ever serve in the United States Senate. In both his public and private life, he has left a tremendous legacy of goodness and strength of character to his descendants," Johnson wrote in October 1972.[324]

The unwavering love, confidence, and support George Bush received from his father inspired him to seek more from life than just financial success. More importantly, the late senator instilled in him the belief that those born into privilege had a responsibility to serve others and make a meaningful impact in the world. The younger Bush had endeavored to follow his father's guidance by seizing every opportunity that came his way.

Throughout his time at the UN, Bush mirrored many of the approaches his father had used throughout his political career. He built relationships with both allies and adversaries of the United States, advancing the administration's interests without seeking attention or recognition. More significantly, his experience at the United Nations introduced him to the complexities of foreign affairs and a deeper appreciation for the diverse perspectives within the international community.

During challenging times, including the defeat on the China vote, Bush followed his father's example by staying positive and gracious, and showing his staff the importance of preparation, discipline, and commitment. "My Dad was the real inspiration in my life," Bush wrote to Nixon on October 16, 1972. "So often we talked, even in the hospital, of your Presidency—he was in great admiration of your ability to make the tough decision."[325]

To cope with his father's illness and death, Bush dedicated himself to securing the president's reelection. As the University of Virginia Miller Center's Ken Hughes writes, throughout the 1972 campaign, Nixon portrayed himself as a statesman, demonstrated by his landmark visit to China and the signing of the Strategic Arms Limitation Treaty (SALT I) with the Soviet Union. At the same time, his decision to mine North Vietnam's Haiphong harbor reinforced his image as a strong, unwavering leader committed to the fight against communism. The diplomacy of Henry Kissinger further enhanced the administration's success when Kissinger announced on October 26, just days before the 1972 election, that 'peace was at hand,' signaling an agreement between the United States and North Vietnam to end the war.[326]

As in 1968, Nixon took advantage of a deeply divided Democratic Party, which had nominated George McGovern, a progressive senator from South Dakota. Like George Bush, McGovern was a decorated navy pilot who later dedicated himself to public service. Since entering the Senate in 1962, he had become an outspoken critic of US involvement in Vietnam. His campaign slogan, "Come Home, America," called for an immediate withdrawal from the war and advocated a liberal domestic agenda, including the establishment of a national health-care system and the expansion of Social Security.[327]

On Election Day, Nixon secured a decisive victory, capturing over 60 percent of the popular vote and winning every state except Massachusetts. Still, despite Nixon's dominance at the polls, the president remained a curious and distant figure. Although Bush served as the administration's connection to the New York establishment, Nixon continued to hold that world in disdain, often referring to its members as "Ivy League bastards." Nevertheless, Bush maintained a public image of unwavering support and optimism.

Privately, however, as 1973 progressed, he became increasingly unsure about what the future held and whether Nixon would keep his word about giving him a role within the new administration.[328]

CHAPTER 9

The Dark Side of Politics: Chairman, Republican National Committee

Chairman of the Republican National Committee, George Bush, in a meeting with President Nixon and others in the Oval Office. May 22, 1973.

On July 25, 1973, Republican National Committee Chairman George Bush received a handwritten letter from a former House of Representatives colleague, Democratic Congressman Donald Riegle Jr. of Michigan. The note addressed Bush's continued support for President Nixon amid the escalating political scandal known as Watergate. What had initially begun as a break-in at the Democratic National Committee headquarters in Washington, DC, had since unraveled into a national catastrophe that involved several of Nixon's closest aides and had the potential of implicating the president himself.

Riegle, who had switched parties due to his disapproval of Nixon's handling of the Vietnam War and his 1972 reelection campaign, urged Bush to distance himself from the unfolding crisis. "As a friend who would do just about anything for you—Please don't get sucked into Watergate—even indirectly," Riegle warned. "I doubt that Nixon is going to survive- and I really wish you were completely out of the picture.... You're a straight arrow George—but you're traveling with a lot of people who aren't. It is not far-fetched to expect that [Attorney General John] Mitchell, [Nixon Finance Chairman Maurice] Stans, [Assistant to the President for Domestic Affairs John] Ehrlichman, and [White House Chief of Staff H.R.] Haldeman will be going to prison. In fact, if Nixon is forced out, it is likely he could well be indicted, convicted and sentenced to prison. You're caught in a grave and deteriorating situation—and you shouldn't let yourself get sucked into it in any way," Riegle wrote. But Bush's commitment to Nixon did not waver. "I owed Richard Nixon a great deal.... He came to Texas to campaign for me when I first got into elective politics, then gave me the rare opportunity to represent my country on an international level," Bush reflected in 1988.[329]

***

In January 1973, Bush met with President Nixon at Camp David to discuss several potential opportunities in the new administration. Among the possibilities were roles as undersecretary of the Treasury, a high-profile position at the State Department, or chairman of the Republican National Committee (RNC). Bush enjoyed his time at the United Nations, finding diplomacy rewarding. He mused, "If all the other panting candidates for Secretary of State dropped by the wayside—I might get that—a slot which in my current thinking, would be tops." However, Nixon urged Bush to accept the chairmanship of the RNC. "We have a chance to build a new coalition in the next four years, and you're the one who can do it," Nixon said.[330]

The administration faced intense pressure. Six months earlier, police had thwarted a break-in at the Democratic National Committee's headquarters, located in the Watergate apartment complex just two miles from the White House. As the weeks unfolded, reporters led by Bob Woodward and Carl Bernstein of *The Washington Post* discovered that the burglars were linked to the Committee to Reelect the President (CREEP), an organization distinct from the official GOP party apparatus. Over time, it became clear that the break-in represented only one instance in a broader pattern of illegal activities orchestrated by individuals closely tied to Nixon.[331]

Bush's strong reputation, natural ability to build relationships, and unwavering loyalty to the president made him an ideal candidate for the role. When Barbara Bush expressed concern about his decision to accept the offer, Bush's response was simple: "You can't turn a president down." As he weighed the decision, Bush took the same approach he had used during his time at the United Nations: seeking counsel from seasoned political veterans who could help guide him through the complex landscape he would soon navigate.[332]

The first advice Bush received came from his friend Rogers Morton. A generation older, Morton had chaired the RNC from 1969 to 1971 before being appointed secretary of the interior. "When it came to the inner workings of the White House, I valued Rog's judgment more than anyone else's," Bush wrote. Morton believed that for Bush to operate with full independence, he required direct access to the president, which included a seat at cabinet meetings. Seeking further input, Bush consulted his father's longtime friend, Pennsylvania Senator Hugh Scott. The legislator agreed with Morton's assessment. "Insist on it," Scott advised.[333]

On November 21, the day after his conversations with Morton and Scott, Bush incorporated their advice into his acceptance letter to the president. "I can and will, of course, take orders, but I'd like to retain options on the style in which to carry them out.... each person has his own style, his own methods, and if I get too far out of character.... this will not serve you well," Bush wrote.

The president expressed to Secretary of the Treasury George Schultz his confidence that the former UN ambassador possessed the skills necessary to do the job. "A total Nixon man—first.... Doubt if you can do better than Bush," Nixon told Shultz.[334]

Taking over the RNC in January 1973, Bush applied the same principles of diligence and fiscal responsibility that had guided him in business and at the United Nations. Faced with a budget deficit, he streamlined operations by cutting unnecessary staff, flying coach, and driving his own car. The new chairman also asserted his independence by resisting pressure from the White House to use the committee as a platform for attacking those investigating the Watergate scandal.[335]

While responding thoughtfully to angry letters criticizing Nixon, Bush drew on the lessons he learned from his parents about maintaining an optimistic attitude. "Putting it on a very personal basis, everything that my Father stood for in life seems from time to time threatened by the arrogant behavior of a handful of people, but we must look ahead. We must accentuate the positive," Bush wrote in May 1973.[336]

As months went by, Watergate increasingly overshadowed the political landscape, marked by the resignations of several of the president's staff. Bush urged the administration to be more transparent in its discussions of the scandal with Congress. During a meeting with 1964 GOP presidential nominee Senator Barry Goldwater, Bush agreed with the senior legislator's disappointment that Nixon had not sought advice from those with more seasoned political experience. Bush agreed with Goldwater and mentioned the senator's recommendation to Bryce Harlow, a former counselor to Eisenhower, whom Nixon had kept on as a White House advisor.[337]

In June, as chronicled by *The Washington Post*'s Carl Bernstein and Bob Woodward, Nixon's former counsel, John W. Dean III, testified that the president had been informed on thirty-five separate occasions about plans to cover up the Watergate break-in. Though Dean lacked documentary evidence to support his claims, his testimony stunned the nation. A month after Dean's revelations, Bush compiled his thoughts on the Watergate scandal in a twelve-page, handwritten series of notes, which he intended to develop into an op-ed. "I'm troubled and confused by all of this. Troubled because every value I have has been abused by men I have known and, in some cases respected," Bush wrote at the beginning of the document.[338]

Bush often preferred to channel his anger about a situation onto paper rather than express it publicly. The approach often allowed him to maintain a calm and composed demeanor, even during moments of significant stress. "'The enemy list' is absurd—It's dumb politics, but worse, it's just plain wrong," Bush wrote, referring to a record, kept by the White House, of journalists, intellectuals, entertainers, and politicians who publicly opposed the president's policies.[339]

The RNC chairman—who valued the free exchange of ideas and believed in building relationships even with those he disagreed—found the actions of those surrounding President Nixon appalling. "It's dumb because those idiots that put it together were so 'knee jerk' that they fouled it up—they put people on the list who eventually supported the president. They made 'enemies' out of friends….at a time we needed friends. That's just dumb. It's wrong because there's a fundamental principle involved here…. It offends one's sense of democracy to think that opposition should be equated with enmity," Bush wrote. Despite his anger at the way the media treated the president, he believed their criticism, though harsh, came from a place of patriotism. "I can't stand some of the columnists on the [enemies] list. They hate Nixon and they gut him relentlessly at every turn…. but enemies no," Bush wrote.[340]

While Bush also had a low opinion of those Democrats that opposed the President's policies and "want[ed] desperately to see us Republicans whip those members of Congress who made the list," he believed "they are opponents not 'enemies—and they love America as much as we do." But Bush's anger went beyond the adversarial relationship the administration had developed with the media or the legislative branch. The RNC chairman also found himself "troubled" by the lack of remorse shown by those involved in the scandal. "There was…no judgment, no heart ache, the nagging voice of conscience...seems to have had its vocal cords severed." Bush believed that those who orchestrated the break-in and other illegal activities linked to CREEP not only lacked integrity and were indifferent to the weight of their responsibilities but also lacked humility. "[T]oo much power passed to those who never knew victory nor defeat," Bush wrote.[341]

Even as the scandal continued to intensify, Bush remained steadfast in his loyalty to the man in the White House. On several occasions, Bush had asked Nixon directly if he had any involvement in the cover-up. Each time, Nixon looked Bush in the eye and firmly denied the accusations. "I believe in our President—some of it is because I believe in the Presidency and what it does to a man. I know this man, I know of his strengths, and I guess I know of his weaknesses...." While Bush acknowledged Nixon's flaws, he believed they were no worse than those of others. He admired Nixon for his aspiration to "greatness," driven by both "pride" and a genuine sense of service and respect for office. For these reasons and more, Bush wrote, "I don't believe John Dean III. I do believe President Nixon."[342]

Writing journal entries provided Bush a way to process complex problems like the Watergate scandal. Throughout his career, he also used journaling as a tool to channel his frustrations with the media, political opponents, foreign leaders, and others with whom he disagreed.

On July 16, 1973, the turmoil of Watergate intensified following the revelation from former Nixon aide Alexander Butterfield that the president secretly recorded conversations with aides and associates, on the telephone and in the White House. Despite the stunning news, Bush remained resolute. "This isn't the time to quit, it's not a time to jump sideways, it's not a time for me to wring my hands on the sidelines," Bush wrote to a friend in response to suggestions that he run for governor of Texas.[343]

There is no doubt that Bush admired Nixon deeply, appreciating the kindness and loyalty the president had shown him by offering him a position in the administration after his defeat in the 1970 Senate election. Kindness and loyalty were core values he regarded as fundamental to good character. However, his admiration for Nixon and his reluctance to acknowledge the darker sides of his character clouded Bush's judgment, making it more difficult for him to take Congressman Riegle's warnings to heart, even though they were given with Bush's best interests at mind.[344]

Bush's struggles with Watergate were also influenced by the very drive and discipline that had contributed to his success. A man who rarely chose the path of least resistance, Bush often believed that his perseverance could overcome any challenge. His decision to leave a comfortable life on Wall Street for an uncertain future in Texas, and his dive into politics in a state where the GOP had little presence, were prime examples of that mindset. These same qualities of determination and resilience were traits he admired in his commander in chief.

As Bush continued to display his loyalty for Nixon, those like Riegle worried that the public might perceive Bush as "wittingly or unwittingly – being used to perpetuate the cover-up," a perception that could have serious consequences for his friend's future political career.[345]

By May 1974, the turmoil within the administration led Bush to question whether he could continue supporting a man "to whom I owe loyalty but to whom I can no longer serve with the same sense of inner drive because the tapes have offended me so much," Bush wrote. Like many other dedicated Republicans, Nixon's irrational and hateful language on those recordings deeply disturbed Bush.

With cynicism and negativity consuming Washington, Bush shifted his focus to the accomplishments of his children. At the end of July, he wrote a heartfelt letter to his four sons, emphasizing the importance of love, gratitude, devotion to family and country, and pride in the values they had learned. He was particularly proud that his sons had come to judge people not by their color or creed, but by their character.[346]

Bush emphasized that even amid the growing cynicism, serving the country remained one of the highest callings and sacrifices one could make. "Dad [Prescott Bush] helped inculcate into us a sense of public service I'd like you boys to save some time in your lives for cranking something back in." Bush wrote to his sons, George, Jeb, Neil, and

Marvin. While much of the letter contained Bush's unfiltered thoughts about the president and his associates, it also conveyed the knowledge he had acquired during his time as chair of the RNC. These experiences shaped his understanding of leadership, loyalty, and the importance of staying true to one's values, even in the face of adversity.[347]

Bush's letter contained blunt comments on Watergate, but it also revealed the deep admiration Bush had for Nixon's resilience. Despite intense criticism from both inside and outside the government, Nixon's determination to press on in the face of adversity left a lasting impression on Bush. He encouraged his children to remain steadfast in their convictions, regardless of the challenges they encountered. "Listen to your conscience. Don't be afraid not to join the mob—if you feel inside it's wrong," Bush wrote.[348]

Bush's emphasis on the importance of conscience had played a critical role in his patrician upbringing. As author Richard Brookhiser noted in an article for *Time* in 1993, "When a Wasp thought of his duty to the moral law, the guide he consulted was his own conscience." For Bush and others raised to focus on promoting the common good, one's conscience acted as "a stern interior monitor." But though Bush strongly believed in standing by one's convictions, even in the face of great opposition, his inability to reconcile his view of Nixon until the very end of Watergate placed him in a potentially precarious position.

Bush also believed in seeing the best in people, offering empathy or guidance even when others disagreed with his approach. "Don't confuse being 'soft' with seeing the other guy's point of view." While he firmly believed that individuals were accountable for their actions, Bush also contended that Nixon, despite not being aware of the break-in, had surrounded himself with individuals more interested in using the presidency for personal gain than for the good of the nation. "Power accompanied by arrogance is very dangerous. It's particularly dangerous when men with no real experience have it—for they can abuse our great institutions," Bush wrote.[349]

Bush also emphasized to his children that, beyond family, he viewed friendship as one of life's greatest treasures. "Avoid self-righteously turning on a friend, but have your friendship mean enough that you would be willing to share with your friend your judgment. Don't assign away your judgment to achieve power." Bush likely drew this insight from his observations of Nixon's introverted nature. "He is unable to get close to people. It's almost like he's afraid he'll be reamed in some way. People who respect him and want to be friends get only so close—and then it is clear—no more!" This reflection connects to Bush's earlier conversations with Bryce Harlow, Barry Goldwater, and others in discussing Nixon's hesitance to seek advice, not only from experienced individuals but also long-time allies with whom he had built deep relationships throughout his career.[350]

During the Watergate scandal, while Nixon refused to seek counsel from experienced professionals, Bush found himself relying more on Robert Strauss, the chairman of the Democratic National Committee. The two shared a longstanding friendship; both being Texans, the two men had known each other since the 1950s. A lawyer and colleague of James A. Baker III, as well as a veteran of local and national politics, Strauss understood many of the struggles Bush faced. "It was a friendship made during adversity, and that is what I think makes it so strong and special to me," Strauss said. Over the years, Strauss became a trusted friend and advisor, and in 1991, Bush appointed him ambassador to the Soviet Union.[351]

Throughout the crisis, the Dallas lawyer could be relied on to offer a sympathetic ear or an optimistic perspective, assuring Bush that things would eventually work out. While a prominent opponent of Nixon, Strauss held enough respect for Bush not to publicly criticize him. "He was a friend, but more important, he didn't have any part in Watergate," Strauss said.[352]

On August 5, 1974, Bush listened to a tape featuring a lengthy conversation between Nixon and his chief of staff, H. R. Haldeman. Recorded just six days after the break-in, the conversation revealed Nixon's attempt to use the CIA to obstruct the FBI's investigation. The revelation devastated Bush. "I saw that he had not leveled with the American people. You don't look your cabinet in the eye and say one thing, and then have it turn out to be something completely opposite," Bush recalled in an interview with C-SPAN in 1999.[353]

Outraged, Bush considered resigning and joining many of his GOP colleagues in urging the president to step down. However, his belief in the system the founders had established led him to conclude that "this system must work, should be permitted to work fairly…somebody has got to pick up the pieces." Despite his decision to remain as chairman, Bush ultimately accepted the fact Nixon's presidency was coming to an end. "I do not feel the President can survive," Bush wrote in his journal that evening.[354]

Bush acknowledged that Nixon had achieved significant accomplishments. However, the revelation of "the smoking gun"—the conversation between Nixon and Haldeman—shattered his ability to view the president favorably. "I felt deeply betrayed by his lie of the day before. The man is amoral. He has a different sense than the rest of people," Bush wrote in a journal entry. Disheartened by the actions of a man who had done so much for him, Bush sat down on August 7 and urged Nixon to resign. "My own view is that I would now ill serve a President, whose massive accomplishments I will always respect and whose family I love, if I did not now give you my judgment.… This letter is made much more difficult because of the gratitude I will always have for you." The next day, Nixon announced his resignation.[355]

While Bush's time serving under Nixon represented one of the most challenging periods of his career, it also provided him with valuable experience in several administrative areas. Though he had previously led his own company, his tenure as chairman of the RNC taught him how to manage a large political organization. As chairman, Bush traveled across the country, engaging with numerous GOP members, many of whom held differing views from his own. Like his time at the United Nations, Bush's role allowed him to increase his visibility through editorial meetings with the media and to refine his public speaking skills, including his stump speeches. These experiences proved instrumental in his eventual run for president six years later.

41

Through the Watergate experience, Bush learned the importance of surrounding himself with a broad network of reliable, experienced, and supportive friends. When he became president in 1989, he chose individuals for his cabinet whom he had known for decades—seasoned professionals in their fields, many of whom had also held elective office. "Nixon seemed to have few real friends," George W. Bush later reflected. "A cost of his isolation was that he had no one to keep him grounded or talk him out of his worst instincts. By contrast, my father was extroverted, optimistic, and determined to see the best in people."[356]

Most importantly, America's national crisis did not deter Bush from continuing to seek his next opportunity in public service. In August 1974, Bush's friend, Congressman Gerald R. Ford, succeeded Nixon in the Oval Office. As Bush prepared for an upcoming meeting with the new president, he hoped that, despite the challenges surrounding Watergate, Ford would offer him a position that brought him closer to the White House.

CHAPTER 10

A Whole New World: China and the CIA

George Bush with Henry Kissinger in China. 1975.

In the fall of 1974, now the United States liaison to the People's Republic of China, George Bush clashed with his superior Henry Kissinger, who was serving at the time as both secretary of state and national security advisor. Bush admired Kissinger's deep historical knowledge and command of international affairs. But at the same time, he also expressed discomfort with the nation's chief diplomat's dominant and highly centralized approach to foreign policy. In a diary entry that year, Bush questioned the wisdom of such concentrated authority: "I am wondering if it is good for our country to have as much individual diplomacy.... Isn't the President best served if the important matters are handled by more than one person?"[357]

As the public face of the Ford administration in China, Bush aspired to project a more informal image, opting for camaraderie over hierarchy. Whether playing tennis with colleagues or riding a bike with his first name emblazoned on the back, he saw these gestures as part of a broader effort to build trust and confidence. Bush believed facilitating an atmosphere of ease and openness served as a more effective method than the climate of fear and intimidation Kissinger cultivated among his subordinates. "People on his staff are scared to death of Kissinger. It is unbelievable," Bush observed of the former academic. "Nobody is willing to bite the bullet and speak up."[358]

While Bush observed Kissinger manage the nation's international agenda, he used his time in Peking to reflect on decisions he might make if placed in charge of navigating US foreign affairs. He drew lessons from the nation's failure in Vietnam, concluding the country should avoid conflicts "where we'd have no support from the American people." Though he supported American internationalism, he felt US involvement in the affairs of other nations did not solve every problem. But "we have got to be realistic," We have to have our eyes open," he wrote in early 1975.[359]

***

On August 9, 1974, Bush attended President Nixon's farewell address to his staff in the East Room of the White House. Despite the many acts of kindness Nixon had shown him and the significant positions he had entrusted to him, Bush remained deeply perplexed by the man who had played such a prominent role in American public life for over twenty-five years. His confusion grew as he watched Nixon during his final moments in office, addressing the staff who had stood by him through the years. "One couldn't help but look at the family…and think of his accomplishments and then think of the shame and wonder, what kind of man is this, really." he recalled.[360]

Bush may have owed Nixon for rescuing him from political obscurity six years earlier, but that gratitude could not outweigh the crimes

Nixon had committed or the disdain he had shown for his supporters and the nation. "No morality—kicking his friends in those tapes—all of them. Gratuitous abuse," Bush wrote. After Nixon's departure to California, Bush watched as Gerald Ford adjusted to his new role in the Oval Office.[361]

A graduate of the University of Michigan and the Yale Law School, Gerald Ford had a long and distinguished political career that included the position of minority leader in the House of Representatives. With a moderate temperament and extensive government experience, Ford returned stability and integrity to the presidency. He had known Prescott Bush during his time in Congress, and he was a frequent golf partner of the senator. In 1967, when George Bush first arrived in Congress, Ford also played a key role in helping him secure a spot on the Ways and Means Committee. Bush admired Ford, seeing in him qualities reminiscent of Dwight Eisenhower. "He is an Ike without the heroics but he has that decency the country is crying out for right now," Bush wrote.[362]

During a meeting on Sunday, August 11, Bush thanked Ford for understanding the pressure Bush and his colleagues had endured at the Republican National Committee. Most importantly he appreciated Ford's quiet self-confidence and a refusal to stand on ceremony. "Let's be informal," the new president suggested to Bush as they began their conversation.[363]

Much of the talk during the meeting focused on the selection of a vice president. Aware that Ford had Bush on a list along with several other candidates, he asked Ford if he could "give him my credentials as well as shortcomings and then try to be somewhat objective." As the discussion continued and Ford asked about the merits of other potential candidates, Bush became increasingly uncomfortable. Despite his deep desire for the vice presidency, he struggled to maintain an air of impartiality. "[A]nd in the back of my mind was it sounds like you're building yourself up, making your own case all the time," Bush wrote. He also emphasized to Ford that the nation had suffered a tremendous trauma, and Ford needed to define his presidency by signaling a new direction for the country.[364]

However, despite Ford's famous declaration that "our long national nightmare is over," the Watergate scandal had severely eroded public trust in institutions and the experts who governed them. A poll in 1973 showed the nation's confidence in the executive branch had plummeted from 41 percent in 1966 to just 19 percent. That decline in faith also reflected voter turnout.

Over time, as moderate voters became disillusioned with politics, the ideological wings of both parties filled the void. Voters began increasingly seeking candidates from outside the political establishment and who championed ideology over pragmatism.[365]

Bush believed Ford needed to establish a new tone for the nation. On the matter of the vice presidency, he emphasized the importance of selecting someone who could heal divisions and unite the country. Ford valued Bush's candor and expressed his appreciation by warmly putting an arm around him as their meeting concluded. As Bush left the White House, he reflected, "My God, what a mammoth difference between the man I served…with I hope total dedication and this wonderfully warm, uncomplicated, decent human being. If he gets a break on some of these major issues he will indeed be a great President."[366]

As President Ford conducted a broad search to fill the vice presidency, George Bush emerged as a leading candidate. Young, politically seasoned, and known for his credentials as a mainstream conservative, the Texan drew support from both the GOP's right wing as well as southern Democrats, who still held considerable sway in Congress. Pat Buchanan, a former Nixon speechwriter and briefly an advisor to the Ford White House, favored New York Governor Nelson Rockefeller, a liberal Republican, whom he saw as the strongest choice. Although both Buchanan and Ford advisor Bryce Harlow viewed Bush as a highly credible option, they acknowledged that Rockefeller's national prominence and deep executive experience could offer the administration distinct advantages.[367]

Six days later, Bush received word that President Ford had selected Nelson Rockefeller as his vice president. Though Bush had pledged his full support for whatever decision Ford made, his natural competitiveness made it hard to hide the disappointment of being passed over for the role. "Yesterday was an enormous personal disappointment. For valid reasons, we made the finals (valid reasons I mean a lot of Hill, RNC, & letter support), and so the defeat was more intense," he wrote to James Baker. Yet, even in moments of personal and professional setback, Bush remained grateful for the many friends who had stood by him. "None did more than you to help me with a problem that burned my soul and conscience," he wrote warmly to his friend of nearly two decades.[368]

Two days following Rockefeller's announcement, Bush returned to Washington to meet with Ford about a position within the administration. "What do you want?" Ford asked. Bush raised the possibility of several positions, including secretary of commerce or chief of staff, both of which the president politely rejected. Recognizing Bush's interest in foreign affairs, Ford suggested he serve as ambassador to Great Britain or as a liaison to the People's Republic of China. When Bush mentioned that he had considered returning to private life, Ford interrupted him, saying, "I don't want to lose your talents." After discussing the options with his family, Bush decided to accept the position in China.[369]

Serving as the nation's representative in Peking was not Bush's first choice, but he saw it as an opportunity. He believed the assignment was "important to our future and a bigger diplomatic challenge than even Great Britain or France." More than anything, Bush valued Ford's confidence and warmth. The president's qualities of fundamental decency, self-assurance, and goodwill were critical in guiding Ford's decision to pardon Nixon for his role in Watergate, a choice Bush believed essential in helping the nation recover from one of its darkest moments.[370]

Bush saw China as an appointment with potential. "A new China was emerging, and the relationship between the United States and the People's Republic would be crucial in the years to come, not just in terms of Asian, but of worldwide American policy," he later wrote. Though the position took him far from the nation's center of power, the experience allowed him to immerse himself in a new culture while applying the skills he had honed as a businessman, diplomat, and politician. "Many of the people here...served at the United Nations. I also feel that the Party

Chairmanship didn't hurt a bit. It gives me some insight into our own domestic political matters that can perhaps be passed along to the policy makers," Bush wrote to Reg Murphy of *The Atlanta Constitution.*[371]

Although Nixon's visit to China years earlier had opened a new chapter in American foreign policy, the two nations still lacked formal diplomatic relations. Many Americans harbored deep resentment toward Chairman Mao, for overthrowing Chiang Kai-shek's nationalists and for opposing the United States in the wars in Korea and Vietnam. Many Americans, particularly on the right, held a deep dislike for Mao's brutality during the Cultural Revolution, which targeted intellectuals and anyone he believed opposed his vision of Communism. When Bush arrived in China, the Cultural Revolution, begun in 1966, had yet to reach its conclusion.[372]

For many, an American diplomatic post in China seemed like a dead end. The position lacked ambassadorial status, and under State Department protocol, Bush had no authority to attend official diplomatic events. These restrictions stemmed largely from Secretary of State Henry Kissinger's tight control over US-China policy. While Bush respected protocol, his competitive nature led him to believe that complacency achieved nothing. "[M]y hyper-adrenaline, political instincts tell me that the fun of this job is going to be to try to do more, make more contacts," he wrote at the start of his *China Diary.*[373]

From the moment he arrived in Peking, Bush approached his role with the same strategy he had used at the United Nations. Whether or not he succeeded in forging deep connections with Chinese officials, he believed that action and effort were what truly mattered. "Bar and I have been bicycling around Peking like mad," he wrote to Charles Bartlett. "[B]ut we are going to be hanging in there," he assured the journalist.[374]

After the exhaustion of Watergate, the China assignment gave Bush a renewed sense of energy and purpose. Despite lacking an official diplomatic title, he believed China had the potential to become a major geopolitical force. If he could gain insight into their thinking, the experience might position him for a future high-level foreign policy role. "I am learning and doing in a very important area of our foreign policy. Believe me, it is exciting," he wrote to an acquaintance.[375]

Against Secretary of State Kissinger's recommendation, Bush informed the State Department that he would attend events hosted by foreign embassies to commemorate their national days of celebration. While he knew these formal gatherings offered little insight into Chinese policymaking, he saw them as opportunities to build relationships within the diplomatic community. "You'd get to see what they called a responsible person who was going to be the top guy representing China at the Hungarian National Day…and you'd get to say a few words with him, and sidle up to him," Bush wrote to Congressman John Rhodes.[376]

Bush had no objection to following Kissinger's directives. At the same time, he also had no hesitation in communicating directly with President Ford when he believed political instincts could help resolve a foreign policy issue. "Please pass the following to the President. I hope it will be shared only with SecState…it is pure politics, but I feel strongly about it.… I have a better feel for what is happening at home. It is [Rog Morton's] impression and mine that there is little focus in the US on the political aspects of our trip to China," Bush wrote in the spring of 1975.[377]

Despite being unable to form deep friendships with Chinese diplomats, Bush remained persistent. Bicycling through Peking, he believed that wearing accessories like a People's Liberation Army cap or a Marlboro Country wool jacket helped create a relatable image among the Chinese people. "I get the feeling that the Chinese like the feeling that the U.S. ambassador is not some stuffy guy above everyone else," he observed. Whether effective or not, Bush hoped that his style of personal diplomacy would foster a sense of goodwill between China and the United States.[378]

Despite Bush's affable nature, he made little progress in earning the trust of Chinese officials. Besides a brief interaction with future leader Deng Xiaoping, his overall engagement with China's political class remained limited. Reflecting on his efforts, Bush wrote, "I've tried to give the right impression of America here…tried to move around in the diplomatic community; tried to increase our contacts with the Chinese;

tried to have interesting people from the States here; and tried to learn and make suggestions to Washington."[379]

The challenges Bush faced during his year in China proved both rewarding and intellectually stimulating. Being far from the turbulence of Washington gave him the opportunity to reflect on broad policy questions and explore potential solutions. "Where is our ideology?... Where is our principle? What indeed do we stand for? These things must be made clear," he wrote, grappling with key policy considerations during his time in China.[380]

Bush's understanding of international affairs grew through observing and listening to Henry Kissinger. While he undoubtedly shared the secretary's realpolitik philosophy, that nations act primarily out of their own self-interest, he found Kissinger's unwillingness to consider alternative viewpoints troubling. The experience with Kissinger taught Bush a lesson, one that he carried into his own presidency. "[Bush] wanted open discussion in his presence, and he consciously cultivated as many varied opinions as possible," noted Jeffrey Engel, editor of Bush's *China Diary*. Unlike Kissinger's rigid and intimidating leadership style, Bush's warm and approachable demeanor inspired those around him and encouraged them to speak candidly, sharing their true perspectives.[381]

Bush's recognition that he did not have all the answers and needed to surround himself with experts from diverse backgrounds stemmed directly from observing Kissinger's reluctance to share information with colleagues. "What he [Bush] learned from Kissinger was 'don't' depend on only one single voice, however good that one voice is.... What [Bush] wanted was to hear strong people, knowledgeable people, argue points of view in front of him," National Security Advisor Brent Scowcroft explained in a 2007 interview.[382]

While Bush deepened his understanding of international affairs and diplomatic strategy, he grew increasingly frustrated by his inability to build meaningful relationships with Chinese officials, who remained wary of him. A man of action, he thrived on missions that demanded both responsibility and leadership. That sense of purpose reignited when, on November 1, 1975, Bush received a telegram from Kissinger informing him that Ford intended to nominate him as the new director of the Central Intelligence Agency. Bush recognized that despite formidable challenges that came with the job, it offered another meaningful and potentially rewarding opportunity.[383]

Bush considered the president's offer at a time when the nation's chief intelligence agency had reached a low point. He had followed the recent shocking revelations of the CIA's covert operations, which included assassinations of foreign leaders and the overthrow of governments deemed threats to US interests. Many of these disturbing details emerged during investigative hearings led by Democratic Senator Frank Church. The findings were so damaging that President Ford issued an order requiring the agency to submit to strict congressional oversight, effectively ending its ability to operate independently.[384]

Bush remained uncertain about whether he wanted the position. The CIA post offered valuable administrative experience. But following his tenure at the Republican National Committee, Bush wondered if he wanted to accept the challenge of repairing an organization that had reached its nadir. Another consideration concerned his own political future: He believed the job represented another political dead end. Having harbored presidential ambitions since the 1960s, Bush recognized that the CIA's tarnished reputation could complicate his chances if he ever decided to run for president.[385]

Despite those ambitions, Bush's strong sense of duty ultimately prevailed. "When the cable came in, I thought of Big Dad—what would he do? … I think he would have said, "It's your duty." It is my duty, and I'll do it," Bush wrote to his four siblings.[386]

In his formal response to Kissinger about the new opportunity, Bush again referenced the late senator as the model he aspired to emulate. "Henry, you did not know my father. The President did. My dad inculcated into his sons a set of values that have served me well in my own short public life. One of those values quite simply is that one should serve his country and his President." He noted that during his time at the UN and the Republican National Committee, having access to the president had been crucial to his success. "I would not abuse this access, but I would want to know it is there at all times," Bush wrote to Kissinger on November 2, 1975.[387]

Bush remained concerned about the impact the controversial position would have on his family. The nation's defeat in Vietnam, Nixon's resignation over Watergate, and the disturbing revelations about the American intelligence community had caused widespread cynicism toward the country's institutions. "This new job will be full of turmoil and controversy and Mum and I know that it will not make things easy for you," Bush wrote to his children. "There is ugliness and turmoil swirling around the agency obscuring its fundamental importance to our country. I feel I must try to help."[388]

Bush understood the immense responsibility the position carried but also recognized his lack of experience in the intelligence field. Always valuing knowledge as his most powerful asset, Bush contacted outgoing Director of Central Intelligence William Colby. With over three decades of service as an intelligence officer, Colby's knowledge of how the agency operated, as well as the culture that existed among its employees, made him an ideal person to cultivate. "I would appreciate enormously the chance to have some good long chats with you," Bush wrote to the spymaster in November 1975.[389]

Not everyone held Colby in high regard, including Bush's former boss, Richard Nixon.

In exile at his home in San Clemente, California, the former president advised Bush that he could not "give away the store in assuring members of the Senate Committee that everything the CIA does in the future will be an open book." While progressive voices called for limiting the agency's power, Nixon argued that the United States needed to maintain a strong, effective intelligence network. "We can expect that the covert activities of those who oppose us…will be enormously stepped up in the months and years ahead," the former president wrote. Bush fully supported his old boss's view as he prepared for his hearings before the Senate Intelligence Committee, scheduled for the second week of December.[390]

Despite a tense confirmation process, Bush ultimately received congressional approval after Ford made a formal promise not to consider Bush as his running mate for the 1976 election. Frustrated, Bush understood that he had to prioritize the best interests of the nation over his own political ambitions. "I know it's unfair, but you don't have much of a choice if we are to get on with the job of rebuilding and strengthening the agency," Bush explained to the president. Nonetheless, he remained deeply offended by those who questioned whether he would put politics before the nation's security. "I would simply say that it gets back to character and it gets back to integrity," Bush asserted during his Senate hearing, reaffirming his commitment to the role.[391]

Bush's desire to succeed became evident in remarks following his swearing in as director of central intelligence. "I want this job. I want to do it well," Bush declared on January 30, 1976. While he recognized his lack of intelligence experience, he viewed his primary responsibility as restoring the morale of the men and women dedicated to safeguarding the security of the United States.[392]

During his tenure, Bush consistently praised the agency's employees for their patriotism and pledged to shield operatives from exposure by domestic or foreign sources. He demonstrated his loyalty not just through words but also through concrete actions in support of those he served with. The measures included keeping his office in the agency's compound in Langley, Virginia, eating lunch in the staff cafeteria, and jogging on the agency running track. Bush also visited intelligence stations around the world. At each stop, the director expressed his gratitude to those who were engaged in what President John F. Kennedy called "the long twilight struggle" against totalitarianism. While these gestures may have appeared small, each sent a powerful signal to the members of the intelligence community that the new director supported them and their mission.[393]

As Bush familiarized himself with the intelligence process, he continued to immerse himself in learning about the agency's past and future. In addition to engaging with the agency's skilled staff, Bush sought the guidance of Averell Harriman, a strong supporter of the CIA, inviting

Harriman to lunch in the summer of 1976. During the visit, Harriman delivered a speech to the agency's personnel on the critical importance of their work, also affirming Bush's view that, like foreign policy, intelligence should remain "non-partisan." A firm believer in the integrity of institutions, Harriman expressed his dissatisfaction with what he called "the hysterical tide" of negativity that had threatened to undermine the agency's effectiveness.[394]

Bush also invited Robert Hopkins to attend and speak at the event. The son of Harry Hopkins, a close friend and advisor to President Franklin D. Roosevelt, the younger Hopkins had a reputation as a seasoned agency veteran with extensive experience in covert operations in Europe. By having both Harriman and Hopkins speak to the next generation of intelligence analysts, Bush connected the agency's historical contributions during World War II to its ongoing importance in the Cold War era.[395]

Bush also made a concerted effort to build relationships with members of the Senate Intelligence Committee, who were critical of the agency's methods, objectives, and lack of transparency. Throughout his year as director, he addressed the committee on fifty-one separate occasions. Additionally, he hosted Senator Church and other congressional members at his home to discuss intelligence matters. These informal gatherings, which included other intelligence officials, allowed Church and his colleagues to see Bush's dedication to working across the political aisle, with the goal of ensuring national security.[396]

Committed to remain politically neutral in his role, Bush provided in-depth intelligence briefings to the relatively unknown Democratic presidential nominee, Georgia Governor Jimmy Carter, during the 1976 election. On the Republican side, President Ford faced a nomination challenge from former California Governor Ronald Reagan. Ford, a mainstream conservative, believed in welcoming a diversity of views within the Republican Party, which aligned with the argument Bush had made after his 1964 Senate defeat.[397]

However, many conservatives were dissatisfied with Ford's pragmatic domestic policies and his approach to continuing Nixon's policy of détente with the Soviet Union. Reagan vocalized those concerns at the 1975 Conservative Political Action Conference, when he called for a party composed of "no pale pastels, but bold colors which make it unmistakably clear where we stand on all the issues troubling the people."[398]

To secure the nomination, Ford adjusted his stance on key issues like abortion and other matters that resonated with right-leaning voters. In a further attempt to placate conservatives, he replaced his Eastern liberal vice president, Nelson Rockefeller, with staunch Kansas conservative Senator Robert J. Dole. Although Ford narrowly clinched the nomination, Reagan's strong challenge fractured the party, which played a role in Jimmy Carter's slim victory in the general election.[399]

Like the Goldwater surge in 1964, Reagan's insurgent 1976 campaign represented another significant moment in the rise of the right. As Geoffrey Kabaservice observes, "85% of convention delegates had been bound to candidates in primary elections or conventions in 1976 versus 48% in 1968." The point illustrated the commitment of ideologically driven Republicans who nearly tipped the nomination to "Reagan, due to the Party's shift towards "organizational discipline."[400]

Reagan's campaign, much like Goldwater's, reflected the belief among many conservatives that Ford and Bush represented a Republican Party lacking true conservative principles. Right-wing activist Paul Weyrich captured the frustration of disenchanted Republicans by describing party's moderates as "effete gentlemen of the northeastern Establishment." Weyrich contended that the GOP had forsaken its core principles in favor of compromise over conviction. The criticism reflected longstanding conservative frustrations dating back to Eisenhower's "Middle Way" philosophy, which emphasized party balance and bipartisan solutions to national challenges.[401]

Ronald Reagan's formidable primary challenge, as well as lingering public outrage over Ford's pardon of Richard Nixon, significantly weakened Ford's campaign. Robert A. Strong of the University of Virginia Miller Center also noted that the country's struggle with high inflation led many to question Ford's ability to lead effectively, despite his extensive experience in the House of Representatives. In contrast, Jimmy Carter, the little-known governor of Georgia, gained momentum precisely because he stood outside the Washington establishment. His campaign slogan, "A Leader for Change," struck a chord with voters disillusioned by the Vietnam War and disheartened by the Watergate scandal. Carter's clean-cut image, strong family values, and repeated vow never to lie to the American people proved crucial in securing his victory over Ford in November 1976.

Following Carter's narrow victory, Bush expressed interest in remaining as the director of Central Intelligence. When Carter declined Bush's request, Bush told former President Nixon at the end of 1976 that the new president "should have someone here who has his total confidence and who will have total access to him." As Bush prepared to return to private life, he could look back on a public service career marked by significant achievements.[402]

In Washington and Peking, Bush demonstrated strong leadership, keen analytical skills, and an ability to manage both policy and personnel effectively. Despite the turmoil of Watergate and Vietnam, he had earned the confidence and loyalty of those he worked with. Through personal diplomacy and an insatiable curiosity, he cultivated valuable relationships, deepened his understanding of government administration, and played a key role in restoring the morale and reputation of an agency vital to national security.

Bush developed a deep admiration for the CIA and the dedicated individuals who served within it. Years later, looking back on his tenure there, he remarked, "You learn what the intelligence community really is. You learn what it can do and what it can't, and what it should not be asked to do. You know the importance of human intelligence, and you know the limitations of human intelligence."[403]

As Bush wrapped up his final responsibilities as CIA director, his ambitions for higher office remained. During his last intelligence briefing with the president-elect, the conversation shifted to intelligence issues that potentially could require attention by 1985. With a knowing smile, Carter quipped, "I don't need to worry about that. By then, George will be President and he can take care of it." Bush responded with a good-natured grin. Even as he prepared to return to Houston, Bush already had begun to develop the foundations of a strategy that would eventually turn Carter's comment from a witticism into a reality.[404]

CHAPTER 11

Working with Reagan: Vice President

Vice President George Bush and President Ronald Reagan at a Press Club Dinner. February 5, 1981.

On the final morning of the 1980 presidential campaign, George Bush and Ronald Reagan sat side by side in a television studio, preparing to deliver their closing message to the American people. Though known for his communication skills, Reagan rarely appeared at his best early in the morning. As he began speaking, the former actor immediately realized he lacked the confident delivery the public had come to expect. "I'm awful," he admitted to aides Michael Deaver and Stuart Spencer.[405]

Then, like a great athlete aware of the importance of the moment, Reagan rose to the occasion. Over the next thirty minutes, Bush sat in amazement as Reagan delivered the address without a single mistake. "Bush watched him do it with a look of awe—just awe—on his face," Spencer recalled.[406]

At that moment, the vice-presidential nominee recognized the power of Reagan's ability to connect with the public, a skill that Bush, despite hard work, never achieved. "President Bush was action-oriented and didn't place much emphasis on communication," recalled aide David Bates. While Bush struggled with his oratory, Reagan had honed his speaking skills through years in Hollywood and as a spokesperson for General Electric, where he learned the importance of refining his speeches until they felt effortless. That training, combined with meticulous preparation, allowed Reagan to effectively convey his administration's policies to the public. Although Bush never matched Reagan's oratorical prowess, the two men respected each other for their shared dedication to preparation and hard work.[407]

***

George Bush constructed his 1980 presidential campaign on the pillars of character and competence. Positioning himself as "A President We Won't Have to Train," he highlighted his strong values and judgment, as well as the extensive expertise he had gained in both domestic and foreign policy. "My experience near the center of action—Congress, the United Nations, the Republican National Committee, China, the CIA—had been extensive. I'd seen the inner workings of the White House... and developed my own ideas about how it ought to run," Bush reflected in 1987. While many considered Ronald Reagan, the charismatic yet staunchly ideological sixty-nine-year-old former California governor, as the frontrunner for the Republican nomination, Bush presented himself as a leader who, like his father, believed in governing through consensus.[408]

Bush argued that the nation required a seasoned leader who possessed the necessary skills to tackle the challenges facing the United States. In the aftermath of Watergate and the end of the Vietnam War, public confidence in government institutions remained severely shaken. By 1980, the American people were under siege as violent crime rates soared a staggering 76 percent.[409] Economically, the nation faced a mounting hardship as unemployment rose from just over 4 percent in the early 1970s to more than 7 percent by 1980. Compounding the woes, the cost of goods and services had surged by over 8 percent, more than double the rate of inflation a decade earlier. These challenges, along with the Organization of the Petroleum Exporting Countries (OPEC) decision during the 1970s to reduce the supply of oil, caused gas prices to soar, further increasing public doubts about President Jimmy Carter's ability to effectively manage the nation's domestic affairs.[410]

Carter's difficulties in the Middle East went beyond his struggles with OPEC. In January 1979, supporters of the Islamic radical Ayatollah Khomeini overthrew Mohammad Reza Pahlavi, widely known as the "shah of Iran." Installed with US support following a hostile coup in 1953, the shah served as a crucial Western ally in a region where, except for Israel, many nations aligned with the Soviet Union. Although the shah was a staunch opponent of communism, his regime became notorious for corruption and severe human rights abuses, including the imprisonment, torture, and execution of political dissidents.

Following the shah's exile, President Carter allowed him to enter the United States for cancer treatment. The decision enraged supporters of Ayatollah Khomeini, who, in November 1979, stormed the US embassy in Tehran, taking fifty-two Americans hostage. The new Iranian regime demanded the shah's return to face justice for his alleged crimes, along with the repatriation of the wealth he had amassed. The crisis lasted 444 days and severely damaged Carter's image, casting him as a weak and indecisive leader. Just a month later, Carter faced another major challenge when the Soviet Union invaded Afghanistan. The action sent a powerful message throughout the globe that the United States had become a nation in retreat.[411]

Many on the right believed that the invasion of Afghanistan—in addition to meeting the USSR's objective of strengthening its sphere of influence by ensuring "a friendly and socialist government" along its border—also represented a broader campaign by Moscow to expand its global reach. That strategy involved supporting leftist regimes throughout the Third World, including those in Angola, Ethiopia, Mozambique, South Yemen, and Nicaragua. Carter also faced criticism for what many perceived as a lack of firmness toward the Soviet Union, particularly in arms negotiations. Republicans as well as conservative Democrats voiced opposition to the second Strategic Arms Limitation Treaty (SALT II), which Carter signed with Soviet leader Leonid Brezhnev in 1979. These critics argued that the treaty weakened national security, and as a result, it ultimately failed to gain approval in the Senate.[412]

Announcing his candidacy at Washington, DC's National Press Club on May 1, 1979, George Bush outlined an agenda centered on maintaining strength abroad and stability at home. In defining his vision for the nation, he drew inspiration from another pragmatic leader, Dwight Eisenhower. "There is in world affairs a steady course to be followed between an assertion of strength that is truculent and a confession of helplessness that is cowardly," Bush stated. "There is in our affairs at home, a middle way between the untrammeled freedom of the individual and the demands for the welfare of the whole nation." His remarks were carefully crafted to appeal to the broadest possible constituency, a strategy suggested by Richard Nixon five months earlier. Nixon advised Bush not to focus on simply defeating his Republican primary opponents but presenting himself as the best candidate to defeat Carter in the general election.[413]

Bush had chosen to anchor his campaign on the strength of America's institutions and the resilience of its people. These core principles of presidential leadership, as well as Bush's strong experience in government, helped secure endorsements from prominent figures like Henry Cabot Lodge Jr., former President Gerald Ford, and others. But despite such support and a vast network of friends and family, Bush understood the daunting challenge ahead. "I have no time to think about relaxation. Just this one goal...determined to push on...I don't want to look back and find that I've left something undone," Bush wrote in his journal on October 10, 1979.[414]

41

Yet one of Bush's biographers, Jon Meacham, observed that many viewed Bush as "yesterday's man," a relic of the Eastern establishment, whose perceived elitism and detachment from everyday Americans made him an easy target for conservatives. To them, he symbolized the very leadership they blamed for the nation's domestic and foreign policy decline over the past two decades.[415]

Throughout the campaign, Bush's dedication and relentless effort surpassed expectations. The biggest surprise occurred when he secured a victory over Reagan in the January 1980 Iowa caucuses. The next major challenge arose in New Hampshire, where Bush and Reagan were set to face off in a high-profile contest in the town of Nashua, pitting the two frontrunners against one another. However, the event became embroiled in controversy when, following a protest by candidate Senator Robert Dole, the Federal Election Commission ruled that the *Nashua Telegraph* could not sponsor the debate unless all Republican primary candidates were invited to participate. Following Bush's refusal to share the expenses with Reagan, the governor's campaign stepped in and offered to cover the $3,500 costs of the event.[416]

On February 23, the day of the debate, Bush discovered that the Reagan campaign planned to include the other Republican candidates. He opposed the move, arguing that the *Nashua Telegraph* had initially set the debate rules and that changing them at the last minute made it unfair. Bush also believed that a one-on-one debate with Reagan would give him a better opportunity to articulate his views, a strategy he had struggled to implement in a previous debate earlier in Manchester, New Hampshire, where the presence of multiple candidates limited meaningful discussion.[417]

Bush's steadfast commitment to following the procedures ultimately backfired. When *Nashua Telegraph* editor Jon Breen ordered Reagan's microphone cut off, Reagan seized the moment with a forceful retort: "I am paying for this microphone, Mr. Green!"—electrifying the audience. Meanwhile, Bush, who remained seated in silence throughout the ordeal, appeared weak and indecisive. Harkening back to the incident years later, Bush acknowledged his principled stance but recognized its political cost.

"I had accepted a set of rules, and I'd given my word, and I was going to keep it. Some of my father there, I think, and Mother too. Play by the rules," he later wrote.[418]

Reagan secured victory in the New Hampshire primary, but Bush's persistence led to wins in several New England states, as well as Michigan and Pennsylvania. However, as the campaign progressed toward California, Reagan's momentum continued to build, prompting James Baker to suggest on May 22 that Bush consider exiting the race. "We just don't have the money, I wish to hell we did, but we don't, and I don't see how we can get it," Baker candidly told the candidate during a phone call.[419]

Initially unwilling to listen to Baker's counsel, Bush returned to Texas to seek advice from his family about the possibility of ending his campaign. While on the plane, Bush sat at a table with a writing pad in front of him. He wrote: "I WILL NEVER GIVE UP. NEVER. NEVER." It indicated his inherent competitiveness, rooted in a long-standing principle of doing whatever it takes to win. However, he also understood that if he didn't exhibit restraint and drop out, the growing tension between him and Reagan could make it difficult for the former actor to consider Bush as his vice president.[420]

The decision to withdraw from the race on May 26 represented one of the most painful moments of Bush's life. "It hurt like hell," he recalled. Despite his defeat, Bush never expressed anger or resentment over his political loss. George W. Bush believed his father's choice to remain gracious, even in the face of great disappointment, sent a message to his family: "[T]he critics were not getting to him, so we shouldn't let them get to us either," the younger Bush wrote.[421]

After failing to secure the presidential nomination, Bush "pledged [his] wholehearted support…to defeat Jimmy Carter." Bush approached his endorsement of Reagan with the mindset of working toward the "common goal of restoring the American people's confidence in their government and our nation's future." Even as Bush spoke of victory in November, he expressed his deep gratitude to all those who had dedicated their time "and personal commitments on my behalf and whom I'll never be able to fully repay for all they've done," he wrote in a statement marking the end of his campaign.[422] Following Bush's decision to leave the race, many speculated that Reagan might consider him for vice president. By 1980, Bush had accumulated significantly more government experience than six years earlier, when President Ford had first considered him for the position. "I am complimented that you want me to be the vice-presidential nominee, but I…am not interested in seeking that position," Bush wrote to a supporter that summer.[423]

Reagan had little interest in selecting Bush as his vice president, either. During the campaign, their relationship had grown strained. As historian Tevi Troy wrote in 2021, Reagan resented Bush both for criticizing his age and for labeling his plan to address the nation's inflation and unemployment crises as "voodoo economics." Reagan also saw Bush as an elitist, indecisive, and not a true conservative.[424]

Bush prepared to attend the Republican National Convention in Detroit, Michigan, uncertain of what the future held, while also focusing on clearing a $400,000 campaign debt. By campaign finance standards, the amount was relatively small, but he decided to resolve the issue before the convention. As the date drew nearer, Bush also seemed open to the idea of becoming vice president. While he may have wanted the position, he also understood the value of humility over aggressively promoting himself. "I really feel it should be Reagan's call, though uninhibited by pressure," he wrote at the end of June 1980.[425]

When discussions with former President Gerald Ford about serving as vice president stalled over Ford demanding a broader role in the administration, Bush accepted Reagan's invitation to take the second spot on the ticket. Reagan's foreign policy advisor, Richard V. Allen, contended in *The New York Times* in 2000 that Reagan had remained ambivalent about selecting Bush. However, in practical terms, the Texan appeared the ideal choice.[426]

In addition to finishing second in the primary process, Bush represented the moderate or establishment wing of the Republican Party. His experience as ambassador to the United Nations, envoy to the People's Republic of China, and member of Congress helped balance Reagan's lack of foreign policy and Washington experience. Bush's pragmatic decision to support Reagan's opposition to abortion and his shift toward favoring supply-side economics ultimately solidified the ticket.

Bush recalled being overjoyed when he received the phone call from Reagan. "I was—and am—an optimist, convinced that no matter how bad a situation might look, something good can come out of it. It's ingrained, part of my nature," Bush wrote years later. On several occasions when he thought his career in public life was over, an unexpected opportunity had emerged, allowing him to continue climbing the political ladder. Ironically, Ronald Reagan, a man who believed his destiny involved reviving the fortunes of the American people, had also revived George Bush's political career. "Out of a clear blue sky. I thought we were done, out of it, just gone," Bush wrote.[427]

Bush knew Reagan had opposed selecting him for the second spot on the ticket. However, once the GOP nominee made the decision, any lingering animosity between the two vanished. "There was never a hint of negative feeling left over from our fight for the presidential nomination because Reagan's instinct, I learned, is to think the best of the people he works with." Bush quickly realized that despite Reagan's intense competitive streak, he also possessed enormous gratitude in having a political partner who brought his own unique strengths to the campaign.[428]

In his remarks to the convention after being selected as Reagan's running mate, Bush showed his deference to the GOP nominee by keeping the focus on the broader goal, rather than on himself. He highlighted the united effort needed to defeat President Jimmy Carter that November and praised Reagan's leadership qualities. Bush invoked the memory of the man who had received the Republican nomination twenty-eight years earlier, Dwight Eisenhower, describing him as "a man of decency, compassion, and strength" who had "led America three decades ago into a new era of peace, prosperity, and progress." As *The New York Times* commented following the remarks, by aligning Reagan with Eisenhower's successful legacy, Bush connected him to a record of achievement, as well as to a pragmatic political style designed to appeal to moderate Republicans and disillusioned conservative Democrats dissatisfied with Carter's leadership.[429]

During the campaign, Reagan capitalized on Bush's foreign policy experience by asking him to deliver a message to Chinese leader Deng Xiaoping. While the GOP ticket supported a strong relationship with Taiwan, Reagan made it clear that he had no intention of destabilizing US-China relations. In a note to American expatriates titled "Republicans Abroad," Bush emphasized that the connections built with Asian leaders during his time as ambassador to the United Nations and liaison officer to China would benefit the nation. "I have known these men for years—we are old friends and we can therefore talk frankly to each other…I am sure that a Reagan-Bush administration will have strengthened relations with China," Bush wrote in the fall of 1980.[430]

On November 4, Bush and Reagan were able to take advantage of the nation's feelings of disorder under Carter to win a landslide victory. After the election, Bush sent a letter expressing appreciation to his defeated predecessor, Vice President Walter F. Mondale. "Thank you for your wire, your call, your just plain decency. I've lost plenty—I know it's no fun," Bush wrote on November 8.[431]

Bush's letter also requested a meeting with Mondale to discuss what the longtime Minnesota senator had learned about the vice presidency. Mondale's advice reinforced the lessons Bush had gained throughout his years in public service. Among them was the importance of unwavering support for the president, even when decisions were unpopular. Mondale also emphasized the need to manage the relationship with the media carefully, ensuring that all interviews given by the vice president were on the record.[432]

That strategy protected Bush from being misquoted or embarrassing the administration. Most importantly, Mondale emphasized the key to earning the president's trust concerned maintaining strict confidentiality and never leaking their conversations. He also stressed that the vice president had a duty not only to offer the president unwavering loyalty but also to provide the most thoughtful and honest counsel possible.[433]

Mondale further warned Bush about the bureaucratic infighting that could arise, even when a vice-presidential initiative had the full backing of the president. He referred to these potential challenges as "line responsibilities." Bush had become familiar with this issue from his experience in the Ford administration.[434]

During a conversation with Gerald Ford's vice president, Nelson Rockefeller, Bush had gained insight into the challenges of the position. As governor of New York from 1959 to 1973, Rockefeller had wielded significant political power across the Empire State. However, upon becoming vice president, he found himself at odds with those close to Ford. "My relations with the president are good, but that damned staff has cut me off at the knees," Rockefeller told Bush. The discussions with Mondale and Rockefeller proved valuable, helping Bush better define his role in working with Reagan.[435]

On November 10, two days after requesting the meeting with Mondale, Bush also expressed his gratitude to the president-elect and Mrs. Reagan for their kindness and inclusiveness toward him and his family. In a note, he reaffirmed his commitment to loyalty, assuring Reagan of his unwavering support throughout the administration. "I will never do anything to embarrass you politically…and you'll see no leaks in [columns by reporters] Evans and Novak bitching about life," Bush wrote while he and Barbara vacationed in Florida.[436]

Unlike previous chief executives who maintained a cordial but distant relationship with their vice presidents, Reagan viewed Bush as a vital part of his administration. In addition to their private weekly lunches, Bush joined the president in most of the meetings he attended and received copies of any documents Reagan reviewed. These interactions provided Bush with invaluable insight, shaping his own approach to the vice presidency. He later adopted a similar structure with his own vice president, Dan Quayle.[437]

Bush also deeply admired the kindness Reagan showed to others. While the vice president always sought to remain humble and considerate, he remained impressed by Reagan's consistent respect for people, regardless of their position. "There was a kindness there that taught me a good lesson—don't get to be a big deal, don't bawl out the airline stewardess, don't throw your weight around. Contain your anger. Smile a lot.

Laugh. Be kind to people. Those values I learned from Ronald Reagan," Bush recalled to Hugh Sidey about the fortieth president.[438]

While Bush and Reagan came from different backgrounds, their personalities shared striking similarities. Both men had a warm demeanor that naturally drew people to them, as well as a great sense of humor, never taking themselves too seriously. As *US News & World Report*'s Kenneth T. Walsh wrote in 2011, that warmth and camaraderie were often evident during their weekly Thursday luncheons, a tradition that began with President Carter and Vice President Mondale. "There was no agenda, so Reagan could talk about whatever he pleased without aides hovering in the room and without being channeled toward topics that were important to others. The goal was just to talk privately in a natural way," Bush recalled of those interactions.[439]

Bush valued his private moments with the president, and Reagan, in turn, appreciated his discretion in keeping their conversations confidential. Bush had learned this principle from his father's relationship with President Eisenhower. This same trustworthiness also extended to Bush's meetings with foreign leaders. "As Vice President, Bush would meet with individuals who shared their most closely held views, knowing that the message they were sending would go directly and only to President Reagan," recalled the vice president's chief of staff, Craig Fuller.[440]

Bush's discretion played a key role in developing a close relationship between him and Reagan. "Bush appreciated the trust Reagan had in him right from the start, and he was determined to earn it, letting no daylight get between them over the eight years," Fuller said. While Bush certainly had presidential aspirations, he remained focused solely on serving Reagan, never using his position for personal political gain. "I don't believe a President should have to be looking over his shoulder, wondering if the Vice President was out there carving him up to undermine his programs in one way or another," Bush wrote to Richard Nixon.[441]

Bush also admired Reagan's ability to place complete trust in his chief of staff, James A. Baker III, and counselors Michael Deaver and Edwin Meese III. That confidence allowed Reagan to delegate the details of policy and scheduling to others, giving him the freedom to focus on the larger issues. "I know I have to operate more like President Reagan, but I can't go all the way," Vice President Bush told Fuller in February 1985.[442]

Bush believed that "one of life's enjoyments involved diving into the details." However, he learned from Reagan the importance of having "trust in the people to whom he had delegated responsibility." This trust allowed Reagan to focus on "moments" where he could create "the most favorable impact," as Fuller put it in a conversation with the author.[443]

Ironically, Bush's belief in finding a balance between delegating certain responsibilities and focusing on others proved correct following the revelations of the 1986 Iran-Contra scandal. The controversial episode involved the Reagan administration's decision to secretly sell arms to Iran, hoping that the Iranian government would assist the United States in freeing seven hostages held by the Middle Eastern terrorist group Hezbollah. Additionally, members of the president's national security staff covertly used the proceeds from those arms sales to support the Nicaraguan resistance, fighting to overthrow the communist government of Daniel Ortega, all without congressional authorization or knowledge.

A 1987 report on the investigation, led by Republican Senator John Tower, harshly criticized Reagan for his "hands-off" management style. It remains unclear whether Bush agreed with the Tower Commission's assessment of the president. However, the situation may have reinforced Bush's concerns about the potential risks of allowing too much autonomy to subordinates in the daily activities of the administration.[444]

There were clear weaknesses in the manner Reagan managed the executive branch. However, the process he employed during cabinet meetings became an effective strategy for stimulating debate among his advisors. Rather than dominating discussions, Reagan preferred to hear from members of his administration who had strong opinions on a particular issue. Listening to alternative points of view contributed to the president's ability to make the most thorough and informed decisions possible.[445]

During many of these discussions, Bush saw himself as an honest broker, with the sole agenda of ensuring that President Reagan received the best possible advice. The vice president understood his role within the administration and did his best not to give anyone the impression that he knew more than he did. "He wasn't trying to impose an agenda, he just wanted to make certain that the President, and frankly some of the rest of us, understood what the implications were," Craig Fuller commented during an oral history in 2004.[446]

By watching Reagan address the people and issues he deemed priorities, Bush came to understand what Fuller described as "laying out an agenda in an organized, logical way." In the past, Bush's vice-presidential schedule was contained in a disorganized spiral notebook, leaving much of his staff uncertain about his daily agenda. The revised approach allowed Bush, much like Reagan, to meet only with individuals specifically associated with the issue he was addressing that day. "He learned that you have to really guard your time.... You can't have all the contact you might want to have with all the people who might want to have contact with you. I think he learned that from President Reagan," Fuller said.[447]

Throughout the administration, Bush found himself surprised by the president's political pragmatism. Initially viewing Reagan as highly ideological, the vice president marveled at Reagan's willingness to negotiate on certain cultural issues critical to his right-wing constituency. "The President is a darn good compromiser...and, yet his adherence to a position comes through loud and clear," Bush wrote in his diary. Reagan "would hold out until he thought he had the best deal possible and then accept it."

According to Fuller, "It was George Bush's instinct to want to find a way to resolve a conflict, but he witnessed the value of waiting, allowing the President to draw people in his direction."[448]

That same gradualist strategy applied to Reagan's approach toward the Soviet Union. Reagan rose to political prominence as a committed anti-communist. During the presidency he continued to criticize the USSR for its totalitarian ideology, its disregard for human rights, and its efforts to weaken democracy globally. However, Reagan also sought to reduce the escalating arms race between the two superpowers, a competition many feared could lead to nuclear Armageddon.[449]

In that respect, while Reagan had no qualms about referring to the Soviet Union as "an evil empire," he also recognized the importance of direct communication with Soviet leaders, such as Leonid Brezhnev. "Should we not be concerned with eliminating the obstacles which prevented our people from achieving their most cherished goals?" Reagan wrote to the Russian leader. Reagan's pragmatic approach to the Soviet Union surprised Bush, revealing a depth and complexity that differed from the ideologically rigid image Bush had formed of Reagan during the 1980 campaign. "I spent sixteen years fighting the man and what he stood for. But I didn't know him," Bush said in February 1981.[450]

Bush admired Reagan's ability to maintain what Bush aide David Bates described as a strong sense of "equilibrium." While the vice president always treated those around him with respect, he was also occasionally prone to moments of anger. Reagan, in contrast, exhibited a calm and composed demeanor, rarely allowing emotions to dictate his actions. This sense of balance became something Bush deeply respected and sought to emulate in his own leadership style.[451]

Reagan also had a remarkable ability to stay upbeat, a trait Bush admired and sought to apply during his time in the White House. In moments of tension, Bush would often use humor, laughing with his colleagues to ease the situation and calm himself. That upbeat and humorous nature endeared Bush to Reagan, allowing him to become a trusted friend and confidant. "I do feel close, and he makes you feel totally relaxed," Bush wrote in his diary. This sense of optimism and calmness would prove invaluable when, on March 30, 1981, following an address at the Washington Hilton, a gunman targeted Reagan for assassination.[452]

Upon learning of the attack on the president, the vice president, traveling on Air Force II bound for Austin, Texas, immediately prepared to return to Washington. Aware that the media would be waiting for him to make a statement, Bush knew the importance of gathering all the facts before speaking publicly. As he prepared to confront the crisis, Bush recognized his extensive experience and deep knowledge of government made him better equipped than anyone to handle the situation.[453]

Despite his deep apprehension that the president "could die," Bush kept his concern hidden from those around him. "He seems so calm, no signs whatever of nervous distress," Texas Congressman Jim Wright, traveling with Bush, noted in his journal that day. As biographer Jon Meacham suggests, Bush's ability to control his anxiety may have stemmed from his near-death experience during World War II, where he learned to remain composed in the face of life-threatening situations.[454]

As the plane approached Washington's Andrews Air Force Base, discussion began about the quickest way Bush could reach the White House. Driving would take too long. When a Bush aide, John Matheny, suggested Bush and his team land on the South Lawn next to the White House, the vice president grew apprehensive. Having studied the presidency and strongly aware of the symbolism of the office, Bush disagreed with the idea. "Only the President lands on the South Lawn," Bush told Matheny.[455]

Understanding that "the country can only have one President at a time, and the Vice President is not the one," Bush declined to take charge in the immediate aftermath of the assassination attempt. The decision reflected Bush's entire identity, which discouraged drawing unnecessary attention to himself. "*The President in the hospital.... Marine Two dropping out of the sky, blades whirring, the Vice President stepping off the helicopter to take charge.* Good television, yes—but not the message I thought we needed to send to the country and the world," Bush reflected.[456]

Bush realized that putting himself front and center would give the nation the impression that he reflected the qualities of a strong and decisive leader. However, the vice president believed that such a display put himself in direct opposition to the values his mother had imparted, a belief that braggadocio, showing off, and being one of the "la de dahs" was not the way to conduct oneself.[457]

Bush believed such a self-centered gesture would embarrass both the president and Nancy Reagan. No, Bush thought. Despite the urgency of the situation, his staff would simply have to land the helicopter at the Naval Observatory and then drive to the White House.[458]

Throughout Reagan's recovery, Bush remained deeply concerned with any appearance of supplanting the president. For that reason, he refused to sit in Reagan's chair in the Cabinet Room and the Situation Room. Those moments, and others like them, displayed Bush's unwavering belief in the presidency, and in the principles of virtue and humility that the founders had so strongly cherished. Remaining steadfast in his loyalty, Bush was determined to avoid giving even the slightest impression that anyone but President Reagan was in charge of the nation.[459]

The way Bush had handled his position caused President Reagan to value Bush's counsel and friendship even more than before. "Did it help me with President Reagan? Sure.... He was the president, I wasn't. A president has enough to worry about without having to worry that his vice president...[is] trying to make himself look good at the president's expense. I'd decided that he deserved my total loyalty, and he got it," Bush recalled.[460]

As many in Washington remained uncertain about whether Reagan would run for a second term, former governor of New Hampshire Hugh Gregg encouraged Bush to position himself for a bid at the 1984 GOP nomination. While Bush appreciated Gregg's suggestion, he had made a promise to remain loyal to Reagan, and it was one he intended to keep. "I will do nothing at all of any kind that could even marginally be considered as moving around for '84. I am too devoted to the Prez to do this, and it would be wrong," Bush wrote to Gregg in the summer of 1982.[461]

Bush enjoyed his time as vice president, though it was not without its challenges. Accustomed to making executive decisions, he often found it frustrating to "hold back" his opinions. Despite the lack of autonomy, he appreciated his close relationship with President Reagan. He valued the opportunity to offer honest assessments and feedback, something he believed was crucial to their partnership. Being able to observe Reagan up close also provided Bush with insights into the qualities and approaches he believed necessary when he sought the presidency again.[462]

Learning from Reagan also helped Bush understand the importance of balancing pragmatism with firmness. "Resist pressures to compromise all the time; be willing to talk, but do it from strength," Bush noted in his journal as he observed Reagan navigate the complexities of political issues like Social Security and tax reform. Despite the improving economy, the vice president remained concerned about the nation's fiscal health. Bush disliked deficits and believed that if a solution did not develop, "there will have to be more revenues raised," he wrote in a journal entry that July, as the 1984 Republican convention approached.[463]

He had little reason to worry. While those on the president's right flank continued to distrust Bush, Reagan's unwavering support for his less ideological colleague ensured that both men were easily re-nominated. On August 23, 1984, in Bush's second speech accepting the GOP nomination for vice president of the United States, he once again invoked the memory of Dwight Eisenhower, emphasizing the importance of steady leadership and national unity in the face of challenges. The speech served as a reminder of Bush's respect for past Republican ideals, as well as his continued commitment to supporting Reagan's agenda.

Four years earlier, Bush had compared Eisenhower's character to Ronald Reagan's, highlighting their shared qualities of leadership and vision. During remarks on August 24, 1984, Bush connected the administration's theme of promoting democracy worldwide to Eisenhower's 1957 inaugural address, which championed an internationalist agenda and the importance of alliances and institutions. "May a light of freedom flame brightly, until at last the darkness is no more," Bush said, echoing the words of the thirty-fourth president, reinforcing the continuity of American ideals and the Reagan administration's commitment to advancing freedom on the global stage.

The vice president concluded his remarks with a prayer by Eisenhower that called for humility and fairness, qualities that were central to the character of Dwight Eisenhower but also resonated deeply with George Bush. "May we grow in strength without pride in self. May we, in our dealings with all the people of the earth, ever speak truth and serve justice," Bush said, according to *The New York Times*. The prayer encapsulated Bush's own values and vision for the future, blending reverence for past leaders with a commitment to principles of integrity and justice.

As Bush entered his second term as vice president, he began seriously considering another run for the presidency. With 1988 in mind, he deliberated about why he wanted to occupy the White House and about the qualities he believed were essential for a chief executive. Many of these insights stemmed from his own experiences, as well as lessons he had absorbed from others throughout his political career.

Bush placed a strong emphasis on knowledge as a critical factor in decision-making. He firmly believed in surrounding himself with a diverse range of opinions, especially from those with whom he disagreed. "If you can't listen, you can't lead," he wrote to his speechwriter Victor Gold, underscoring his commitment to open dialogue and thoughtful leadership.[464]

Bush also considered himself a conservative with a gradualist approach to solving the nation's problems. While he did not possess a strong ideological streak, he believed that his deep familiarity with domestic and international issues, along with his extensive relationships with key figures in government, positioned him well to navigate the challenges of the presidency.

By the late 1980s, Bush felt that his confidence had grown significantly. He had come to appreciate Reagan's advice about the importance of focusing on the big picture rather than getting immersed in unnecessary details. That lesson, he believed, was pivotal to effective governance and would help him lead with both pragmatism and strength.[465]

As Bush prepared for the 1988 campaign, he faced scrutiny over the 1986 Iranian arms sales and the role he played in advising the president. Bush had supported the arms-for-hostages deal, believing that the transaction not only secured the release of seven American hostages but also created an opportunity for the United States to cultivate a relationship with Iranian moderates who might gain power once the aging Ayatollah Khomeini passed from the scene.

However, the deal contradicted the principles set forth by the Bush-led anti-terrorism task force, which opposed negotiating with hostage-takers. Despite Secretary of State George Shultz's strong objections, Bush chose not to challenge Reagan's decision, aligning himself with the administration's approach even as the controversy unfolded.[466]

After the Iran-Contra affair became public in November 1986, Bush attempted to distance himself from the controversy by stating in a televised interview that "it [is] ridiculous to even consider selling arms to Iran." The statement was not just inaccurate; it also revealed a lapse in judgment. As vice president, Bush had expected to provide wise counsel, particularly in foreign policy matters. His decision to remain largely silent when Reagan needed critical input did neither himself nor the president any favors.[467]

Despite intense scrutiny, the Tower Commission investigating the Iran-Contra affair found no evidence to implicate Bush in any criminal wrongdoing. However, the controversy raised questions about his leadership and judgment, issues that would resurface as he prepared for his 1988 presidential campaign.[468]

Bush's belief in loyalty and his determination to succeed were the two key factors that influenced his actions during the Iran-Contra scandal. "My gut instinct is to run to the President's defense and jump into the fray," he wrote in November 1986, soon after the scandal broke. For Bush, loyalty to Reagan remained paramount, even when it meant aligning himself with a politically damaging situation.[469]

The vice president's commitment to discretion also played a role in his handling of the crisis. Bush understood from his father's experience with Eisenhower that true allies of the president did not reveal private conversations or distance themselves from an administration's agenda when it became politically inconvenient. The approach, while rooted in a sense of duty, also meant that Bush remained publicly tied to the controversy as he prepared for the 1988 campaign.

During Bush and Reagan's private luncheons, the vice president often voiced disagreements and provided alternative solutions on policy and legislative matters. However, Bush firmly believed that his role required confidentiality. "Bush did not want to break his longstanding rule of keeping his advice to the president confidential, almost whatever the cost," writes biographer, Jon Meacham. That steadfast commitment to private counsel reinforced his reputation as a loyal deputy, though it sometimes came at the expense of his own political standing. Bush saw his primary duty as supporting Reagan, even when that meant absorbing criticism for decisions in which he may or may not have played a behind-the-scenes role.[470]

The other factor influencing Bush's decision-making during the Iran-Contra scandal concerned his intense competitiveness, his relentless drive to win and conquer any challenge, regardless of the circumstances. Throughout his life, that determination sometimes clouded his judgment. Examples include his hospitalization during his junior year at Andover after refusing to moderate the intensity of his schedule, as well as his 1964 Senate campaign, when he compromised his values in a failed attempt to secure victory.

Bush believed he possessed the experience and knowledge necessary to become president. He believed he had gone above and beyond in his service to those in power, and the moment had finally arrived for him to captain the ship of state. However, the Iran-Contra scandal posed a significant problem, as it brought his defining qualities, loyalty and service, into "direct conflict" with his relentless ambition to reach the pinnacle of political power.[471]

During his seven and a half years working alongside Ronald Reagan, Bush deepened his understanding of government and policy while also receiving an invaluable lesson in presidential leadership. Observing Reagan's emphasis on not just oratory but also presentation and discipline, Bush came to appreciate why the president remained such an effective communicator. As his White House Chief of Staff John Sununu later explained, "Bush understood Ronald Reagan's style of simplified leadership: identify big issues, target them, give them an image, and characterize them for what you want to accomplish. And repeat, repeat, repeat, repeat until everybody follows."[472]

Bush also admired President Reagan's pragmatism in negotiations. As *The Wall Street Journal* wrote in 2015, those who mistook Reagan's casual demeanor for a lack of strategic acumen did so at their peril. Reagan firmly believed that "if you got seventy-five or eighty percent of what you asked for…you take it and fight for the rest later." Yet, he also believed in doing whatever necessary to secure the best possible deal, demonstrating a shrewd and calculated approach to leadership that Bush came to respect and internalize.[473]

Bush took that lesson to heart. Announcing his candidacy for president on October 12, 1987, he demonstrated the insights he had gained from watching Reagan negotiate an arms agreement with the Soviet Union. "It didn't come free, it didn't come easy. We waited them out; we increased our strength. We refused to budge until the agreement was good. Some people used that against us, saying we didn't want an agreement at all…when the truth was, we just didn't want a bad one," Bush said.

More importantly, Bush had observed Reagan's ability to take both victories and setbacks in stride, always maintaining a sense of gratitude for the opportunity to serve his country.

"I never once in eight years, no matter how difficult the problem, heard [Reagan] appeal to me or to others around him for understanding about the toughest, loneliest job in the world," Bush reflected several months into his own presidency.[474]

During the 1988 campaign, Bush faced more than just scrutiny over his involvement in the arms-for-hostages scandal. Despite his efforts to align himself with the Reagan Revolution, many conservatives continued to question the depth of his ideological commitment. "He can't really disassociate himself from his Connecticut heritage," noted Vermont Senator Robert Stafford, capturing a broader unease among the party's right wing. Bush encountered the strength of this conservative skepticism early on, finishing third in the Iowa caucuses behind televangelist Pat Robertson and the winner, Senator Bob Dole of Kansas. Nevertheless, his steadfast determination, President Reagan's support, and a series of timely political advantages ultimately propelled him to secure the Republican nomination.[475]

As the GOP convention in New Orleans approached, Bush recognized that the moment had come to define himself on his own terms. For the last eight years, the nation had viewed him through the prism of

Reagan's presidency. Now, after decades of hard work and perseverance, he had the opportunity to articulate the vision, values, and lessons he had learned throughout his long career in public life.

PART II
TAKING COMMAND

CHAPTER 12

Setting the Tone: President

Bush Presidential Inauguration. January 20, 1989.

In March 1989, during a luncheon with journalists in the East Room of the White House, President George Bush reflected on the former presidents he most admired. He named Theodore Roosevelt and Dwight D. Eisenhower, praising both for their leadership and lasting impact on the nation. Of Roosevelt, Bush spoke with fondness, calling the New York patrician a personal role model. With a hint of humor, he noted that they shared privileged upbringings but also a deep dedication to public service and a strong interest in the complexities of policy.[476]

However, when asked which president he felt the strongest affinity with, Bush expressed his greatest admiration for Eisenhower. "I have great respect for Eisenhower…he was a hero," Bush told the assembled reporters. "He was a fair-minded person, a strong leader, and earned the respect of the people. And I think he was given credit for being a compassionate individual." Like Bush himself, Eisenhower's leadership developed through years of experience, giving him a profound understanding of the complexities within a vast bureaucracy. The military man's long apprenticeship under seasoned mentors like George S. Patton Jr. and George C. Marshall prepared him for pivotal moments in both his career and in world history. In his comments about Roosevelt and Eisenhower, Bush revealed his deep admiration for those who guided the nation with strength and confidence, tempered by empathy, wisdom, and a dedication to public service.[477]

***

On the evening of August 18, 1988, Vice President George Bush stood on the stage of the Louisiana Superdome in New Orleans to formally accept the Republican Party's nomination for president of the United States. The moment represented a culmination of decades of public service, yet Bush knew that the occasion symbolized more than just celebration; it meant the opportunity to define his leadership and vision for the future. Bush understood the weight a successful convention speech carried in shaping the campaign's trajectory. He needed to reassure conservatives still skeptical of his ideological commitment while also appealing to the broader electorate. "I felt calm but not bashed and not hyped for the event. I knew what I had to do," Bush reflected in his journal after the convention.[478]

Less than a year earlier, in October 1987, as Bush officially announced the beginning of his presidential campaign, he set out to establish a tone of unity and optimism, declaring his vision for "a greater harmony" and "a new tolerance" in American life. Standing before a crowd near his home in Houston, Texas, the vice president detailed his plans to strengthen the economy and promote global security by limiting the use of nuclear weapons.

But Bush's message went beyond policy. Channeling the spirit of Theodore Roosevelt, he urged Americans to embrace a sense of duty and purpose beyond personal success. "We diminish our triumph when we act as if wealth is an end in itself," he told the audience, encouraging them to contribute to the greater good rather than simply celebrating prosperity.

The moment underscored Bush's belief in service, responsibility, and the idea that leadership required not only political ambition, but a commitment to pursuing an idea larger than oneself.[479]

In a series of remarks Bush referred to as "prosperity with a purpose," he emphasized that those who were fortunate enough to enjoy privilege had a duty to serve as role models for others. "The fact is, prosperity is not an end but a beginning. It has a point. It gives us time to think and care. It frees us up to learn and grow, to be better than we are, to develop the things of the spirit and the heart. Prosperity with a purpose means giving back to the country that has given you so much," he declared.[480]

In that moment, Bush embraced Theodore Roosevelt's call to live a "strenuous life" rooted in a reverence for America's past. But his words also echoed a lifelong lesson from his father: Wealth is meaningless unless it is used to nourish the greater good. "You have got to live by values if you want to live a life of meaning," Bush said, underscoring his belief that true success required service, integrity, and a deep commitment to something beyond material gain. "Increasingly we see those who dropped their standards along the way. As if ethics are too heavy and slowed their rise to the top," Bush said, emphasizing the themes of greed and avarice that defined the decade of the 1980s.[481]

Those themes of sacrifice, service, and character played a central role in Bush's address to the GOP convention ten months later. Throughout his speech, Bush framed his life as a series of missions, missions that had taken him from the battlefields of the Pacific to the oil fields of Texas and ultimately to positions of public responsibility at home and abroad. "Everything I learned from history, from my father, Prescott

Bush, everything I valued from my service in the US Navy reinforced the words duty, honor, country," Bush later reflected in a memoir written with Brent Scowcroft, *A World Transformed*.[482]

During remarks as the GOP nominee, Bush positioned himself as a symbol of the "Greatest Generation," embodying the millions of Americans who confronted life's most significant challenges and persevered. "And this has been called the American Century because, in it, we were the dominant force for good in the world. We saved Europe, cured polio, went to the moon, and lit the world with our culture," Bush declared to the packed venue in New Orleans.[483]

By aligning himself with the legacy of American resilience and achievement, Bush sought throughout his address to inspire confidence in his leadership and in his extensive experience across both the private and public sectors. He celebrated the nation's past triumphs while reinforcing its ongoing responsibility to strive for greatness in the years ahead. The themes he articulated in his address crystallized his argument that values, experience, and steady leadership were exactly what the country needed as it approached the final decade of the twentieth century.

As Bush concluded his address, he reaffirmed the themes he had first introduced in 1980, presenting himself as a leader of character and experience, with the steady temperament and expertise needed to guide the nation. He positioned himself as a reliable statesman—one whom Americans could trust in the White House because of his deep knowledge of government and also because of his proven ability to lead in times of crisis.

At the same time, Bush worked to reassure conservatives who had long questioned his ideological convictions. As part of this strategy, he selected Dan Quayle, a young, staunchly conservative senator from Indiana, as his running mate. He also set aside his personal concerns about the growing deficit to better align with the party's right wing. His emphatic promise, "Read my lips, no new taxes," drew the most enthusiastic applause of the night, solidifying his support among conservatives and setting the stage for the general election ahead.[484]

Many considered the speech a resounding success. Commentators across the political spectrum hailed it as the finest of Bush's career. In 2024, Peggy Noonan, the author of Bush's convention address, reflected in *The Wall Street Journal*, "He had never worked harder on a speech, and I'm not sure he ever did again." The widespread praise underscored a crucial lesson Bush had absorbed from Reagan, about the power of a well-crafted address to shape public perception on a national scale. "I knew it was good," Bush wrote in his diary, marking the moment as a personal and political triumph.[485]

Despite the speech being well received, Peggy Noonan does not exaggerate in implying that Bush had a distaste for speechmaking. While Bush recognized his new role placed him at the center of national attention, the values instilled in him discouraged displays of personal self-importance, creating a tension with the demands of the presidency. As biographer Jon Meacham put it, "He had these competing imperatives of competitiveness and humility in his head." Despite the internal conflicts and competing impulses surrounding the race, Bush remained resolute to win the election.[486]

Bush and his Democratic opponent, Governor Michael Dukakis of Massachusetts, competed in a fierce and bitterly contested campaign. Bush's chief political advisor, Lee Atwater, framed Dukakis as an unpatriotic liberal, weak on crime and lacking the extensive experience and leadership qualities that Bush had cultivated throughout his career. One of the campaign's most controversial strategies concerned a television advertisement that targeted Dukakis's record on law and order. The controversial TV spot produced by the National Security Political Action Committee, a conservative group unaffiliated with the Bush campaign, highlighted the case of Willie Horton, a convicted murderer who committed rape and assault while on a weekend furlough from a Massachusetts prison. Although a Republican governor had implemented the furlough program, Atwater seized on the issue with the objective of tying Dukakis to what many viewed as a critical lapse in public safety.[487]

The ad's racially charged undertones were evident, as it disproportionately focused on the image of a black criminal while painting

Dukakis's policies in a negative light. Critics saw it as an example of the "Southern Strategy" pioneered by Richard Nixon, which sought to exploit racial tensions to gain political advantage. Atwater understood the power of fear-based messaging and successfully tapped into public concern surrounding crime and lawlessness, reinforcing a broader narrative of Democratic ineffectiveness in protecting American citizens.[488]

The campaign's focus on Horton, while highly effective in influencing public opinion, also stirred significant controversy and became a symbol of the negative tactics that defined the 1988 presidential race. Bush, despite his initial calls for a "gentler" tone," found himself deeply enmeshed in the attack-driven politics of the campaign, marking a stark contrast to the message he had championed in his recent convention address.[489]

While the Bush campaign didn't directly produce the Willie Horton ad, it certainly leveraged its message with great effect. Following the ad, the GOP nominee repeatedly cited the case to highlight Dukakis's weakness on crime. The ad tapped into the national anxieties around law and order, reinforcing the idea that Dukakis's policies were both ineffective and potentially dangerous. As Josh King, analyst of the 1988 campaign, told *The New York Times* in 2018, while Bush may not have designed the Horton strategy, he believed it necessary to hire people "who would use the barest of knuckles in pursuit of the goal of humiliating and destroying the opposing candidate." The GOP nominee's earlier calls for a "kinder, gentler" approach were indeed overshadowed by the campaign's aggressive tactics, particularly in this instance. The Bush campaign faced criticism for shifting from a more hopeful message of unity to one that played on racial and class-based fears.[490]

Bush remained unapologetic about the ad, believing that to create a new harmony he had to win. "If you want to be President—and I do—there are certain things that I have to do. Politics isn't a pure undertaking—not if you're going to win, it's not." The vice president understood that politics was a contact sport and understood that morality often faded into the background during a high stakes political battle. "To serve, he had to succeed, to preside he had to prevail," Jon Meacham stated during Bush's eulogy in December 2018.

Years later, Dukakis acknowledged Bush's perspective. "This was politics, pure politics. We were in a tough campaign. He needed to make me look too 'liberal', so he used what was at hand and the Horton case was in the public record." Bush's strategy, built on extensive experience in government, combined with the popularity of the Reagan Revolution, all contributed to Bush winning the presidency with 53.4 percent of the vote.[491]

Shortly after winning the election, Bush sought to fulfill his promise of creating a "new harmony" by arranging a meeting with congressional leaders. While eager to meet with the head of the GOP majority, Robert Michel, Bush recognized the importance of establishing a strong working relationship with Jim Wright, the Democratic Speaker of the House, especially given the divided Congress. "Wright offered to come down to the White House. I said no, that I would go and see him," Bush wrote to his transition chair, Craig Fuller.[492]

As Bush prepared to select his foreign and domestic policy team, he ruminated about how he could become the most effective president. His thoughts frequently returned to the core traditions that had guided him throughout his life and contributed to his personal and professional success. "Family, faith, friends, do your best, try your hardest, rely on your innate good sense, kindness, and understanding of the American people.... No one can have instant success, no one can make this nation kinder and gentler overnight, but we can try," Bush wrote in his diary just days before being sworn in as the nation's forty-first president.[493]

Upon taking the oath of office on January 20, 1989, Bush honored a tradition established by Dwight Eisenhower by reciting a brief prayer he had selected for the occasion. This inaugural prayer symbolized both Bush's strong commitment to faith and how he viewed Eisenhower as a presidential model. Longtime aide David Bates recalls Bush emphasizing the significance of beginning each cabinet meeting with a prayer. "I want to do it the way Ike did," Bush remarked to Bates.[494]

In his inaugural address, Bush revisited the themes he highlighted during his speech at the Republican convention six months earlier. He called on Americans to look beyond material wealth and instead focus on the fundamental values of family and community. "In our hearts we know what matters. We cannot hope only to leave our children a bigger car, a bigger bank account. We must hope to give them a sense of what it means to be a loyal friend, a loving parent, a citizen who leaves his home, his neighborhood, and town better than he found it," Bush stated, alluding to his parents' belief in the puritan sense of frugality.[495]

Bush's speech articulated a vision of conservatism centered on the idea that the nation thrived through interconnected communities, where individuals took responsibility for supporting one another, rather than relying on the government to drive change. "The old ideas are new again because they are not old, they are timeless: duty, sacrifice, commitment, and a patriotism that finds its expression in taking part and pitching in," Bush declared. The remarks also celebrated the accomplishments of Bush's generation, who fought in World War II, then played a crucial role in revitalizing the postwar world.[496]

By suggesting that kindness and camaraderie were inherent in every American, Bush portrayed the United States as a unified community where people joined forces to achieve the greater good. These values had shaped Bush's own life, reflecting the lessons from his parents, who had taught their children to live by the golden rule of "do unto others as you would have them do unto you."

The president did more than urge citizens to support one another; he called on Washington to join him in bridging the partisan divide. Bush encouraged members of both parties to collaborate in finding solutions that served all Americans. "To my friends—and yes, I do mean friends—in the loyal opposition—and yes, I mean loyal: I put out my hand. I am putting out my hand to you, Mr. Speaker. I am putting out my hand to you, Mr. Majority Leader. For this is the thing: This is the age of the offered hand," Bush declared, turning toward the Democratic leadership seated on the reviewing stand.[497]

41

The day after his public appeal to Congress, Bush followed up with a personal note to Speaker Wright. In extending a formal invitation to the Texas Democrat, Bush sought to initiate discussions on reducing the national debt. He expressed his eagerness to build a strong relationship with his fellow Texan, emphasizing that "the American people expect that concerns of such national import should be tackled in a spirit of bipartisan cooperation." Bush admitted later he had learned that strategy from Ronald Reagan. "He was an example of how you can be a strong leader and yet still be a kind and gentle man, something I spoke of as a goal for the nation," Bush later reflected in his memoir.[498]

From the outset of his administration, Bush prioritized building relationships with Congress. "Just start working on them, get time on my schedule, and we're going to do stuff up in the residence," he instructed his director of legislative affairs, Fred McClure. As part of this strategy, Bush committed to meeting weekly with members of Congress, along with a few of their constituents, at the White House.[499]

Loyalty and mutual support were central to Bush, especially in shaping foreign policy. Emphasizing the idea that "a new breeze is blowing," he underscored his belief that freedom is an inherent force that benefits nations both large and small. While urging Americans to stand by one another, he also reaffirmed his conviction that the United States remained a beacon of hope for people around the world.

The president reaffirmed the nation's commitment to its allies and the international institutions essential to global stability. This included a determination to bridge the gap between the United States and the USSR, striving for a world free from the threat of nuclear catastrophe. "While keeping our alliances and friendships around the world strong, ever strong, we will continue the new closeness with the Soviet Union, consistent both with our security and with progress," Bush declared. Having observed his predecessor's efforts to collaborate with Mikhail Gorbachev in pursuit of a nuclear-free world, Bush aimed to leverage his own skills in personal diplomacy to forge a strong relationship with the Soviet leader.[500]

As Bush outlined his agenda for the nation, he also gave careful thought to the makeup of his administration. From Richard Nixon, he had learned the risks of surrounding oneself with unfamiliar advisors, while Ronald Reagan had shown him the importance of assembling a strong first-term team capable of providing the best possible counsel. Bush also knew he did not have the desire to fully delegate control of the administration's daily operations to his subordinates.

"I was fortunate to have served under three Republican Presidents.... I had observed Lyndon Johnson...and later, from afar, Jimmy Carter. Through their experiences, I came to understand how foreign affairs and national security policy-making should function...and the challenges of the presidency itself," Bush reflected in a history of his administration's foreign policy.[501]

As Bush's first appointment he named longtime friend and confidant James A. Baker III as secretary of state. Although the Texas lawyer had limited foreign policy experience, he possessed exceptional negotiating skills, a deep understanding of how Washington operated, and the president's full trust. More importantly, as Education Secretary Lamar Alexander noted, "each man appeared perennially aware of what the other was thinking and doing." The Tennessee politician's observations were correct. "I don't believe I could do this job without trusted close friends nearby," Bush wrote to Baker in the summer of 1989.[502]

Some argued that Baker believed Bush should adopt the structure of the three-person leadership team that had worked for Reagan. However, Bush never considered this approach.

"I do believe that one of George H. W. Bush's fears was, to use his word, being 'handled.' He tolerated the closely coordinated process involving Jim Baker, Bob Teeter, Lee Atwater, and me because he felt it was necessary for the election. But he clearly wanted to break away from us as he prepared to govern," recalled presidential transition chief Craig Fuller. While Reagan's system had complemented his personality, Bush had a different style. He took pleasure in the details of governing and administration. "I intended to be a 'hands-on' President," Bush reflected years later.[503]

The president's chief of staff, former New Hampshire Governor John Sununu, understood Bush's desire to stay closely connected to the happenings within the White House.

"I never, never freelanced a single thing, and knew it and was comfortable with that.... But I asked him everything.... Nothing was too important and nothing was too trivial," Sununu explained. A former engineer, Sununu deeply respected Bush and was committed to doing whatever it took to help him succeed. "Like a good chief of staff, he is not afraid to be the SOB so that the Boss can be the good guy," Richard Nixon wrote to Bush in April 1989.[504]

For national security advisor, Bush chose his longtime colleague, Lieutenant General Brent Scowcroft. A former Air Force officer, the reserved West Point graduate had served as deputy to Henry Kissinger before becoming national security advisor under Gerald Ford. Bush became acquainted with Scowcroft while serving as Nixon's ambassador to the United Nations, and their relationship had deepened during Bush's time as US representative to China and director of the CIA. The two grew even closer during the Reagan administration, when Scowcroft served on the president's Commission on Strategic Forces and the Tower Commission investigating the Iran-Contra affair.[505]

Bush and Scowcroft had both witnessed the exclusion of Secretary of State William Rogers from Nixon's and Kissinger's management of the administration's foreign policy. Bush also appreciated Scowcroft's company and his experience as a former miliary leader. During his time as chairman of the Republican National Committee, Bush additionally had built a close relationship with Alexander Haig. In watching the former NATO commander manage the National Security Council, Bush concluded that, given the office's involvement in foreign and defense matters, the national security advisor should have a military background. Scowcroft's experience made him the perfect fit for the job. "He would not try to run over the heads of cabinet members, or cut them off from contact with the president," Bush noted, perhaps thinking about his past experience with Henry Kissinger.[506]

The president valued Scowcroft's extensive understanding of the geopolitical landscape as well as his gracious manner. Though Bush had held several key foreign policy positions, he admired the depth of knowledge Scowcroft brought to the administration, particularly regarding the Soviet Union and arms control. Although they were contemporaries, Bush saw his friend as someone whose expertise and experience helped him grow intellectually. "On other important matters, like missiles, NATO, and [German Chancellor Helmut] Kohl and [British Prime Minister] Margaret [Thatcher], you've steadily showed me the way," Bush wrote to Scowcroft after a trip to Europe in June 1989.[507]

Beyond his strong credentials, Scowcroft had a solid working relationship with James Baker, a quality President Bush believed essential for effective collaboration among the three. In the early days of the administration, Bush and Scowcroft carefully considered additional figures who could strengthen the president's foreign policy team. With Scowcroft's recommendation, Bush appointed Robert Gates as deputy national security advisor. Like Scowcroft, Gates had an Air Force background and had served on Ford's national security staff. Most importantly, he possessed an intelligence background, having begun as a CIA analyst and worked his way up to deputy director of the agency during the Reagan years.[508]

Bush also chose to retain Judge William Webster as director of central intelligence, believing that the jurist performed admirably under Reagan. Appointing Gates to the National Security Council also gave Bush the opportunity to consult someone who shared his deep interest in intelligence analysis. As a former CIA director, Bush had a profound appreciation for the vast knowledge and expertise within the intelligence community and valued the critical role it played in shaping national security policy.

From his own experience as DCI, Bush understood the importance of earning the immediate respect of the intelligence community. That required a leader with deep expertise in the field and who also prevented politics from influencing analysis or decision-making. Given these qualifications, it is not surprising that in 1991 Bush selected Gates to lead the agency.[509]

The remainder of Bush's foreign policy team included Richard Cheney, who became secretary of defense after the Senate rejected Bush's first choice, former Texas Senator John Tower, amid allegations of drinking and womanizing. Additionally, Bush opted to retain Admiral William Crowe as chairman of the Joint Chiefs of Staff. When Crowe decided to step down in October 1989, General Colin Powell, who had previously served as Reagan's national security advisor, succeeded him.[510]

Bush had observed the intense rivalry between Secretary of State George Shultz and Secretary of Defense Caspar Weinberger during the Reagan administration. He had also witnessed how Henry Kissinger had sidelined William Rogers in key foreign policy decisions under Nixon. Additionally, both Bush and Scowcroft were aware of the conflicts between Secretary of State Cyrus Vance and National Security Advisor Zbigniew Brzezinski during the Carter administration.[511]

Bush believed that the success of his foreign policy team depended on prior working relationships. "George Bush was probably the first president since Franklin Roosevelt…who was acquainted with all the members of his cabinet before he named them," recalled Bush Personnel Director Chase Untermeyer. Bush also had a clear understanding of the skills each position required. Recognizing the structure of the executive branch, Bush knew that for his advisors to be effective, they needed direct access to the president.[512]

While expertise remained a priority, Bush's selections were also shaped by loyalty.

Baker and Scowcroft embodied both qualities, as did Nicholas Brady and Robert Mosbacher, who served as secretaries of treasury and commerce, respectively. Additionally, Bush retained as his counsel C. Boyden Gray, whose father had known Prescott Bush during the Eisenhower administration. Beyond their longstanding relationships with Bush, all these men also shared ties to the Eastern establishment. Baker, Brady, Gray, and Mosbacher were, like Bush, mainstream conservatives who all came from elite prep school backgrounds, with three of the four having attended Ivy League universities.[513]

The president's emphasis on assembling a team that not only had deep expertise in domestic and national security matters but also shared a strong sense of loyalty to one another led to minimal tensions or rivalries. "There was an element of trust that made it a delight to go to work every day.... There was a concept that it was a team," recalled Secretary of Defense Cheney. While Bush recognized that disagreements were inevitable, he prioritized ensuring that all voices were heard and every perspective carefully considered.[514]

Cheney's depiction of the White House staff mirrored the collaborative environment Prescott Bush described at Brown Brothers Harriman. The firm's partners and Bush's cabinet shared key traits: mutual respect, a sense of familiarity, aligned values, a confident yet relaxed demeanor, and a commitment to keeping disagreements within the group. Commenting on the qualities of effective leadership, Bush stated, "The secret is to get good people and give credit to them. I think that was a value I got from my mother.... I think that attitude helped get the most loyalty.... You can't take credit and then jump to the side when something goes wrong."[515]

Throughout his presidency, Bush sought to create an atmosphere of relaxed informality. However, he never lost his deep reverence for the White House. While there were plenty of moments filled with laughter and lightheartedness, he remained mindful that he and those around him were treading on hallowed ground. "And that's why when anybody was there I would not ever go in there and have meetings with neckties gone and plastic cups," Bush remarked. "I have great respect for the dignity of the office and for the office of the presidency itself," he told Hugh Sidey in 1996.

The atmosphere of informality extended beyond Bush's relationship with his cabinet. He believed that despite holding the nation's highest office, he should maintain as low a profile as possible. As Peter and Rochelle Schweizer note, the approach included having his motorcade stop at traffic lights and minimize unnecessary noise while traveling through the nation's capital. "I think in part it was an effort to escape some of his past, you know, riding the limousine to the country day school," Press Secretary Marlin Fitzwater explained. The president also made a conscious effort to limit his television appearances, urging his staff to avoid overexposing him to the public.[516]

During Bush's time in office, humor and gratitude were constant priorities. Following Reagan's example, he seized every opportunity to create lighthearted moments. At public events, he never failed to express appreciation, thanking everyone involved, no matter how small their role. While Bush valued communication, he recognized that he lacked Reagan's oratorical flair and never felt entirely comfortable being the center of attention.[517]

As one biographer notes, while Bush believed a speech could inspire the nation, he doubted that rhetoric alone could impact public opinion. The observation recalled the moment when Henry Stimson addressed Bush's graduating class at Andover, urging them to prioritize college over military service. Though Bush admired Stimson's words, he ultimately chose to postpone his studies at Yale to serve in the navy.[518]

Bush recognized he had his own strengths for influencing the public, particularly his ability to use personal relationships to persuade both allies and adversaries to reconsider their positions. To reflect the leadership qualities he admired, he displayed images of two presidents whose example he hoped to follow. In the Cabinet Room, he placed John Singer Sargent's portrait of Theodore Roosevelt. In the Treaty Room of the White House, he hung P. A. Healey's 1868 painting *The Peacemakers* by George Peter Alexander Healy, which depicted Lincoln meeting with his generals on a steamer during the Civil War in 1865.[519]

Bush also sought to foster a less polarized relationship between his administration and the Democratic-controlled Congress. These included gestures of goodwill, such as offering Maine's Senator George Mitchell a plane ride back to Washington after one of Bush's frequent visits to his summer residence in Kennebunkport. On another occasion, he ensured that Speaker of the House Tom Foley was moved from the second row to the front during the signing of the 1989 Clean Air Act. Additionally, Bush continued to maintain a locker in the gym of the House of Representatives, using it as an opportunity to build relationships with members of both parties.[520]

In his efforts to build a more congenial relationship with Democrats, Bush also prioritized strengthening ties within his own party. When Georgia Congressman Newt Gingrich assumed the role of GOP minority leader following Dick Cheney's appointment as secretary of defense in 1989, Bush grew concerned about Gingrich's combative style and fiery rhetoric. "The question is, will he be confrontational? Will he raise hell with the establishment? Will he be difficult for me to work with?" Bush reflected in his diary that March. While Gingrich's aggressive tactics worried Bush and other pragmatic conservatives, the congressman's advocacy for inclusivity within the GOP and his emphasis on the importance of civil rights suggested that Gingrich and the president might share more common ground than initially expected.[521]

The president hoped the Georgia politician would understand the important concept of pragmatism that Bush believed necessary for success. Bush also believed that the president and Congress could only achieve legislative victories by collaborating with one another. Knowing that the two had to work together, Bush invited the new minority leader and his colleague, Minnesota Congressman Vin Weber, for beer at the White House.[522]

During their conversation, Bush emphasized his belief that pragmatic governance was more effective than strict ideological rigidity. "I'm worried that sometimes your idealism will get in the way of what I think is sound governance," he said politely. While Bush may have hoped his optimism would allow him to find common ground with the charismatic Georgian and his young, aggressive Republican colleagues, his earlier concerns about Gingrich's ambition proved accurate. As his presidency progressed, Bush watched as partisan hostility deepened, making the prospect of bipartisan consensus increasingly unattainable.[523]

Bush remained uneasy with Gingrich's confrontational approach to politics, though his aggressive style resonated with the frustrations of many House Republicans. Having been in the minority since 1954, even moderate members were eager for someone like Gingrich to challenge what they saw as a corrupt and entrenched system in need of reform. As scholar Julian Zelizer noted in *Time* in 2020, Gingrich believed, "If you teach [Republicans] how to be aggressive and confrontational...you will increase their abilities to fight Democrats on the floor." Gingrich's combative approach to political discourse energized Republicans, culminating in a major victory when he played a key role in forcing the resignation of Democratic House Speaker Jim Wright over an ethics scandal in 1989.[524]

While Bush acknowledged Wright's troubles during the 1988 campaign, as president he sought to set a more unifying tone, urging the nation to embrace the challenge of helping others rather than focusing solely on themselves. By assembling a team of highly competent and principled advisors, Bush created an atmosphere of mutual respect and collaboration within the executive branch. This environment encouraged open dialogue, ensuring that he received the best possible counsel to guide his decisions. The unity and loyalty he expected from and engendered in his staff proved essential in navigating the many challenges that lay ahead.

CHAPTER 13

A Delicate Balance: The Fall of the Berlin Wall

President Bush and President Gorbachev sign United States/Soviet Union agreements in the East Room of the White House, Washington, DC. June 1, 1990.

On July 6, 1989, President George Bush awarded diplomat George F. Kennan the Presidential Medal of Freedom, recognizing his pivotal role in shaping US policy toward the Soviet Union. At eighty-five, Kennan remained an influential figure in American foreign relations. As he presented the former ambassador with the nation's highest civilian honor, Bush acknowledged the evolving global landscape. "Today we stand on the threshold of a new era, a new era in our relationship with the Soviet

Union, one that looks beyond the successful strategy of containment, which George Kennan did so much to develop," he declared.[525]

Kennan, the last surviving member of the insular group of WASP elites responsible for building the postwar world, accepted the honor, though he remained puzzled by the recognition. President Bush had never sought his counsel or shared his views. Yet, the tribute went beyond politics or policy. For Bush, the gesture signified gratitude for a lifetime of service that helped guide the country through an era of fear and uncertainty. While Kennan liked Bush personally, biographer John Lewis Gaddis notes, Kennan argued that Bush "did better adjusting to the views of others in whom he sensed political influence and authority."[526]

Bush next invited the academic to a White House gathering later that year to discuss developments in the Soviet Union, though the occasion had little to do with flattering Kennan's ego. The president genuinely respected his expertise. For Bush, Kennan's presence offered yet another opportunity to deepen his understanding of a nation the scholar had spent a lifetime studying. This commitment to seeking wisdom from seasoned experts also extended to Bush's continued reliance on his predecessors in the Oval Office.[527]

***

While George Bush strongly believed in personal diplomacy, he remained a realist in his approach to global politics. Despite his generally positive view of Soviet Premier Mikhail Gorbachev's reform efforts, Bush and his national security team remained cautious about the Russian leader's broader intentions. That uncertainty led Bush to task Secretary of State James Baker, National Security Advisor Brent Scowcroft, and their colleagues with developing a comprehensive analysis to determine the direction of US foreign policy. Bush's cautious and deliberate approach mirrored the skepticism President Eisenhower maintained when he took office. "The traumatic uprisings in East Germany in 1953 [and] Hungary in 1956...were constantly on my mind through these tumultuous months," Bush later reflected, recalling the crises that had challenged his predecessor.[528]

Bush's strategy also reflected his deep conviction in the value of international organizations, particularly the North Atlantic Treaty Organization. On May 12, 1989, Bush expressed that commitment when he celebrated NATO's fortieth anniversary in a commencement address at Texas A&M University. In his speech to the graduating class, Bush honored the legacy of Kennan and Secretary of State Dean Acheson, whose policies helped contain Soviet expansion and protect the sovereignty of other nations. The president not only paid tribute to these statesmen, who brought experience and sound judgment to public service, but he also signified a broader "sense of continuity." His remarks underscored a shift by the United States from a strategy of containment to one of engagement, as Bush sought to welcome the Soviet Union as an equal partner in the international arena.[529]

The president believed that thoughtful predecessors like Presidents Harry Truman and Dwight Eisenhower had navigated the early days of the Cold War with great skill. He saw the success of figures like Kennan and Acheson as rooted in their commitment to democratic principles, strong governmental institutions, and humanitarian values that upheld the ideals of a free society. Bush affirmed that the United States hoped to engender a closer relationship with Moscow, by working to dismantle the diplomatic barriers that had divided the two nations for more than four decades.

On the surface, Bush's remarks about the US relationship with Russia conveyed a sense of optimism. However, behind the scenes, he and his national security team continued to remain apprehensive of Moscow's actions. While Bush and Scowcroft were open to the possibility that the Soviet Union had embraced a new path toward democracy and freedom, they were wary of the sincerity of Gorbachev's reforms.[530]

Bush expanded on his Texas A&M remarks during a meeting with NATO leaders in Brussels on May 26. While some within the Republican Party argued that the United States had invested too much money and manpower defending Western Europe, Bush firmly believed that history had proven the alliance's significance. He saw US engagement in global affairs as essential to maintaining world stability. "I always have believed that the United States bears a disproportionate responsibility for peace in Europe and an obligation to lead NATO. In the 1930s, we learned the hard way that it was a mistake to withdraw into isolation after World War I," Bush reflected years later.[531]

Having interacted with many of the attendees during his vice presidency, as well as during his tenures at the United Nations and as US envoy to China, Bush had fully prepared himself to engage in what he referred to as "personal diplomacy." He believed that building direct relationships with world leaders played a fundamental role in communicating the US agenda. "If a foreign leader knows the character and the heartbeat of a president (and vice versa), there is apt to be far less miscalculation on either side," Bush later reflected, emphasizing the message he sought to convey to his European counterparts.[532]

Following the NATO summit, Bush delivered an address on May 31, 1989, in Chancellor Helmut Kohl's hometown of Mainz, Germany. Twenty-four hours earlier, a last-minute technological mishap had erased the speech, forcing speechwriter Mark Davis and his team to reconstruct the text from notes and memory. "Any other president would have fired us," Davis recalled. But Bush took the setback in stride, demonstrating his characteristic patience and good humor.[533]

Bush sought to build on the growing fissures in the Iron Curtain, urging progress toward greater liberty. "But the passion for freedom cannot be denied forever. The world has waited long enough. The time is right. Let Europe be whole and free," he declared in remarks that continued to highlight NATO's historical significance.[534]

Bush's awareness of United States history also shaped his perspective on his own connection to those who had previously occupied the Oval Office. Bush requested NSC advisor Scowcroft visit every living former president, offering them occasional updates on global politics. As Nancy Gibbs and Michael Duffy note in *The President's Club*, these exchanges enabled Bush to draw on the experience of his predecessors, gaining valuable insight into various foreign and domestic challenges. Wanting to have access to those with as much experience as possible,

Bush offered each president a special phone so he could communicate with them directly.[535]

For Bush, a connection with those he had served remained vital. Throughout his presidency, Bush sent his predecessors handwritten memos about subjects that primarily focused on foreign policy. "One of the many things I admired about George Bush was that he was smart enough to use those relationships with former presidents to good advantage and humble enough to seek their advice as often as he saw fit," recalled John Sununu.[536]

As democratic change swept through Eastern Europe, Bush carefully observed the unfolding events to determine how the United States should respond. In the summer of 1989, he watched as Hungary dismantled barriers separating its citizens from the West and Poland's Solidarity movement secured a historic election victory. Visiting both nations in the wake of these upheavals, Bush encouraged continued reforms. At the same time, he recognized the need for a measured approach. "We could support freedom and democracy," he wrote, "but we had to do so in a way that would not make us appear to be gloating over Gorbachev's political problems with Party hard-liners."[537]

Bush believed that bragging undermined Washington's relationship with Moscow and also posed a potential danger. The president understood that the unconventional nature of Gorbachev's reforms had placed him in a precarious position. Years later, Bush admitted he wanted to proceed with caution about any actions he decided to take. He knew that excessive pressure on Gorbachev to push for more reform could alienate the Soviet leader's hardline opponents and destabilize his leadership. This sensitivity was evident during Bush's visits to Poland and Hungary in the summer of 1989. While congratulating the governments of both nations for their reforms in speeches in Gdańsk and Budapest, Bush avoided making grand statements about the Soviet Union's decline.[538]

Even as euphoria spread across Eastern Europe, Bush remained cautious about the unfolding events and believed that the United States needed to take a more active role in controlling the pace of change. As a result, he decided to personally contact Gorbachev and request a convenient opportunity to have their first face-to-face encounter. On July 21, Bush expressed his hope that the two could meet in a personal, unhurried setting, free from the interruptions of large delegations or complicated documents. "I just want to reduce the chances there could be misunderstandings between us," Bush wrote Gorbachev.[539]

Without informing anyone beyond Baker, Scowcroft, and Sununu, President Bush proposed an informal meeting, either at Camp David or at the Bush family's summer home in Kennebunkport. Bush hoped to create a relaxed atmosphere, "with neckties off," where the two men could speak candidly on a wide range of issues. To maintain discretion, Bush suggested that the meeting be timed to coincide with Gorbachev's planned visit to New York for his September address to the United Nations.[540]

The Soviet president responded favorably to the idea of a meeting. Gorbachev mentioned that he had scheduled a visit to Italy and proposed a meeting with Bush at the end of November. After further discussions, Bush and Gorbachev agreed to gather in December aboard two military ships off the coast of Malta. Bush appreciated the event's historical significance. Scowcroft had mentioned the first conference between Franklin D. Roosevelt and Winston Churchill had occurred on board a ship off the coast of Newfoundland in 1941. The idea also resonated with the president because the intimate space prevented the inclusion of media and personal staff.[541]

Averse to formal gatherings, Bush preferred more casual encounters and believed a private meeting with Gorbachev allowed both leaders to openly clarify their positions on various issues. While he considered including Scowcroft and Baker, he felt they were not essential to the meeting. "I knew exactly what I wanted to do, and I knew how I wanted to go about doing it," Bush recalled.[542]

Meanwhile, he faced ongoing criticism that his administration had not done enough to accelerate the pace of change in Eastern Europe. However, Bush's careful monitoring of events, and his awareness of the risks associated with too rapid a transformation, led him to believe that the critics were speaking from a position of ignorance. "I think it's crazy," he wrote in his journal on November 8, 1989. "If we mishandle this and get way out [in front] looking like [the rebellions are] an American project—you would invite crackdown, and invite negative reaction that could result in bloodshed. The more I'm in this job, the more I think prudence is a value and experience matters."[543]

No sooner had Bush written those words than an event unfolded that shocked the world. On November 9, 1989, as Bush sat at his desk in the Oval Office, Scowcroft informed him that East Germany had opened the Berlin Wall. The development, sparked by the introduction of a new East German visa program, appeared to allow unrestricted travel between East and West. With many believing the policy applied to Berlin as well, crowds gathered at the iconic barrier that had divided Germany since 1961.[544]

White House Press Secretary Marlin Fitzwater urged the president to make an immediate statement. However, Bush remained cautious. He understood that any remark would reflect on Gorbachev's leadership. Weighing the potential consequences, Bush believed "this was not the time to gloat about what many in the West would interpret as a defeat for Gorbachev." As Baker and others received information, Bush shared his concerns with Fitzwater of his reluctance to make any sweeping statement before fully considering all the factors involved in the unfolding events.[545]

After he and his staff had absorbed the latest developments, President Bush addressed the Washington press corps in the Oval Office. Displaying what James Baker later called 'heroic restraint,' Bush voiced measured satisfaction while cautioning against premature celebration.

"As I answered questions, my mind kept racing over a possible Soviet crackdown, turning all the happiness to tragedy," he later recalled. Reporters, however, seemed more struck by his lack of exuberance than by his caution.[546]

The Democratic Senate leader, George Mitchell, voiced similar criticisms, suggesting that Bush make a celebratory trip to "dance on the Wall," a proposal Bush found absurd. "I think publicly I simply do not speculate…but it is a reason to be prudent and be cautious, and to stop short of the euphoria that some are exhibiting," Bush said while dictating his thoughts.[547]

A less experienced, more self-centered leader might have seized the moment to boost their own popularity. Recognizing the historic significance of the event, Bush opted to keep his comments measured. His thoughtfulness proved to be the right approach. Shortly after the Berlin Wall collapsed, Gorbachev cautioned Bush "not to overreact." Bush understood that offering quiet support to Gorbachev strengthened their trust, allowing them to collaborate on issues that promoted global safety and security.[548]

In his communications with Gorbachev, Bush consistently made gestures aimed at developing a sense of trust between Russia and the United States. The president believed in doing whatever was necessary to encourage Gorbachev to collaborate with him in creating a more peaceful and stable world. Bush contended that the situation could only be achieved through the natural process of change, leading to the evolution of democratic principles where citizens gained greater political autonomy.[549]

As the effects of the Berlin Wall's fall continued to reverberate through Eastern Europe, the president prepared for his first extensive meeting with the Soviet leader. Bush had to limit his intake of information due to the demands of his daily responsibilities, but the upcoming meeting provided an opportunity for him to fully immerse himself in data and briefing papers. "Brent [Scowcroft] offered me about twenty topics to choose from: I took them all. I wanted to be prepared for everything," Bush wrote.[550]

While Bush believed that significant progress could be made in private exchanges with Gorbachev, he understood that any advances would ultimately enhance the security of the entire continent of Europe. In a strategy that Assistant Secretary of State Robert Zoellick called "alliance diplomacy," Bush communicated with each NATO member, asking them to identify the key issues they felt should be raised with Gorbachev and promising a follow-up meeting with all involved after the Malta summit. Bush recognized that every nation acted in its own self-interest. However, the president hoped to cultivate a sense of camaraderie and trust, one that would allow Gorbachev to eventually see the United States as an ally to turn to in times of adversity and crisis.[551]

On Thanksgiving Day, Bush sent Gorbachev a handwritten agenda outlining several key issues he hoped to discuss, including arms control, human rights, and Soviet involvement in Central America and the Middle East. Above all, Bush aimed to build a rapport with the Soviet leader, which he believed was essential for building a trusted friendship. "Success does not mean deals signed in my view. It means that you & I are frank enough with each other, in a confidential setting, so that our two great countries will not have tensions that arise simply because we don't know each others innermost thinking," Bush wrote to his Russian counterpart.[552]

Recognizing the challenges Gorbachev faced, Bush conveyed his hope that their upcoming meeting would set a constructive tone for the future. "I will give thanks that you are pressing forward with glasnost-perestroika, for you see, the fate of my own precious grandkids and yours is dependent on perestroika's success," Bush wrote in closing.[553]

During their meeting aboard the Soviet cruiser *Maxim Gorky*, Bush stressed his commitment to a relationship of goodwill with Gorbachev. The Soviet leader, despite Bush's measured response to the fall of the Berlin Wall, remained concerned that the United States sought to exploit Soviet instability for economic and military advantage. Seeking to reassure him, Bush stated, "I hope you have noticed that as dynamic change has accelerated in recent months, we have not responded with flamboyance or arrogance that would complicate Soviet relations."[554]

Realizing that the men were unfamiliar with one another, Bush prioritized building an atmosphere of trust and confidence. Aware of the Soviet Union's turmoil, Bush recognized that exploiting Gorbachev's weakened position accomplish little. "All his life, George Bush had been a humble man. He wasn't trying to score points for himself.... And he knew the best way to achieve results was to think about the situation from the other person's perspective," George W. Bush later wrote.[555]

In his discussions with Gorbachev, Bush proposed a range of economic incentives, including granting Russia "most favored nation" trading status. According to Marlin Fitzwater, the suggestion made "Gorbachev's face light up like sunshine." But Bush's economic commitments were more than just proposals, they were a demonstration of trust in the Soviet leader and a clear endorsement of the reform agenda Gorbachev aspired to achieve for his nation.[556]

Over the next two years, the trust forged between Bush and Gorbachev at Malta laid the foundation for an ongoing dialogue, with the two leaders meeting on five separate occasions. As their relationship grew stronger, they successfully negotiated arms control agreements and held substantive discussions that ultimately led to the 1990 reunification of Germany. Diplomatic historian Tizoc Chavez notes that Bush's prudence and restraint transformed "US-Soviet summits" into "a routine affair." When Gorbachev resigned as president of the Soviet Union in December 1991, he called Bush on Christmas Day to express his gratitude for the trust and respect that had defined their relationship. "I value greatly our cooperation together, our partnership, and friendship," Gorbachev told him.[557]

President Bush's experience, humility, and self-confidence were essential in guiding the United States through the precarious aftermath of the Berlin Wall's fall. He recognized the fragile nature of Gorbachev's position and the challenges posed by the sweeping changes in Eastern Europe. Understanding the importance of stability, Bush prioritized building a personal relationship with the Soviet leader during a pivotal moment in history. These same principles earned Bush the respect of NATO allies, including French President François Mitterrand and Canadian Prime Minister Brian Mulroney. "They trusted his tactics and strategy, and most importantly, they trusted that he would ensure they shared in the credit for the success of this world-changing effort," John Sununu remarked.[558]

As Bush reviewed a challenging year, he understood that presidents are ultimately judged by their ability to navigate historic moments. "I'm certainly not seen as visionary, but I hope I'm seen as steady and prudent and able," he wrote in his journal. Recognizing the fragility of Gorbachev's position and the sweeping changes unfolding in Eastern Europe, Bush prioritized stability. He focused on building a personal relationship with the Soviet leader based on trust during a transformative moment in history.[559]

CHAPTER 14

Not for Self: The 1990 Budget Negotiations

President Bush signs Executive Order Ethics Package as C. Boyden Gray, Counsel to the President, looks on in the Oval Office of the White House. April 12, 1989.

On the afternoon of May 6, 1990, President Bush invited congressional leaders to the White House for a lecture by historian David McCullough on the early life of Theodore Roosevelt. Bush and the "Rough Rider" shared much in common. Both were well-born who chose lives of public service with the aim of improving society for the better. Additionally, they were both committed in using government to enact gradual, meaningful change for the benefit of all Americans.[560]

Bush and Roosevelt identified as Republicans; however, both were ambivalent with many of the policies championed by their party. During McCullough's lecture, the historian noted how fortunate the country had been to have strong presidential leadership during some of its most pivotal moments. As the group gathered under the shadow of Roosevelt's portrait, Bush hoped that, like TR, he might find the political magic necessary to build a bipartisan consensus on the nation's fiscal challenges.[561]

Throughout McCullough's presentation, Bush found himself feeling nostalgic for the simpler world of the early twentieth century. "…oh to be President in those less complicated times where you could finish work at 4:00, and go for a ride." Bush wrote in his diary. After the lecture, when meeting with congressional leaders, Bush recognized that he had little choice but to consider some form of tax increase or face the risk of a government shutdown. Many respected leaders, such as Federal Reserve Chairman Alan Greenspan and former Presidents Nixon, Ford, and Carter, believed that the only way to restore the nation's fiscal stability was through spending cuts or tax increases. According to John Sununu, Bush envisioned a future in which, with the Cold War behind them and the nation moving toward fiscal discipline, the United States "would enter an era of surpluses, growth, and prosperity—and peace."[562]

***

Throughout his political career, George Bush skillfully balanced campaign rhetoric with the realities of politics. However, his 1988 convention pledge, "Read my lips: no new taxes," became a defining moment that constrained his presidency. Seeking to secure support from the right and finally claim the office that had eluded him eight years earlier, Bush made a resolute commitment against tax increases. Yet, once in office, his deep concern over rising deficits forced him to choose between ideological loyalty and fiscal responsibility. While his decision demonstrated a commitment to sound governance, it also highlighted the political cost of the willingness to work across the aisle to reach a decision mutually beneficial to both parties. Bush's pragmatic philosophy represented a defining trait of the GOP establishment wing at a time of growing partisan polarization.[563]

One of Bush's deepest convictions concerned his aversion to deficits. During the 1980 campaign, he had criticized Ronald Reagan's economic policies as "voodoo economics." In January 1987, Richard Nixon shared his concerns, telling Bush, "George, you know you were right about voodoo economics, don't you? We've got to handle the deficit. You know there is going to have to be a tax increase." Like Dwight Eisenhower, Bush came from a family who believed in the values of frugality and gratitude for one's possessions. Both men saw deficits as a serious threat to the nation's economic stability. Reflecting that belief, Bush emphasized fiscal responsibility in his 1987 campaign autobiography, writing, "On day one…I intend to name a team of negotiators to represent the executive branch in top-level budget sessions with the Congress."[564]

Bush's declaration, "Read my lips, no new taxes," became the most notable moment of his 1988 GOP acceptance speech. As reported by *The Washington Post*'s Bob Woodward in 1992, many within Bush's inner circle opposed its inclusion, including his budget director, Richard Darman. On multiple occasions, Darman urged speechwriter Peggy Noonan to remove the line, but she refused, arguing that its clarity left no room for "misinterpretation." White House Chief of Staff John Sununu also had reservations, recognizing the potential political risks of such an unequivocal pledge. As a former governor, Sununu understood the dangers of making such a statement, particularly on the contentious issue of taxes.

Years later, Bush admitted that the pledge had been a mistake. "I felt uncomfortable with some of that. But it was persuasive—the convention loved it," he recalled. Despite his no-tax pledge, Bush entered office determined to rein in the deficit, believing that unchecked spending threatened the nation's long-term economic growth. "If it weren't for the dammed deficit, I'd be kicking up my heels and feeling like a Spring colt," the president wrote to his friend, writer Willie Morris.[565]

Bush's decision to break his promise on raising taxes reflected his tendency to separate politics from policy. As academic Martin Medhurst writes, Bush viewed politics as...the narrow, self-interested activities that one had to engage in to get elected to office," but once elected, he prioritized broad consensus and national benefit over partisan loyalty. While his decision to raise taxes ultimately strengthened the economy in the long run, it alienated a conservative base crucial to his reelection. By breaking his pledge, Bush reinforced the skepticism within his party that he lacked any ideological convictions. It also fueled the perception that he symbolized the arrogant elitism of the establishment, who casually disregarded promises, believing voters had elected them solely for their judgment and expertise.[566]

Bush began his presidency facing a daunting $152.1 billion budget deficit. Determined to cut spending, he found himself in a struggle against a Congress controlled by the opposing party, making his goal increasingly unrealistic. The General Accounting Office delivered an even starker assessment. As historian John Robert Greene notes, the nonpartisan government agency concluded that "new taxes would be needed as a part of any 'credible' effort to lower the deficit." In the end, Sununu and Darman were right: The "read my lips" pledge had left the president with few viable options.[567]

On principle, Bush remained reluctant to break the commitment he had made at the convention. Yet he also believed that raising taxes represented the only workable path to achieving a balanced budget. Still, he remained hopeful that his experience in the House of Representatives would help him negotiate a solution with Democrats. With that idea in mind, Bush leaned on his close friendship with an influential Democrat congressman from Illinois, Ways and Means Committee Chairman Dan Rostenkowski. The Chicago politician gave Bush his word he would wait a year before raising the issue of a tax hike.[568]

Rostenkowski kept his promise. The first budget from the Bush administration passed through Congress in just nine weeks. While Bush aimed to keep taxes low, he also firmly believed that free trade could serve as a powerful engine for economic growth. "The goal of competition is not just simply to disadvantage the competition, it's to better deploy the advantages we have to create new ones," Bush said in an address to businessmen.[569]

Despite the appearance of progress with Democrats on the budget issue, the reality proved more challenging. With the deficit projected to rise to $171 billion in the next fiscal year, Bush also faced the looming challenge of the Gramm-Rudman-Hollings Act. Passed in 1985, the legislation mandated a reduction of the deficit to $91 billion by October 1, 1991. If these targets were not met, automatic cuts of 40 percent were imposed across all domestic expenditures, including national defense, housing, education, and other vital programs.[570]

The ideological divide between the two parties in reaching a budget agreement was more pronounced during Bush's presidency than during Eisenhower's. When Ike balanced the budget in 1960, the Democratic-controlled Congress included a significant number of Southern conservatives who strongly advocated fiscal discipline. Even Midwestern liberals, such as Senator Hubert H. Humphrey from Minnesota, recognized the importance of consensus in addressing the nation's political challenges. The cooperative spirit helped facilitate solutions, a stark contrast to the more polarized environment Bush faced.

By the time Bush arrived in the White House, maintaining that consensus had become more challenging. According to a 2022 analysis by the Pew Research Center, when Bush served in the United Nations in 1971, there were a combined one hundred and sixty moderates in both the House of Representatives and the Senate. By 1990, the parties were no longer seeking what Arthur Schlesinger called "the vital center" but moving in increasingly ideological directions. That growing rigidity made it increasingly difficult for Bush to forge a bipartisan agreement on the deficit.

On January 29, 1990, with inflation rising and the stock market showing volatility, President Bush presented his 1991 fiscal-year budget to Congress. Totaling $1.23 trillion, the budget included reductions in capital gains taxes and defense spending. Bush recognized that these cuts alone would not be enough to meet the $64 billion target set by the Gramm-Rudman-Hollings legislation. To bridge the gap, Darman and his team inserted a provision for $14 billion in "user fees." Although not labeled as taxes, the measure reflected Bush's understanding that additional revenues were necessary to prevent cuts to essential programs that served the general welfare.[571]

Democrats argued that the administration's budget measures were insufficient. As reported by *The New York Times,* in the second week of April 1990, House Democrats responded by calling for deeper cuts in defense spending, along with increased funding for education, childcare, and the environment. With a budget totaling $1.2 trillion, Democrats, backed by the Congressional Budget Office, claimed that the administration had underestimated the budget's impact on the deficit by $70 billion.

Bush recognized the need for negotiations to find a viable solution. The following day, aware that his willingness to break the "no new taxes" pledge would draw criticism, he issued a statement agreeing to budget talks with no preconditions. Republicans on his right condemned him. Despite that political pressure, Bush tried to take solace in the advice his mother had given him during her recent visit: to maintain a positive outlook. "I can't let the bastards get us down.... Push forward," he wrote in his diary.[572]

The president recognized that rigid adherence to principles could lead to deadlock. "When you're are faced with...the practical reality of shutting down the government or dealing with a hostile Congress, you get something done," Bush said. While he believed that raising taxes remained a necessary evil, he did not take the decision to break his 1988 promise lightly.[573]

Bush valued keeping his word above all else. Personal integrity and adherence to his principles were fundamental to his character. At the same time, he believed in the convictions expressed by his father, about making decisions and initiating policies that would best serve the nation's long-term interests. The decision to raise taxes, while painful, represented one such choice aimed at ensuring the country's fiscal stability. But Bush also recognized the political toll it took on his prospects for reelection in 1992. "It did destroy me," he recalled decades later.[574]

While Bush ultimately made the decision to increase taxes, he received poor assistance from Sununu, Darman, and Secretary of the Treasury Nicholas Brady. The trio had prematurely issued a statement in Bush's name, announcing that he had agreed to a tax hike before a budget deal became finalized. Additionally, Bush made the misstep of waiting several days to explain his reasoning to the American people, further complicating the political fallout.[575]

Never known as a great communicator, Bush may have understood that making remarks about his decision to raise taxes would do little to shift public opinion, particularly among those who opposed it. He believed leadership required tough choices, and with a potential government shutdown looming, Bush believed the time for easy answers or short-term thinking did not solve the problem. "He truly believed that the country was going to judge him on results…and how it turned out—not on what he said in a speech," Vice President Dan Quayle recalled.[576]

Bush biographer Jon Meacham argues that his weakness as an orator represented a significant obstacle to his success as president. Meacham contends that despite years of close association with Reagan, Bush had little interest in perfecting a compelling verbal delivery. However, Bush did learn from Reagan in other ways: He recognized the power of a well-delivered speech, as demonstrated by the positive reception of his 1988 convention address. Focusing mainly on the substance of his speeches, oratory remained a skill he never fully acquired.[577]

He also showed little interest in using the presidency like Theodore Roosevelt, as a means of gathering support for a particular issue. The president's reluctance to employ oratory to clearly justify his decisions, or to strategically prepare the public in advance, frustrated members of his own administration.

"I didn't know it was going to happen until it happened," White House Communications Director David Demarest recalled about Bush's tax-increase decision. "Ronald Reagan raised taxes a bunch of times—nobody thought he was the great tax raiser. Well, he positioned it properly.… We did none of it. We posted it on a bulletin board. It was horrible." Despite having a front-row seat during the Reagan years, Bush's aversion to rehearsed or overly polished rhetoric mirrored his broader distaste for politics, an approach that clashed with the demands of the office he held.[578]

The president was a competitive man, but not a combative one. While he understood the differences people had with his decisions, he refused to whine, complain, or twist himself into knots trying to please everyone. A self-assured individual, Bush understood that doing something right did not always mean taking the popular position.

"I truly feel that George is doing what is responsible and right for the country, and to heck with politics. There is life after the White House," Barbara Bush wrote in her diary.[579]

While Bush may not have enjoyed speechmaking, he tried to convince the nation of the prudence of his actions when he delivered an address to a joint session of Congress on September 11, 1990. Iraq had invaded Kuwait a month earlier, and the president believed it necessary to update the nation on the steps being taken to prevent Saddam Hussein from advancing further into the Middle East. "I just hope that Iraq and the country's unity...can now be parlayed into support for the budget agreement," Bush wrote several days before the speech.[580]

During his remarks, the president argued that efforts to remove Iraq from Kuwait, and the determined push to reduce the deficit, were both crucial to advancing the national interest, domestically and abroad. "Our world leadership and domestic strength are mutual and reinforcing; a woven piece, strongly bound as Old Glory," Bush stated. While the war had not begun, Bush sought to use his rhetoric to inspire patriotism, urging the nation's representatives to unite behind a cause that would benefit the country in the long run. "In the final analysis, our ability to meet our responsibilities abroad depends upon political will and consensus at home," Bush said, calling for unity to address the nation's fiscal challenges.[581]

The speech made little progress in bridging the gap between the two parties. On October 30, Bush addressed the media to announce the administration's revised budget. While the "marginal" tax rate remained unchanged, the new budget included additional taxes on gas, tobacco, and alcohol.[582]

More importantly, the new budget aimed to cut the deficit by $500 billion over four years, while it also introduced a "pay as you go" system, requiring those who proposed new programs to specify how they would be funded. While Bush was frustrated about breaking his promise on taxes, he recognized that prioritizing the fiscal health of the nation remained essential. "Sometimes you don't get it just the way you want.... But it's time we put the interest of the United States of America first and get this deficit under control," the president stated when announcing the agreement.[583]

Bush anticipated backlash from the Right, and it came as no surprise when Congressman Newt Gingrich and his colleagues expressed their fury over the president's decision. On the other side, liberal Democrats felt that Bush had placed too much emphasis on spending cuts, leading them to believe that additional concessions were necessary. Despite Bush's efforts, the agreement failed to gain traction in Congress. Since no consensus had been reached by October 1, the severe cuts mandated by the Gramm-Rudman-Hollings Act were triggered.[584]

Following a three-day partial government shutdown, Bush signed a resolution on October 9 to allow the government to continue functioning. He lamented the failure of many to understand that successful governance reflected the collective good, not individual interests. "It will not be as good a budget deal as I want or as good as what we have proposed: but it is essential that we get a deal," Bush wrote to Republican Congressman Jim Lightfoot in the second week of October 1990.[585]

Recognizing the need for compromise, Bush agreed to eliminate the gasoline tax in exchange for higher taxes on the wealthiest Americans. When he signed the Omnibus Budget Reconciliation Act at the end of October 1990—which included measures to reduce the deficit by $492 billion but also raised the nation's top tax rate from 28 percent to 31 percent—he understood the political risks for both him and the GOP. Yet, his decision reflected a fundamental principle: prioritizing the nation's long-term stability over partisan concerns. Bush had no intention of harming his party politically; rather, he believed true leadership was not about preserving personal popularity but about ensuring the nation was in a stronger position for the future. Looking back on Bush's choice, President Bill Clinton later remarked, "I thought he did the right thing."[586]

Robert Zoellick, president of the World Bank from 2007–2012, argues that the 1990 budget agreement played a crucial role in Clinton's ability to reduce the deficit during the 1990s. "Bush's deal saved about 2 percent of GDP; Clinton's subsequent deals saved 1.5 percent and then 0.5 percent. But in creating that positive economic climate, [Bush] paid a big political price," Zoellick explained in an email exchange with the author.[587]

While Bush expected criticism from the Right, he grew upset by the intense backlash against officials who had helped negotiate the tax increases. One prominent target, the administration's budget director, Richard Darman, faced harsh attacks from fellow Republicans, who blamed him for leading the president toward political disaster. Bush saw things differently. "I know you've been hurt by some unkind, unfair arrows aimed at Dick's back," he wrote in a letter to Darman's wife, Kathleen. In the note, Bush strongly defended Darman's role, emphasizing the positive impact of his contributions in securing the budget agreement.[588]

The president wanted to convey his deep appreciation for Darman for his expertise and competence, but also for his commitment to making a courageous choice: "The politicians want to be sure they emerge blameless, unscathed, untouched by compromises. But Dick and others were trying to do something for our country & to help me *govern*—to make something happen," Bush wrote.[589]

Additionally, GOP economic advisor Bruce Bartlett suggested that another factor influenced Bush's decision to align with Democrats on the budget. The negotiations were taking place during Iraq's invasion of Kuwait, and Bush's growing realization of the gravity of the international situation led him to understand that "we were almost certainly going to war shortly," and that the costs of such a conflict should be accounted for financially.[590]

Bush's signing of the budget bill in the fall of 1990 reflected his commitment to tackling complex challenges rather than deferring them to others. While many Republicans saw his decision as a betrayal of conservative principles, Bush remained convinced that forging consensus meant achieving the greater good. Throughout his political career, Bush had observed Presidents Ford and Reagan make difficult choices they believed were necessary for the country's well-being. "I think he's a traditional American. I think he believes in compromise…who wants to solve problems…and that angers real ideologues on both sides as we're learning today," said Bush advisor and Fox News founder Roger Ailes.[591]

The decision to raise taxes may not have carried the same historical weight as Ford's pardon of Nixon or Reagan's willingness to set aside ideology in building a relationship with Mikhail Gorbachev. However, Bush's commitment to fiscal principles were deeply rooted in the puritan philosophy of conserving resources for the future. While Bush saw the tax increase as a necessary step for economic stability, it ultimately came at a political cost, jeopardizing his chances for reelection.

While Bush suffered politically from his reversal on the "no new taxes" pledge, his decision demonstrated a level of presidential leadership that has endured over time. As Harvard economist Jeffrey Frankel noted in 2018, Bush's focus on reducing the deficit made a lasting positive impact on the nation's economic future. When Bill Clinton defeated Bush in the 1992 election, he carried forward Bush's "pay-as-you-go" policy at the recommendation of Treasury Secretary Robert Rubin, using it as a tool to continue deficit reduction. Passed on a party-line vote, the legislation upheld Bush's fiscal restrictions throughout Clinton's presidency. These measures contributed to economic growth while leading to budget surpluses from 1998 to 2000. In that regard, Bush's decision reflected not just his commitment to fiscal conservatism but also his dedication to the founders' vision of governance—one that prioritized the good of the nation over political expediency.

CHAPTER 15

The Triumph of Experience: Operation Desert Storm

President Bush walks with Saudi Arabian Foreign Minister Prince Saud Al-Faisal, at Walker's Point, Kennebunkport, Maine. August 16, 1990.

On Christmas Eve, 1990, the Bush family gathered at Camp David. As President Bush continued to ready the nation for possible military action against Saddam Hussein, in response to Iraq's unlawful and unjust invasion of Kuwait, he spent much of his time reading letters from servicemen and sending holiday greetings to members of his staff. The night before, Bush had dreamed of visiting his father. "We embraced, and I told him I missed him very much.... I could see him very clearly: big, strong, and highly respected."

In that moment, Bush may have contemplated what his father, Prescott Bush, would have done under such grave circumstances. Awaiting a performance of Christmas carols, the looming January 15, 1991, United Nations deadline pressed heavily on the president's mind. If Saddam Hussein did not withdraw Iraqi forces from Kuwait by then, Bush had threatened to unleash the full power of a thirty-five-nation coalition against the Iraqi regime. "I'm getting older, but does that make it easier to send someone's son to die? Or does it make it more difficult? All I know is that it's right," he reflected.[592]

***

In the final days of the Vietnam War, George Bush sat in Peking, China, pondering the conflict that had caused so much turmoil within the United States and throughout the international community. Far from the daily bustle of Washington, Bush spent his spare time considering what actions he might take if faced with a situation requiring the deployment of US military forces. "I am wondering what I would have recommended if I had been in a position of major authority," Bush wrote. A strong believer in the domino theory, Bush shared the views of Dwight Eisenhower and others, believing that if international communism gained a foothold in Vietnam, it could eventually spread throughout the entire region.[593]

Bush firmly believed in the strategic use of American power. However, from watching his country's involvement in Southeast Asia, he learned that any military action needed to have clear, focused objectives, backed by domestic support and international alliances. The insights he recorded in his 1975 journal, combined with his extensive experience in both foreign and domestic policy, laid the foundation for how he managed the campaign to remove Iraq's Saddam Hussein from Kuwait fifteen years later.[594]

On the evening of August 1, 1990, National Security Advisor Brent Scowcroft informed the president that Iraqi dictator Saddam Hussein was about to invade Kuwait. True to his strong belief in the importance of international institutions, Bush immediately contacted UN Ambassador Thomas Pickering. "While I was prepared to deal with this crisis unilaterally if necessary, I wanted the United Nations involved as part of our first response.... Decisive UN action would be important in rallying international opposition to the invasion and reversing it," Bush wrote in his memoir.[595]

Thinking back to the events of that period, Bush acknowledged that while he believed in the importance of the United Nations, he remained uncertain about its effectiveness in condemning international aggression. Having served as the US representative to the UN during the 1970s, he possessed a strong understanding of the organization's deep divisions, which were exacerbated by Cold War tensions. Even with the collapse of the Soviet Union, Bush questioned whether the divisions within the international community had truly faded enough to generate unanimous support against Iraq's aggression.[596]

Bush believed that his long-standing relationships with many of the world's leaders were crucial in addressing the crises in the Middle East, including his growing partnership with Soviet leader Mikhail Gorbachev. The Soviets had a historical alliance with Iraq, but Bush hoped that his strong rapport with Gorbachev could persuade the Russians to support a condemnation of Iraq by refraining from using their veto in the UN Security Council.[597]

As Jeffrey Engel has noted, no security treaty existed between the United States and Kuwait. However, Bush viewed any threat to the flow of oil between the region and the West as a direct and imminent danger to US interests. At the time of the invasion, the administration remained uncertain whether Saddam Hussein simply sought to control Kuwait or had broader ambitions to expand into other Gulf states.[598]

On August 2, the United Nations Resolution 660 passed with a unanimous 14–0 vote, calling for Iraq to immediately withdraw its forces from Kuwait. Additionally, Bush had ordered the freezing of all Iraqi and Kuwaiti assets and the deployment of American naval vessels in the Persian Gulf. Despite these initial measures, Bush remained uncertain about what further actions to take. "There is little the US can do in a situation like this," Bush wrote as events continued to unfold.[599]

Determined to secure Hussein's withdrawal from Kuwait through diplomatic means, Bush remained composed when addressing the media. Later admitting he "had no idea what our options were," Bush understood that whatever he said, especially concerning the potential use of troops, would have immediate consequences both at home and among international allies. Bush also recognized the significant threat Hussein posed to the West's access to oil. "I did know for sure that the aggression had to be stopped, and Kuwait's sovereignty restored," Bush wrote.[600]

As the president met with his national security team—Defense Secretary Dick Cheney, Deputy Secretary of State Lawrence Eagleburger, and National Security Advisor Brent Scowcroft—all were united in their belief that "the stakes in this for the United States are such that to accommodate Iraq should not be a policy option." Director for Near East Affairs Richard N. Haass formally reinforced that view in a memo, stating that allowing Hussein to remain in Iraq "would be setting a terrible precedent—one that would only accelerate violent centrifugal tendencies in this - emerging post Cold War era...that also raises the issue of US reliability in a most serious way."[601]

The fact that Haass could write such a blunt assessment without fearing how the president would react spoke volumes about Bush's leadership style. Bush believed in listening to everyone before sharing his own thoughts, a method he felt essential to the success of the National Security Council staff. The approach allowed all involved to offer their honest assessments without feeling pressured to please the president. In Haass's view, when Bush decided to develop an initiative to remove Iraq's army from Kuwait, his extensive experience, as well as his "judgment and character," played a pivotal role in managing the crisis.[602]

General Colin Powell shared Haass's assessment, agreeing that Bush's approach epitomized the experience and measured temperament acquired over years in public life. Never one to react impulsively, Bush had a reputation for analyzing issues methodically. He relied on a vast network of contacts to gather as much information as possible before making any decisions. While recognizing the end of the Cold War as a cause for optimism, the president also understood that such profound change could create instability to various parts of the globe.[603]

Those developments, if not closely monitored, could empower those hostile to the global spread of freedom. "These threats...can arise suddenly, unpredictably, and from unexpected quarters. US interests can be protected only with capability which is in existence and which is ready to act without delay," Bush stated in an address at the fortieth anniversary celebration of the Aspen Institute on August 2, 1990. Haass's concerns added emphasis to the dilemma: If the United States chose to ignore Iraq's aggression, nations worldwide would question whether they could still view the US as reliable to lead the campaign against those who sought to undermine democracy.[604]

In the days following Iraq's invasion, Bush leveraged his long-standing relationships with leaders in the Middle East to gauge their views on the crisis. He had an in-depth understanding of the region, including its diplomacy, military dynamics, and economic interests. According to Peter and Rochelle Schweizer, Bush recalled discussing the Suez Canal crisis of 1956 with his father. Additionally, Bush had gained valuable experience in the region during his years in the oil industry, further enriching his understanding of Middle Eastern affairs.[605]

During his time at the United Nations, the Central Intelligence Agency, and as vice president, Bush had built strong relationships with key leaders in the Middle East, including Saudi Arabia's King Fahd, Jordan's King Hussein, and Egypt's President Hosni Mubarak. In addition, Bush tapped into his extensive global network, reaching out to more than sixty world leaders to gather their perspectives on Iraq's actions. In Brent Scowcroft's view, Bush possessed the ideal experience to navigate the crisis due to the deep relationships he had cultivated during his time at the UN. "I think that was just invaluable preparation," Scowcroft said.[606]

In a conversation with Saudi leader King Fahd, Bush expressed his concern that Iraq might expand its influence by moving from Kuwait into

Fahd's kingdom. He suggested supplying Saudi Arabia with American air power as a precautionary measure. Fahd, however, hesitated, asking for time to speak with Saddam Hussein. Given his extensive experience in the region, Bush feared that the Saudi leadership, believing they could prevent a wider conflict, might be inclined to appease Iraq's aggression. He remained uncertain about the decision the Saudis would make, believing any successful operation to remove Hussein's forces required not only Fahd's cooperation but also the support of much of the Arab world.[607]

King Fahd initially resisted the idea of allowing a military presence in Saudi Arabia. However, after numerous discussions and a visit from Dick Cheney, coupled with a guarantee that US forces would leave as soon as the crisis resolved, Fahd ultimately agreed to the deployment of American troops on Saudi soil. Fahd's decision to accept military aid demonstrated his recognition of the situation's gravity and the respect he had for President Bush.[608]

Following his conversation with King Fahd, Bush ordered the deployment of the 82nd Airborne. In addition, aircraft carriers and American ground troops were positioned around Saudi Arabia. The United States also succeeded in securing a vote from the United Nations that approved financial sanctions against Iraq. The president recognized that if the United States were to engage in military action, it would require the full support of the international community.[609]

Without question, developing of an alliance of that size represented a formidable challenge. However, Bush's lengthy experience and his talent at cultivating relationships made him the ideal president to develop an international coalition to confront Saddam Hussein. Advised by an old friend, Canadian Prime Minister Brian Mulroney, to consult French President François Mitterrand, the president arranged for the White House operator to call him at 2:45 a.m. EST, so that he could place a call to Mitterrand at 9:00 a.m. in Paris. When the Frenchman stated emphatically, "We will be there," Bush expressed his appreciation.[610]

Like King Fahd, Prime Minister Mulroney, and many others, Bush made a concerted effort to build personal relationships, including with the French president, who visited Kennebunkport in the spring of 1989. "He cultivated those friendships; they weren't just acquaintances for him... he called when there was no purpose to call, when he wasn't asking for anything," recalled Deputy National Security Advisor Robert Gates.[611]

King Fahd also asked President Bush to secure regional support for Saudi Arabia, which led Bush to call Egyptian President Hosni Mubarak at 2:55 a.m. Mubarak gave permission for American warships to pass through the Suez Canal, allowed US planes to fly through Egyptian airspace, and granted them refueling access at local air bases. Defense Secretary Dick Cheney witnessed the power of Bush's global network firsthand when he arrived in Rabat to consult with Morocco's King Hassan. "You show up in Morocco and the king is waiting for you. His old buddy, George Bush, has talked to him, and yes, he'll send troops. The strength of [Bush's] personality, his experience, the fact that he dealt with these guys over the years and they liked him and trusted him," Cheney recalled.[612]

On August 8 at 9:00 a.m., two days after his conversations with King Hassan, President Mubarak, and François Mitterrand, Bush addressed the American people from the Oval Office. "I knew I was not nearly as good as Ronald Reagan in these situations, so I read through my copy a time or two," Bush recalled. The president wanted to emphasize to the American public the importance of not repeating the mistakes of World War II. At the same time, Bush remained concerned that the painful memory of Vietnam would lead many of his viewers to fear that the United States had begun heading toward another quagmire, this time in the deserts of the Middle East.[613]

Consulting with Vietnam veterans, including Colin Powell, the chairman of the Joint Chiefs reminded Bush that while coalition building played an important diplomatic role, years earlier the United States had developed a similar coalition of more than thirty countries with the objective of sustaining the South Vietnamese government. Powell contended that the key reason for the failure of that coalition's success centered on President Lyndon Johnson's decision to neither use overwhelming force nor clearly define the limits of America's mission. "I'm convinced that they'll support us—the Congress—provided it's fast and surgical," Bush wrote, outlining his vision for the military campaign.[614]

During the address, the president outlined the objectives of the nation's involvement in the Middle Eastern crisis. He stressed that the United States could not stand by while a dangerous dictator threatened the world's oil supply. While Bush emphasized that the United States would play a central role in the campaign, he made it clear that it was not a unilateral action but one coordinated with a global coalition. "We agree that this is not an American problem, or a European problem, or a Middle East problem: It is the world's problem," the president declared.[615]

Bush linked the international campaign to liberate Kuwait with the Allied coalition that had defeated Germany, Italy, and Japan during World War II. Even with the apparent end of the Soviet Union, Bush believed the United States remained a symbol of hope in the face of threats to liberty from international despots. "We succeeded in the struggle for freedom in Europe because we and our allies remained stalwart. Keeping the peace in the Middle East will require no less," Bush stated.[616]

In practicing personal diplomacy, Bush reached beyond the larger nations in the region to smaller states, including Oman and the United Arab Emirates. These gestures mirrored his approach during his time at the United Nations, when he took the time to visit small member states of the General Assembly to show them that the United States valued their opinions on global affairs.

As Bush worked to assemble the thirty-five-nation coalition for "Operation Desert Storm," those close to him, including Condoleezza Rice, recognized that only Bush possessed the talent and skill to develop such a diverse coalition. "They trusted George Bush. They believed in his will and his resolve, and they knew that he could achieve the goals he set out to do." That trust and experience resonated with Gorbachev and Chinese President Yang Shangkun, resulting in Bush's ability to secure support of both the Soviet Union and China.[617]

During the first week of August 1990, Bush worked tirelessly to rally support for the mission to liberate Kuwait. As the summer wore on, some on the White House staff began to question whether he should take his annual summer vacation at Walker's Point in Kennebunkport. Bush loved the outdoors and time spent at sea, and he continued the presidential tradition of enjoying retreats in rural, tranquil settings—much as Presidents Ronald Reagan (Rancho del Cielo), Franklin D. Roosevelt (Hyde Park), and Theodore Roosevelt (Elkhorn Ranch) found physical and spiritual renewal in such environments. "I think [Kennebunkport] gave the president the kind of connection to his roots and restored his strength and self-confidence," said Brent Scowcroft.[618]

By taking a vacation, Bush realized a media firestorm would arise from the perception that he was neglecting his duties during a time of crisis. He also understood the importance of demonstrating that he had not become overwhelmed by the unfolding events. "I remembered all too well the international and domestic perception of the Carter Administration during the Tehran hostage crisis. It had appeared that America's hands were tied, and that the attention of its president was controlled by thugs." Bush believed that projecting confidence and demonstrating that he and his advisors had the situation under control would resonate with the American public. That determination to display a sense of normalcy during great turmoil represented the strength Bush admired in Ronald Reagan, who never appeared rattled by external pressures and maintained an unflappable demeanor.[619]

By sticking to his regular vacation schedule in Maine, Bush aimed to set a standard for the nation. "Life had to go on as normally as possible, not just for the president but for the country as a whole," Bush wrote years later. First Lady Barbara Bush reinforced that sentiment in her decision to fly on an airplane, even when many feared that Iraq's hostilities might lead to hijackings. "We had to show our people that the United States was still in charge and that they had nothing to fear," the president recalled.[620]

That outward confidence, reminiscent of FDR, Eisenhower, and Reagan, resonated deeply with the nation. From August 9–12, Gallup registered the president's approval rating at 74 percent. Despite the high poll numbers, Bush noted that some of his advisors believed he needed to further clarify the objectives he had laid out in his Oval Office address.

However, Bush felt that his actions would ultimately speak louder than words.[621]

Challenges persisted, even as Bush sought to recharge with moments of fishing and golf at Walker's Point. During a visit with King Hussein, the Jordanian ruler frustrated Bush by continuing to believe a peaceful settlement with Saddam Hussein remained possible. Bush grew increasingly concerned. If military action were delayed, Saddam might take hostage the twenty-five hundred Americans trapped in Kuwait. Recalling the difficult days when President Carter struggled to free American hostages held by militants in Iran, Bush wrote, "I am determined that I could not be a Jimmy Carter—an impotent flicking US impotence in the eyes of the world."[622]

Bush's concerns were confirmed when Hussein issued a chilling warning to the president: "You are going to receive some American bodies in bags." As historian Herbert Parmet notes, the statement allowed Bush to frame the conflict not as a battle over oil but as a confrontation with a dictator reminiscent of Hitler, bent on dominating the Middle East. "As was the case in the 1930s, we see in Saddam Hussein an aggressive dictator threatening his neighbors," Bush told an audience. "America will not stand aside."[623]

As Jeffrey Engel observes, while Bush did not always explicitly compare Hussein to Hitler, the Nazi leader was clearly on his mind. "I'm reading...a great, big, thick history about World War II...and there's a parallel between what Hitler did to Poland and what Saddam Hussein has done to Kuwait," the president remarked, referencing historian Martin Gilbert's extensive work, *The Second World War*. Even in the face of State Department criticism, Bush continued making the comparison between Hussein and the Nazi dictator. Chief speechwriter Chriss Winston recalls that even when the word "Hitler" was not in the official speech text, Bush inserted it himself.[624]

Bush's repeated argument that Saddam Hussein represented totalitarian figures of the past drew sharp criticism from the media. However, Bush's own war experience, particularly the loss of two of his crew members over Chichi Jima more than forty years earlier, remained a significant influence on his perspective. He believed those deaths were preventable if the West had acted decisively to stop Hitler at Munich before he unleashed widespread destruction. "It's only the United States that can lead. All countries in the West clearly have to turn to us," Bush wrote on September 7. The quote—echoing Franklin D. Roosevelt's 1940 description of America as the "arsenal of democracy"—underscored Bush's belief that in times of global crisis, the United States alone bore the responsibility to defend freedom around the world.[625]

Bush remained steadfast in his commitment to military action against Iraq, but he continued to listen to those advocating for moderation. After news broke that Hussein had sent ships to Yemen, violating the UN embargo, the president, along with Gates, Scowcroft, and Cheney, discussed the possibility of ordering the American navy to fire on the vessels. However, at the urging of James Baker, Bush chose to reconsider his position and pursue a more measured approach.[626]

Baker cautioned that launching military action without a broad UN Security Council resolution authorizing the use of force could jeopardize the coalition's fragile support, particularly from France and the Soviet Union. He urged Bush to pursue a second resolution, one that authorized an international naval blockade of Iraqi shipping. "Jim had convinced me that the additional effort for international cooperation made sense, and I wanted the Soviets totally on our side," Bush later recalled. Baker's advice proved wise: The passage of UN Resolution 665 on August 25 helped preserve coalition unity and deepened international engagement in confronting the crisis.[627]

As the prospect of military action against Iraq grew imminent, Bush hoped to maintain national unity. On September 11, 1990, he addressed Congress, stressing the importance of liberating Kuwait from Iraq's occupation. "If there ever was a time to put country before self and patriotism before party, the time is now," Bush declared to a packed House chamber. [628]

Bush emphasized that the world had entered a new era of international relations, one no longer defined by an "East-West confrontation." While he did not dismiss the idea that the conflict was about securing the world's oil supply, he believed the developing coalition symbolized an opportunity for "a new world order." The new dynamic, he envisioned, offered all nations the chance to live in an era marked by friendship, peace, and harmony."[629]

Bush emphasized that the mission symbolized more than just about freeing a nation from the grip of a dictator. It also reinforced the belief in universal human rights, the rule of law, and the importance of international institutions. "We stand today at a unique and extraordinary moment. The crisis in the Persian Gulf, as grave as it is, also offers a rare opportunity to move toward an historic period of cooperation…freer from the threat of terror, stronger in the pursuit of justice, and more secure in the quest for peace," Bush stated.[630]

The president recognized that nations would inevitably act in their own self-interest. Nevertheless, he remained hopeful that the end of the Cold War would create conditions for realizing the vision Franklin D. Roosevelt had expressed after World War II—a vision in which the Soviet Union and China, shedding rigid ideological positions, would take a more pragmatic path and join the United States in efforts to promote global stability.[631]

To help sustain public approval, Bush wanted to secure full congressional support for the potential use of military force against Iraq. While he believed his address had achieved some success, he wanted to ensure that the nation's representatives were fully invested in the campaign. Bush recalled Lyndon Johnson's success in gaining complete congressional backing for the 1964 Gulf of Tonkin Resolution. However, he also remembered how LBJ later faced scrutiny for withholding key details about the naval confrontation between the North Vietnamese and the United States, which led to the resolution's passage.[632]

Bush's meeting with congressional leaders on September 21 yielded mixed results. While both parties supported the measures taken so far, they wanted to give the UN-imposed economic sanctions more time before endorsing military action. Speaker of the House Tom Foley also called for another resolution explicitly authorizing military action to remove Iraq from Kuwait. On October 1, as reports of atrocities committed by Iraqi troops against Kuwaiti citizens began to surface, the House of Representatives passed a nonbinding resolution, 380–29, that supported the administration's goal of expelling Iraq from Kuwait.[633]

As Bush, Powell, and others debated the strategy for a detailed military campaign against Iraq, memories of the combat horrors Bush had witnessed as a young man remained vivid in his mind. The painful recollections of so much loss of life made him cautious about the use of American troops to defeat Hussein's brutal Republican Guard. At that point, 107,000 US troops were preparing for combat in Saudi Arabia. "I think my wartime experience does condition me as Commander in Chief and makes me cautious, but it also makes me understand the importance of winning," Bush wrote on October 12.[634]

Congress remained hesitant to grant the president full support for a potential military campaign, but Bush still hoped to secure a resolution. On November 14, he met once more with the leaders of both parties. Members like Tom Foley believed that Bush would proceed with an offensive even without congressional authorization. However, Bush understood that the more unity he could muster in support of the mission, the more confidence he would gain from the nation.[635]

Bush feared that if he went to war without congressional authorization and found himself in a situation like Vietnam, impeachment was a possibility. "If it drags out and there are high casualties, I will be history, [but] no problem—sometimes in life you've got to do what you've got to do," he wrote in his diary.[636]

The anxiety Bush felt about deploying troops became more evident following a Thanksgiving visit to those in uniform in Saudi Arabia. "How young they all are," he dictated to himself. "They seemed ready to fight, ready to do the job and then go home.... And I wonder what will happen if and when the battle begins?"[637]

Having personally witnessed the devastation of war, Bush viewed the use of force as a last resort. He had seen President Reagan deploy troops during his tenure and understood the pain and uncertainty families faced when their loved ones were sent into combat. Bush never took the decision to deploy troops lightly and had no desire to put them in harm's way any longer than necessary.

Days before Bush returned from the Middle East, the United Nations passed Resolution 678, which gave Iraq a deadline of January 15, 1991, to withdraw from Kuwait. If Saddam Hussein failed to comply, the member states had the right to use force. The vote by the Security Council was 12–2. "I felt a huge burden had been lifted from my shoulders," Bush wrote of the council's decision.[638]

With the Soviets agreeing and the Chinese abstaining, the vote represented another victory for Bush and the United States. The president once again convinced Gorbachev to change his mind by agreeing to one final warning rather than two. "While [the resolution] would be passed [in November], it would become operative only around the first of the year, allowing sanctions five months to work," Bush wrote in describing his negotiations with the Russian leader.[639]

Despite the new UN resolution, Bush continued pressing Congress for full backing of a potential military offensive. "How do we fully involve Congress?" he asked in a memo to White House Counsel Boyden Gray. On December 20, he met with Democratic leaders, urging them to pass a resolution endorsing his enforcement of UN mandates. Still, figures like Senator Paul Simon of Illinois urged patience, hoping sanctions might compel Iraq to withdraw. But Bush remained unconvinced. "I don't think we have six months to wait," he wrote Senator Robert Byrd two days later.[640]

The president believed that congressional support would improve his favorability with the public while manifesting his deep respect for the American system of government. Having served in the House, Bush strongly admired those who occupied it. He also believed that following the constitutional process set out by the nation's founders was the most effective way to make an executive decision.

While Congress wavered, the British did not. In November 1990, following turmoil within the British Conservative Party, John Major replaced Margaret Thatcher as prime minister. Bush had not yet met Major, but on the advice of Scowcroft, he decided to present the detailed facts for the potential military operation. "How about 0400 on the morning of the sixteenth?" Bush suggested to Major during a meeting that December at Camp David. The president anticipated that Major would request time to consider the proposal. However, the new prime minister "never flinched." Without hesitation, Major offered his nation's full commitment, continuing the long-standing tradition of the special relationship between the United States and the United Kingdom.[641]

As the year came to an end, Bush put pen to paper in a letter to his children. He admitted he was under intense pressure. "When I came into this job I vowed that I would never ring [*sic*] my hands and talk about the loneliest job in the world.... I have been concerned about what lies ahead." That New Year's Eve, as he rested in his cabin at Camp David, the lessons he had received from Henry Stimson half a century earlier still resonated deeply. "How many lives might have been saved if appeasement had given way to force earlier on in the late '30s or earliest '40s?" Bush wrote. "How many Jews might have been spared the gas chambers, or how many Polish patriots might be alive today? I look at today's crisis as good vs. evil—Yes, it is that clear."[642]

Bush believed he had done his best. He was gratified by his efforts to engage other nations and work with international institutions to gain their support. Still, the president understood that the decision to send young people into battle was the toughest he would ever have to make. "And so I shall say a few more prayers, mainly for our kids in the Gulf... And I shall do what must be done, and I shall be strengthened every day by our family love which lifts me up every single day of my life," he wrote on the final evening of 1990.[643]

Bush remained committed to using force if Iraq did not withdraw from Kuwait by the United Nations' deadline. As Secretary Baker prepared to meet with Iraq's foreign minister, Tariq Aziz, on January 9, 1991, Bush wrote a personal letter to Saddam Hussein, which he wanted Aziz to convey to the Iraqi leader. In it, he urged Hussein to comply with the United Nations resolutions or face the prospect of war. "The international community is united in its call for Iraq to leave all of Kuwait without condition and without further delay. This is not simply the policy of the United States; it is the position of the world community as expressed in no less than twelve Security Council resolutions," he told Hussein.[644]

"But unless you withdraw from Kuwait completely and without condition, you will lose more than Kuwait. What is at issue here is not the future of Kuwait…but rather the future of Iraq," Bush wrote, signaling his resolve that any further delay would come at a greater cost for Hussein and his nation.[645]

After a seven-hour meeting with Baker, the Iraqi diplomat left without taking Bush's letter with him. For Bush and Baker, the gesture spoke volumes about Hussein's refusal to engage in meaningful negotiations. The president had exhausted every diplomatic channel and procedure to convince Hussein to withdraw his forces from Kuwait, but all efforts had failed. The situation evoked Bush's lasting memories of Europe's failure to confront German totalitarianism. "I do think that World War II shaped my thinking on the Gulf. I have Saddam Hussein now as clearly bad and evil as Hitler as the Japanese war machine that attacked Pearl Harbor." Bush wrote in his diary.[646]

On January 8, Bush wrote a detailed letter to House Speaker Tom Foley, urging a full congressional vote on a resolution supporting the United Nations' demand for Iraq's withdrawal from Kuwait. "I can think of no better way than for Congress to express its support for the president at this critical time," he stated. Three days before the UN deadline, on January 12, the resolution was approved by the House with a vote of 250–183 and by the Senate with a vote of 52–47.[647]

The president felt a sense of relief, knowing the vote had sent a clear signal to the world that the nation stood united behind him and the coalition. Reflecting years later, Bush acknowledged that even if Congress had voted against the resolution, "I would have acted and ordered our troops into combat." The decision had already been made, and he was determined to carry it out, regardless of the political fallout. "I know it would have caused an outcry, but it was the right thing to do," Bush wrote in 1998.[648]

With diplomatic efforts in place and solid support from both the international community and political leaders, Bush and his national security team set the time for the initial airstrike on Kuwait: 3:00 a.m. on January 17. As the time neared, Bush relied on his years of experience and preparation. "I kept saying to myself, stay on track, do what you have to do, ask the right questions, make the proper changes, if you need to make them, and then be firm." With just hours before the invasion, Bush remained concerned about how the process of withdrawing troops would unfold once the coalition had achieved its objectives. "I have trouble with how this ends," he remarked into a Dictaphone as he walked alone on the White House grounds.[649]

Bush carried the immense weight of the decision on his shoulders. He had done everything he could to avoid armed conflict. Now, he prepared to assume full responsibility, no matter the outcome. "It is my decision—my decision to send those kids into battle, my decision that may affect the lives of innocence [*sic*].... It is my decision to stand and take the heat.... And yet, I know what I have to do this Sunday night. This man is evil, and let him win and we rise again to fight tomorrow," the president wrote days before the offensive began.[650]

As Bush prepared for his national address on January 16 to announce the beginning of hostilities, he read passages from books that featured words from Thomas Paine and Robert Lowell but found little comfort in what he read. Later that evening, while watching television, he saw a news broadcast showing a young soldier embracing his father before heading off to war in the Gulf. The moment transported Bush back to 1942, when he, as an eighteen-year-old, said goodbye to his own father at Grand Central Station. "I didn't know one single soul, and I was off for an experience into the unknown, and it shaped my life," he recalled.[651]

During his address, Bush stressed that he had made the decision to strike Saddam Hussein because failing to act would lead to a wider conflict and even greater loss of life. As he outlined Iraq's numerous violations against Kuwait, Bush's words inevitably evoked the memory of past global inaction, recalling a time when a dictator, indifferent to international law, was allowed to roam unchecked. "While the world waited, Saddam Hussein systematically raped, pillaged, and plundered a tiny nation, no threat to his own," Bush declared. "While the world waited,

Saddam Hussein met every overture of peace with open contempt.... While the world prayed for peace, Saddam prepared for war."[652]

Aware of the public's concerns about becoming entangled in a prolonged conflict in the Middle East, Bush reassured the nation that his goal was to fulfill the mission authorized by the United Nations and bring American forces back home as swiftly as possible. "I've told the American people before that this will not be another Vietnam, and I repeat this here tonight. Our troops will have the best possible support in the entire world, and they will not be asked to fight with one hand tied behind their back."[653]

"It was as if his whole life—from his time in uniform to his service on Capitol Hill to his diplomatic experience—had prepared him for the moment," George W. Bush wrote of the moment his father sent the nation into battle.[654]

Determined to avoid any protracted conflict, Bush listened carefully to Colin Powell and others who stressed the importance of using overwhelming force to secure a swift and decisive victory. Bush soon learned that the air campaign had exceeded expectations. The planes involved in the initial mission over Kuwait had returned safely to their bases in Saudi Arabia. It quickly became clear that the coalition had achieved near-total air supremacy. "We own the skies—practically own the skies," Bush noted in his diary, though he tried not to let himself become overconfident, even privately.[655]

Even as the military campaign appeared to be progressing smoothly, Bush's diplomatic skills were once again put to the test when Iraq began launching Scud missiles at Israel. Recognizing that a retaliatory strike could escalate the conflict into a wider war, Bush leveraged his strong relationship with Israeli Prime Minister Yitzhak Shamir, convincing him not to respond militarily. "I put on the hardest sale I have ever used.... God, I hope I made headway on that," Bush later recalled. His argument—that the American military would focus on eliminating Iraq's missile capabilities—ultimately proved successful. Despite Iraq's continued missile attacks, Shamir honored his commitment and refrained from retaliation.[656]

Bush's emphasis on thorough preparation, along with his decision to surround himself with advisors of expertise and deep experience, led to swift success: The coalition forces drove Iraq out of Kuwait in just under five days. The American casualties were remarkably light, with the United States losing only 148 men during the campaign, a figure far lower than the Pentagon's initial expectations.[657]

After the quick victory, many began questioning whether Bush should expand the mission to include removing Saddam Hussein from Iraq. Bush appreciated the confidence many had in his leadership, but he remained opposed to going beyond the UN mandate. Despite his high approval rating, he did not let his popularity cloud his judgment. "To occupy Iraq would instantly shatter our coalition, turning the whole Arab world against us and make a broken tyrant into a latter-day Arab hero," Bush said.[658]

The military campaign to remove Iraq from Kuwait marked the first major international crisis since the fall of the Berlin Wall. Brent Scowcroft viewed Bush's decision to focus solely on following the UN mandate as "a groundbreaking development." "It was the President applying long-term, thoughtful strategy that built upon current circumstances to create a better future," Scowcroft remarked.[659]

Many viewed Iraq's withdrawal from Kuwait on February 27, 1991, as a triumphant restoration of American confidence and power. Bush expressed his gratitude to the troops and the coalition that had stood with the United States throughout the months of challenge and trial. However, the president remained humble and understated. "This is not a time of euphoria, certainly not a time to gloat," he said.[660]

While the victory in Kuwait represented the efforts of countless dedicated individuals, George Bush possessed qualities critical to its success. His triumph over Saddam Hussein represented a victory driven by experience, not only as a leader but also through his deep understanding of Congress, the national security apparatus, and the United Nations. Bush's personal relationships, cultivated over decades of public service, proved to be invaluable, as well. Although the successful military campaign could never erase the painful memories of Vietnam, Bush delivered a powerful message to the nation: The American military had the ability to effectively execute a mission abroad. The success of Operation Desert Storm stands as yet another testament to how George Bush's long apprenticeship in public life played a central role in his success as president.

CHAPTER 16

A More Perfect Union: Domestic Matters

President Bush gives the commencement address at Yale University. During the ceremonies he is presented with an honorary degree by Yale President Schmidt, New Haven, Connecticut. May 27, 1991.

On an overcast day on August 7, 1989, President George Bush addressed thirty-six thousand members of the Boy Scouts of America at the organization's Twelfth National Jamboree at Fort A.P. Hill in Bowling Green, Virginia. Wearing a light-brown suit, white shirt, and dark tie, Bush spoke fondly of his deep appreciation for nature, fishing, and the outdoors. While *The New York Times* emphasized that the speech stressed the importance of the Boy Scouts' efforts in combating the dangers of drug abuse, the president also highlighted a set of guiding principles that echoed both the Scouts' code of conduct and the core values that shaped his own life.

"Your Scout law commands you to be trustworthy, loyal, helpful, friendly, courteous, kind, obedient, cheerful, thrifty, brave, clean, and reverent," he reminded them. For Bush, these were not just words, they were enduring ideals that governed his actions and leadership. "As Chief Scout Citizen Teddy Roosevelt put it: "The full performance of duty is not only right in itself but also the source of the profoundest satisfaction that can come in life."[661]

***

Many viewed George Bush's legacy as defined by his role in overseeing the end of the Cold War and leading the liberation of Kuwait from Saddam Hussein's expansionist ambitions. However, Bush also entered the White House with a strong commitment to advancing domestic policy. His initiatives—ranging from promoting volunteerism and environmental protection to advocating for legislation that safeguarded the rights of individuals with disabilities—were all part of his broader vision of fostering a kinder, gentler America.

One of Bush's key domestic achievements, reflecting his commitment to a more just and inclusive society, was the signing of the 1990 Americans with Disabilities Act. The landmark legislation ensured that no individual could be denied equal treatment due to a disability or functional impairment. Speaking at the signing ceremony on the White House lawn, Bush drew a powerful parallel between the ADA and the fall of the Berlin Wall, emphasizing that the law would grant millions of Americans greater freedom and independence. "Let the shameful wall of exclusion finally come tumbling down," he declared to resounding applause.[662]

For President Bush, the bill symbolized more than just a legislative achievement. He understood firsthand the challenges faced by those with physical or cognitive ailments. Bush's older brother, Prescott, suffered from a visual impairment that prevented him from serving in the military during World War II. In 1950, Bush's uncle, Dr. John M. Walker, a highly skilled physician, retired from his medical practice after being diagnosed with polio. These experiences reinforced Bush's commitment to ensuring equal opportunities for all Americans, regardless of their physical abilities.[663]

President Bush deeply revered Dr. Walker. A distinguished physician affiliated with New York's Memorial Sloan Kettering, Walker became a pillar of strength for the Bush family following Robin Bush's diagnosis of leukemia. Bush saw him as a "strong and purposeful man," whose unwavering encouragement guided him and Barbara through their daughter's illness. "You have no choice—none at all—you must treat this child. You must do all you can to keep her alive," Bush recalled telling a constituent in 1967, echoing Walker's firm belief in fighting for Robin's life. Forever grateful for his uncle's support, Bush made it a point to telephone him weekly.[664]

The Bush family's experience with disabilities also extended to Bush's son Neil and his struggle with dyslexia, a condition that challenged his ability to read. The younger Bush's difficulties with literacy underscored his own perseverance and also the unwavering dedication of Barbara Bush. Rather than transferring her son from Washington's St. Albans School, she spent countless hours working with him to strengthen his reading skills. Her commitment paid off, and Neil Bush graduated alongside his classmates. The experience left a lasting impression on the First Lady, inspiring her to champion literacy as a key issue during her husband's presidency.[665]

In 1985, Bush's youngest son, Marvin, received a diagnosis of ulcerative colitis, a life-threatening condition that ultimately required the removal of his colon and the use of an ostomy pouch. Understanding that the illness impacted millions of Americans, Marvin Bush embarked on a high-profile speaking campaign in partnership with the Crohn's and Colitis Foundation. Embracing his family's commitment to service, he used his platform to encourage others not to let their condition define them, offering hope and inspiration to those facing similar challenges.[666]

The Bush family had extensive experience facing and overcoming disabilities. However, it was not until Bush's years in the Reagan White House that he had the opportunity to address the issue legislatively. While campaigning on a platform of reducing government spending, President Reagan tasked Bush with identifying ways to cut unnecessary regulations. Many within the administration viewed two pieces of disability rights legislation as prime candidates for elimination.[667]

The first concerned a 1975 law that guaranteed every child with a disability the right to attend public school. The second prohibited organizations receiving federal funding from discriminating against individuals with disabilities. Reagan and Bush had pledged to reduce government spending, but the mere consideration of eliminating these essential protections sparked a fierce backlash from disability advocates, who viewed the proposals as an attack on fundamental rights.[668]

A massive letter-writing campaign ensued, with more than forty thousand letters flooding the White House in opposition to the administration's plan. Recognizing the intensity of public concern, Bush began meeting disability advocates to clarify the administration's position. However, he came to understand that these laws were not viewed as handouts or special treatment, but as essential tools for achieving independence and self-sufficiency. As the public outcry grew and testimonies before Congress echoed these sentiments, Bush realized these protections were instrumental in empowering individuals to lead productive and autonomous lives.[669]

His 1983 announcement that the administration would exempt disability regulations from the deregulatory process marked a turning point in his perspective on disability rights. Over time, he came to see government support for individuals with disabilities as a fulfillment of the principles outlined in the nation's founding documents. The issue also resonated deeply with his counsel, Boyden Gray, a dedicated Washington lawyer who viewed expanding disability rights as a meaningful opportunity to contribute to a cause that could improve the lives of millions.[670]

Following the disability lobbies' campaign, the National Council on the Handicapped began crafting a broader bill aimed at securing "equal opportunity for people with disabilities." The campaign for a comprehensive legislative support was led by two men who were both confined to wheelchairs: Lex Frieden, the council's director, paralyzed following a car accident, and Justin Dart Jr., a polio survivor whose father a was longtime friend and fundraiser for both Reagan and Bush.[671]

In January 1986, Frieden and Dart met with Bush to discuss a detailed report outlining ideas for the new bill. "When we met with the vice president," Frieden recalled in a 2018 Vox interview, "he mentioned at the beginning of the meeting that he and [his wife] Barbara had reviewed the report the night before. He said they could both relate to it because of the child with a disability whom they had lost."

When Bush launched his 1988 presidential campaign, he made it clear that passing the Americans with Disabilities Act would be a key focus of his agenda. "I am going to do whatever it takes to make sure the disabled are included in the mainstream. For too long, they've been left out. But they're not going to be left out anymore," Bush declared in his acceptance speech for the presidential nomination.[672]

After Bush's election, it became clear that his seven-point margin of victory occurred partly due to support from many Democratic voters who appreciated his commitment to improving the lives of the disabled. However, as the administration got underway, the president faced the complexities of crafting a bill that would satisfy both the Democratic-controlled Congress and the GOP's business constituency. "We have got to get it right," he told John Sununu and Boyden Gray.[673]

Drafting the right language for the bill proved challenging. Negotiations were difficult, but with the support of Massachusetts Senator Edward Kennedy, the administration developed a bipartisan bill requiring both sides to make key compromises. Democrats agreed to limit the types of damages that disabled individuals could claim in lawsuits, while the administration expanded the "public accommodations" section of the bill to include a wide range of institutions, such as hotels, motels, banks, grocery stores, and many others.[674]

One of the key reasons many on both sides of the aisle were willing to engage in bipartisan negotiations was the personal impact of the issue on key legislators. That included Kennedy, whose sister was mentally disabled, and Senator Tom Harkin, whose brother suffered from deafness. Additionally, two congressmen had faced their own struggles with epilepsy, and Senator Bob Dole had severely injured his arm during World War II. These experiences fueled a shared commitment by many in Congress to advance the rights of those with disabilities.

On August 26, 1990, President Bush signed the Americans with Disabilities Act, with over two thousand people attending the historic ceremony on the White House lawn. Bush "understood that he would be remembered forever as the president who made people with disabilities a part of their community, the president who changed the landscape of America, and he was incredibly proud of that," Lex Frieden said on National Public Radio's *Morning Edition* in December 2018.

In a 1994 symposium discussing the Bush administration's domestic accomplishments, many contended that Bush's signing of the ADA was a transformative moment for a significant portion of the American population. The bill represented "fundamental principles of free enterprise democracy…[and] simply mandates a culture which is designed to provide equal opportunity for all to work and live," Justin Dart Jr. said."[675]

Bush's passage of the legislation also manifested the belief that the government had the capacity to provide people with the opportunity to help themselves. The legislation did not focus on "quotas" or "welfare," but aimed to make it easier for the disabled to integrate into the larger community.

In Bush's later years, following his own confinement to a wheelchair due to Parkinson's disease, the president came to fully appreciate the profound significance of the bill. Like so many who face disabilities, Bush refused to let his illness define him. Despite his increasing infirmity, he demonstrated that one could still live a full and active life. Bush's desire to experience adventure remained evident when he skydived to celebrate on both his eightieth and ninetieth birthdays. That showcased more than Bush's resilience; it also celebrated the drive and competitiveness that had been defining traits throughout his life.

George Bush's advocacy for those with disabilities represented part of his larger objective of fostering equality for all, his commitment to helping those in need, and his strong belief in extending a hand to others through volunteerism. Bush's phrase "a kinder, gentler America" truly resonated with him. He believed that the nation's growth and success depended on the public's willingness to care for and support one another.[676]

Bush's belief in using the presidency to inspire a sense of national purpose mirrored the ideals of his predecessors, Theodore and Franklin Roosevelt, as well as John F. Kennedy.

"We need a Good Society built upon the deeds of the many, a society that promotes service, selflessness, action," Bush declared during a commencement address at the University of Michigan in May 1991. He believed true progress could come from authentic acts of human virtue. By striving to improve the communities around them, Bush felt people could strengthen their connections with one another and also experience personal and spiritual renewal.[677]

An earlier expression of that volunteerism occurred between 1933 and 1942, with Franklin D. Roosevelt's New Deal Civilian Conservation Corps. The initiative supported four million Americans working to rejuvenate the nation's forests, roads, and bridges, especially in rural areas. While the program did not directly replace the loss of jobs, it provided the unemployed with the opportunity to restore their confidence and self-worth. Most importantly, the members of the CCC formed a support system, encouraging each other to persevere through the challenging days ahead.[678]

That spirit of volunteerism also resonated with President John F. Kennedy. JFK's iconic call to action, "Ask not what your country can do for you—ask what you can do for your country," urged citizens to embark on careers of service. Kennedy's vision, exemplified by the Peace Corps and Volunteers in Service to America, empowered individuals with a strong sense of public spirit to help the disadvantaged, both at home and abroad. These initiatives, which inspired many to dedicate themselves to public service, directly influenced the formation of President Bush's campaign of volunteerism, known as the "Points of Light" initiative.[679]

According to Richard Benedetto, political correspondent for *USA Today*, Bush first spoke the words "points of light" during a San Francisco campaign event in 1988. While the phrase received national notice during Bush's GOP acceptance speech, the president's clearest articulation of his concept of volunteerism occurred during an appearance in June 1989 at an event for the New York Partnership and the Association for a Better New York.[680]

During his remarks, Bush quoted a 1788 letter from Alexander Hamilton to George Washington highlighting the profound impact Washington could have on the nation by accepting the presidency: "The point of light in which you stand will make an infinite difference." For Bush, this "point of light" symbolized the power of the individual to make a meaningful impact in the lives of others.[681]

Bush's emphasis on volunteerism embodied his belief in the spirit of American ingenuity and self-reliance. It also reflected his view that a president had a responsibility to inspire a sense of virtue and service in the nation's citizens.

His emphasis on the importance of public service in American life had little to do with running for public office, but rather in contributing to the betterment of society, where one could. "Emerson once said, the greatest gift is a portion of thyself," Bush quoted. Emerson's words also echoed the Phillips Academy mantra of "not for self," which shaped much of Bush's philosophy on service and community.[682]

Bush played a pivotal role in reviving the concept of national service—especially when government redirected funding for earlier public-service programs to other priorities, after the idea of national service faded in the 1980s. In 1990, using his passion and political influence, the president revived volunteerism with the passage of the National Community Service Act. The legislation led to the creation of the nonprofit Points of Light Foundation and initiated government funding to foster state programs focused on community service. "Government cannot rebuild a family or reclaim a sense of neighborhood, and no bureaucratic program will ever solve the pressing human problems that can be addressed by a vast galaxy of people working voluntarily in their own backyards," Bush said when signing the bill into law.[683]

The legislation led to the creation of over two thousand programs designed to encourage young people to channel their talents into serving their communities. The president also utilized the Points of Light Foundation to recognize and honor individuals who made the effort to improve the lives of others, taking time from their own busy lives to make a meaningful difference. Bush's belief in the idea of "a thousand points of light" did not represent a vision of moral utopianism, but a distinctly American ideal. He believed people had the power to unite as a community and use their God-given abilities to drive positive change. "If we've learned anything in the past quarter century, it is that we cannot federalize virtue," Bush stated during his commencement address at the University of Michigan in 1991.[684]

Bush's life reflected a commitment to serving and helping others, regardless of race, color, or creed. Whether raising millions for cancer research; teaching Sunday school in Midland, Texas; risking his life in service to his country; or supporting causes like the United Negro College Fund and the Boy Scouts of America, his actions consistently reflected his belief in the power of service. These endeavors directly influenced his goal of making service a central part of the nation's life. Bush believed that the president's responsibility extended beyond preserving, protecting, and defending the Constitution. His vision of volunteerism echoed that of Theodore Roosevelt, who used the presidency to promote the common good as envisioned by the founders.

Bush hoped principles of community service would help reduce the polarization that had come to dominate the country. By expressing faith in the American people's ability to engage in selfless and generous actions to support their friends and neighbors, the president also sought to inspire a new generation to pursue careers in political leadership.

Bush had grown up admiring his father and other public figures who chose to use their talents not solely for personal gain but also to serve the greater good. The gentlemen statesmen, including Prescott Bush, Averell Harriman, and Henry Cabot Lodge Jr., believed they had an obligation to use their God-given abilities to better not just their nation but the world. President Bush understood that politics could be contentious and, at times, deeply unpleasant. However, he never lost faith in the inherent goodness of people and their ability to make a meaningful difference.

Bush's deep modesty often made it difficult for his policies to capture the full attention of the media and the public. Initiatives such as the Americans with Disabilities Act and the Clean Air Act, along with his advocacy for service and volunteerism, gained greater importance after his presidency. Starting with the Clinton administration and continuing through the administrations of his son, George W. Bush, and Barack Obama, each president made national service a central part of their legacy. While Bush's accomplishments on the international stage have received rightful recognition, his efforts to enact policies that contribute to a more perfect union have grown in significance over time.

CHAPTER 17

Gracious in Defeat: The 1992 Campaign

President Bush waves from the back of a train car during his campaign whistlestop in Bowling Green, Ohio. September 26, 1992.

On January 20, 1993, as the sun shone in the nation's capital, President Bush prepared to leave the White House after serving one term in office.

Just over two months earlier, he had lost his bid for reelection to a young former governor from Arkansas, Bill Clinton. Despite Bush's personal disappointment, he remained committed to a smooth transfer of power, doing everything he could to ensure Clinton and his team were well supported during their transition. President Clinton recognized and deeply appreciated these efforts. He held great respect for Bush, especially for the grace and generosity shown by both him and Mrs. Bush on Inauguration Day. As the Bushes prepared to leave behind the role that had defined their lives for the past four years, Clinton was struck by the dignity with which they carried themselves.

"It was a difficult day for them, a tough day. But they were very kind and very generous," Clinton later reflected in a documentary about Bush's life. "I remember watching them drive away from the Capitol after the ceremony and thinking how challenging it must have been for them, yet how gracious they were—brave and dignified. I really admire the way they handled it."[685]

***

George Bush accomplished a great deal during his single term as president. On the international stage, he secured an arms agreement with Soviet Premier Mikhail Gorbachev and successfully led a multinational coalition to liberate Kuwait from Saddam Hussein's Iraq. Domestically, his presidency saw significant achievements, including progress on climate change and the signing of the Americans with Disabilities Act. However, despite these successes, they were not enough to sway public opinion for another four years in office. "Bush passed more major domestic legislation that any American president other than Lyndon Johnson and Franklin Roosevelt. He promoted and signed into law more than a dozen major bills during his single term," Chief of Staff John Sununu wrote in *Politico* in 2018.[686]

In June 1992, as President Bush fought for reelection, he faced a series of challenges that ultimately led to his defeat five months later. An economic downturn, a primary challenge from within his own party by former Nixon aide Pat Buchanan, an independent run by dynamic Texas billionaire H. Ross Perot, and a strong challenge from Democratic Governor Bill Clinton of Arkansas all contributed to a dramatic drop in Bush's Gallop approval rating, from a high of 89 percent in February 1991 to a low of 29 percent a year and a half later.

Though Bush's decision to raise taxes angered many on the right, the success of Operation Desert Storm initially pushed the controversy into the background. However, the president's aversion to politics led him to neglect his political base, a misstep that became significant when the nation faced a brief recession. As economic concerns grew, many conservatives blamed Bush's broken tax pledge for the downturn, further deepening their discontent.[687]

Even before the Gulf War began, economic troubles loomed. By January 1991, the nation's unemployment rate stood at 6.1 percent, rising to 7 percent by June. Economic disparity between the rich and poor also became more pronounced, as many Americans grew frustrated with declining wages while corporate executives amassed greater wealth.[688]

Bush's unpopularity deepened when he refused to extend unemployment benefits beyond twenty-six weeks, citing concerns about "busting the budget." After vetoing Congress's second attempt to allocate $5.8 billion in aid for the unemployed, he attempted to counter the criticism by proposing a capital gains tax cut. However, as *The New York Times* columnist Tom Wicker observed, such a move did little to help "an unemployed shoemaker in New Hampshire."

The perception that Bush appeared unaware of his declining popularity grew in 1991 when those around him grew increasingly worried that he seemed uninterested in focusing on his reelection campaign.[689]

Bush remained steadfast in his commitment to fulfilling the mission entrusted to him by the American people. In his campaign speech on August 20, 1992, at the Republican Convention in Houston, he revisited the themes that had driven his political success. He highlighted his achievements in uniting Germany, restoring Kuwait's sovereignty, and bringing an end to the global threat of communism. Looking back on his role in concluding the Cold War, Bush took a moment to express his gratitude to Ronald Reagan and Gerald Ford for their leadership and skill in steering the nation toward a more secure and independent world.

President Bush then sought to draw a sharp contrast between himself and his opponent, Arkansas Governor Bill Clinton. Clinton, often compared to President John F. Kennedy for his oratorical skills and political instincts, possessed powerful charisma and a natural ability to connect with the public. Bush, however, used his address to highlight their differences in character. Focusing in his speech on his own life of sacrifice and service, he revisited his decision during World War II to answer the nation's call in its time of need. "I was scared, but I was willing. I was young, but I was ready. I had barely lived when I began to watch men die," Bush said during his convention address.

Emphasizing his war service reinforced the president's image as a dedicated patriot, as well as a leader firmly rooted in the values of family, faith, and community. By contrast, Bush cast Clinton as someone who prioritized personal interests over national duty.

The GOP campaign elaborated the contrast, comparing Bush's military record with Clinton's decision to avoid military service during the Vietnam War by securing a student deferment to study at Oxford University. While many of his peers served and died in Southeast Asia, Clinton protested the war from the safety of England.

Besides contrasts in character, Bush and his youthful, dynamic challenger presented a stark contrast in styles. Bush maintained a quiet, formal demeanor, embodying a reserved and composed approach to leadership. Clinton, much like Lyndon Johnson, thrived on personal contact, eagerly shaking hands, hugging supporters, and engaging with voters at every opportunity. He also proved to be a masterful self-promoter. Whether playing the saxophone on *The Arsenio Hall Show* in sunglasses or openly discussing his birth sign and childhood struggles with an alcoholic father on the popular video music channel MTV, Clinton's approach could not have been more different than Bush's more traditional and dignified style.

The Bush campaign argued that, despite his reserved and formal demeanor, the president embodied the values and sensibilities of the American people—unlike Bill Clinton, who, in addition to avoiding military service, faced allegations of infidelity with multiple women.[690]

However, Bush also faced a strong challenge from Patrick J. Buchanan, a former Nixon speechwriter whose insurgent primary campaign resonated with many conservative Republicans and disaffected voters. The conservative commentator tapped into frustrations over issues like illegal immigration and job losses, which, he contended, were exacerbated by Bush's support for the North American Free Trade Agreement. His rallying cry of "take back our country" struck a chord, propelling Buchanan to a significant showing in the New Hampshire Republican primary, where he captured 40 percent of the vote.[691]

Buchanan argued that with the Cold War over, the United States should prioritize domestic affairs over global commitments. In a late 1991 article, Robin Toner of *The New York Times* quoted a sample of Buchanan's pugnacious campaign rhetoric. "Mr. Bush…is a globalist, and we are nationalists," he proclaimed when announcing his candidacy. "He believes in some *pax universalis*; we believe in the old republic. He would put America's wealth and power at the service of some vague new world order; we will put America first." The latter phrase, which came to define Buchanan's insurgent campaign, was originally popularized by a group led by famed aviator Charles Lindbergh, who opposed Franklin D. Roosevelt's efforts to increase US involvement in the fight against European fascism.

Buchanan, who wrote his own speeches, brought a style of politics that reminded Bush of the divisive rhetoric once associated with Alabama Governor George Wallace. His strong performance in the New Hampshire primary secured Buchanan a prime speaking slot at the 1992 Republican National Convention, where he delivered a fiery speech criticizing the LGBTQ community and political correctness. Buchanan framed the nation's cultural conflicts as being just as consequential as the battle to win the Cold War—all a stark contrast to Bush's more measured and unifying approach.[692]

Despite trailing by thirteen points in September, Bush remained confident in his experience, character, and determination to win a second term. "But you can't feel sorry…keep plugging away, keep working hard.… I can make it; I can out-hustle Clinton, out-work him, out-jog him, out-think him, out-campaign him, and we'll win," he wrote in the second week of September.

However, the portrayal of Bush as an out-of-touch elitist, coupled with his discomfort with the performative side of politics, came into sharp focus when he glanced at his wristwatch during a debate with Bill Clinton and independent candidate H. Ross Perot. Looking back on that moment in a 1999 interview with PBS *NewsHour* broadcaster Jim Lehrer, Bush revealed his disdain for the spectacle of presidential campaigns, recalling his thoughts at the time: "Only ten more minutes of this crap." The remark captured his deep frustration with the theatrical and often superficial nature of modern politics.[693]

Despite pouring his energy and optimism into the race, Bush could not overcome divisions within the GOP and the public's dissatisfaction with the economy. When the votes were tallied in November, Bill Clinton and Al Gore defeated the Bush-Quayle ticket with a margin of 44,909,889 to 39,104,545. Ross Perot's independent candidacy, which garnered 19,742,267 votes, also played a significant role in preventing the president from winning a second term. While Bush viewed the defeat as a personal disappointment, he experienced a deeper sense of sadness because of the dedication and hard work of those who had supported him. "My problem was the feeling of letting people down, letting the people around you down.... That was the sad part for me, and I felt very strongly about that. I still do," he reflected years later.[694]

Conceding the election to Governor Clinton, the president went beyond offering congratulations to his opponent. He also expressed his deep respect for "the majesty of the democratic system." Bush held the electoral process in high regard, and he recognized his responsibility to ensure a seamless transition from one president to another.

"I want the country to know that our entire Administration will work closely with his team to ensure a smooth transition of power. There is important work to be done and America must always come first. So we will get behind this new President and wish him well," Bush said, according to a transcript of the speech published in *The New York Times*.

Throughout his political career, Bush had consistently sought to demonstrate a spirit of bipartisanship. Despite the sting of disappointment, the president called on his supporters to help ensure the success of the incoming administration. "Now, I ask that we stand behind our new President. Regardless of our differences," Bush said. In the tradition of his many speeches, Bush spent much of the evening expressing gratitude to his staff, his cabinet, and, most importantly, his family, for their unwavering dedication during the four years he had spent working to build a stronger nation and a safer world.

Bush could have easily shifted the blame for his defeat onto others, criticizing the media, pointing fingers at his staff, or attributing his lackluster performance to medication he had received for a thyroid condition. But blaming others for his missteps was simply not in Bush's character. On November 18, when President-elect Clinton visited the White House, the outgoing president welcomed him with an extended hand. "He's very friendly, very respectful, asked my advice on certain things," Bush noted in a diary entry.[695]

Over the course of two hours, Bush and Clinton discussed a wide range of foreign and domestic issues. Bush also took pleasure in showing his successor parts of the executive mansion, including the pool and the horseshoe pit. As the visit ended, the president reassured Clinton that he would not do anything to make his time in office more difficult. "Bill, I want to tell you something. When I leave here, you're going to have no trouble from me. The campaign is over, it was tough, and I'm out of here. I will do nothing to complicate your work, and I just want you to know that." During their conversation, Bush also advised Clinton not to let the demands of the office cause him to become too distant from friends and family. This advice struck a chord with Clinton, who, like Bush, found energy and joy in the camaraderie of those closest to him.[696]

The president did ask one favor of his successor. He requested that Clinton continue the Thousand Points of Light Program, a signature initiative of Bush's presidency. The president-elect, who had also championed volunteerism during his time as governor of Arkansas, readily agreed. While Bush's competitive drive pushed him to excel in every challenge, service remained the central theme of his life. "There are no magic outside solutions to our problems; the real answers lie within us. We need more than a philosophy of entitlement. We need to all pitch in, lend a hand, and do our part to help forge a brighter future for this country," Bush said in a radio broadcast to the nation on November 7, 1992.

Bush may have disagreed with Clinton's policy agenda and been troubled by aspects of his opponent's character at certain points in his life. But the president understood that the voters had made their choice for the leader of the nation for the next four years. Bush respected that decision and prepared to do everything in his power to support the man who would soon succeed him as commander in chief.

Bush used his final days in office to express both his personal gratitude and that of the nation. One of his final acts, on January 13, 1993, was honoring his predecessor, Ronald Reagan, with the Presidential Medal of Freedom. In addition to his role in shaping Bush's years as vice president, Reagan had delivered a powerful address at the 1992 GOP convention, highlighting Bush's lifelong commitment to public service and character. As Bush presented the award, the moment represented more than simply one president rewarding another for his service; it symbolized an expression of deep love and respect for a man Bush admired as a mentor and as a cherished friend.

Following the conclusion of his administration, Bush remained optimistic about the future. In his transition note to President Bill Clinton, Bush acknowledged that although he and the new president came from different political parties and backgrounds, they shared a common goal: to improve the nation for all its citizens.

After Bush's passing, Clinton contemplated about his predecessor's legacy. Writing in *The Washington Post* on December 1, 2018, he declared that George Bush "was an honorable, gracious, and decent man who believed in the United States, our Constitution, our institutions, and our shared future."

CONCLUSION

George H. W. Bush's funeral. US Capitol viewing. December 3, 2018.

Throughout his public and private life, the man affectionately known as "Poppy" had strived to fulfill every responsibility entrusted to him. During his final hours in the Oval Office, George Bush remained disappointed by his inability to complete his mission as president, but he took pride in the way he had conducted himself. He believed he had upheld the dignity that the office demanded and deserved. "I've tried to serve here with no taint or dishonor; no conflict of interest; nothing to sully this beautiful place and this job I've been privileged to hold," Bush wrote on his final day as president of the United States.[697]

George Bush possessed as competitive and driven a nature as any man who has occupied the presidency. However, his restrained personality often limited his ability to promote his political accomplishments at the expense of others. This included his decision not to overshadow Mikhail Gorbachev after the fall of the Berlin Wall. It was also demonstrated in his choice to ignore those who urged him to use the liberation of Kuwait as an opportunity to topple Iraq's Saddam Hussein.

While Bush may not have radiated the warmth of Bill Clinton, the magnetism of John F. Kennedy, or the charisma of George W. Bush, the forty-first president possessed what historian Gordon Wood describes as a persona characterized by "a certain moral, virtuous, and civilized manner." This ideal of bipartisanship, political courage, knowledge, judiciousness, and humility were qualities Bush sought to instill in the nation throughout his time in office.[698]

The qualities of character and ability that defined Bush's life also embodied the ideals that the nation's founders believed a president should personify. This vision, shared by John Adams and Thomas Jefferson, advocated for a "natural aristocracy"—a group of men who possessed not only natural ability and talent but also principles aimed at achieving the common good. These ideals were realized by presidents like James Monroe, John Quincy Adams, Theodore Roosevelt, and Franklin Roosevelt, who each called on the nation to uphold the standards set forth by its founding documents. The qualities Bush shared with these predecessors are described by author Adam Bellow as "combining the privileges of birth with the iron rule of merit." And writer John Dickerson contends, "Bush was the epitome of what the framers wanted in a president."[699]

Many of George Bush's critics echoed the sentiments of Texas Agricultural Commissioner Jim Hightower, who remarked, "He is a man who was born on third base and thinks he hit a triple." It is true that Bush, born into privilege, received opportunities most could only dream of. Yet, the risks he took and the greatness he achieved were entirely his own.

His parents bequeathed to him a deep sense of humility, which led the forty-first president to never take anything—or anyone—for granted.[700]

While Hightower insinuated that Bush had simply benefited from familial nepotism, allowing him to coast through life, that claim holds little weight. The idea of complacency or resting on one's laurels is incompatible with the values Prescott and Dorothy Bush taught their son. They believed that reputation and accomplishment were essential for a successful life, and their lessons drove Bush to relentlessly prove he was worthy of the positions he held in both business and government.[701]

George Bush may not have attained the same level of greatness as Theodore and Franklin Roosevelt, but he shared key qualities with those predecessors that are essential to a person who occupies the Oval Office. Like the patrician leaders before him, Bush possessed a deep respect for those from all economic and social backgrounds, a genuine love of people, and an optimism about the American spirit—an outlook that inspired his supporters to believe that the nation existed to ensure life, liberty, and happiness for all. Bush, like the Roosevelts, possessed a strong ambition and a powerful work ethic that set an example for others.

In addition, each of these men shared a profound curiosity and an understanding that there were no simple answers when it came to addressing the complex challenges of the presidency. But none were afraid to surround themselves with those who had greater knowledge of specific issues. Most importantly, all three believed in the importance of listening and considering different points of view. They understood that the success of the Republic relied on constructive debate, ultimately leading to a consensus that benefited all Americans.

Although George Bush served only a single term in the White House, he became an exceptional president through what scholar Alvin Felzenberg describes as "the extension of liberty." The idea encompassed the president's ability to bring freedom to millions, by overseeing a peaceful end to the Cold War and through the liberation of Kuwait from Saddam Hussein. Domestically, Bush's signing of the Americans with Disabilities Act provided millions of people once marginalized by society the opportunity to pursue the American Dream.

None of these achievements came easily; they required patience, discipline, hard work, and a deep respect for the nation's founding principles. These successes may never have materialized without Bush's use of privilege—an advantage that allowed him to observe, listen, and learn from leaders like Dwight Eisenhower, Lyndon Johnson, Richard Nixon, Gerald Ford, Ronald Reagan, and others from the older generation of the American political establishment.[702]

The qualities of leadership that Bush had displayed throughout his life and political career were articulated by *The New York Times* following his death in 2018. In an editorial, the publication noted that the late president represented a time "when government attracted people of talent and integrity for whom public service offered a purpose higher than self-enrichment." Bush embodied these ideals during an era when such virtues were integral to the nation's civic life. He, along with others from the patrician class, was shaped by what authors Walter Isaacson and Evan Thomas describe as "a noble style of leadership, both for their country and for themselves."[703]

Since Bush departed Washington in 1993, the values he and his patrician peers once championed have receded from the forefront of American life. Once defining features of the national character, the ideals Bush so valued have diminished in influence and resonance. As civic virtue appears to wane amid a rise in individualism and intensifying political polarization, many have come to believe that the broad sense of optimism that once shaped the American spirit has all but vanished. In the past, the WASP elites that Bush represented were drawn to public service by a strong sense of conscience and a deep-rooted familial tradition of serving others. The commitment to civic duty further shaped by their education at institutions such as Phillips Academy and Yale, as well as other elite preparatory schools and Ivy league universities. This training gave Bush and his generation a sense of mission and a desire to leave the world in a better condition than before.[704]

That sense of public obligation has largely disappeared in the age of Donald Trump. Although many of his advisors were educated at institutions where values like integrity, community, and service were once central to leadership, Trump and his circle have demonstrated that such ideals have been increasingly eclipsed by personal ambition and self-interest.[705]

However, while there is little doubt that Trump represents that ethos, he and those who surround him are not the cause of this problem, but rather a symbol of a much larger crisis of character within American society. The lessons of the "Groton Ethic," rooted in selflessness and service as defined by the school's headmaster, Endicott Peabody, have largely been replaced by an individualistic pursuit of high grades and test scores, and marked by a decline in empathy, integrity, and the inclination to prioritize others over oneself. The shift from prioritizing the common good to pursuing self-gratification is not so much the failure of a particular group or institution, but rather a reflection of society's broader evolution that has come to focus on the individual rather than the community. Henry Stimson foresaw this change in 1947 when he wrote, in his memoir *On Active Service in Peace and War*, "The American lawyer should regard himself as a potential officer of his government and a defender of its Constitution. If the time should ever come when this tradition had faded out and the members of the bar had become merely the servants of business, the future of our liberties would be gloomy indeed." That warning has, in many ways, become reality. As historian Richard Brookhiser asks, "How can you reasonably expect a man to spend time in Washington, D.C., when there are such pots of gold to be found along Broad Street?"[706]

Wall Street's, and recently Silicon Valley's, appeal to individuals who might have otherwise pursued a career in government lies both in the promise of financial gain and in the increasingly unpleasant nature of public service itself. Today, seeking public office often means exposing every aspect of one's life to invasive scrutiny and relentless criticism. Many aspiring public servants are discouraged by the deep political polarization among the two major parties, the constant pressure to raise exorbitant campaign funds, the widespread public distrust of and low regard for elected officials, and the viciousness of the twenty-four-hour media world. As a result, the nation has seen a growing number of candidates who view public office as a platform to advance their own interests rather than to serve the constituents who elect them. As of March 2025, a Gallup poll reported that over 63 percent of Americans disapprove of the way Congress is handling its responsibilities.[707]

Most importantly, institutions such as education, religion, and community organizations like the Boy Scouts—which once played a central role in what David Brooks referred to, in a 2023 *Atlantic* article, as the nation's "moral education"—no longer carry the same influence or relevance. These institutions were instrumental in creating a sense of community and instilling values centered on service, responsibility, and prioritizing the greater good over personal, short-term success.

As society places greater value on individual achievement, the credibility of traditional moral and cultural leaders in education, religion, and politics has become steadily undermined by scandal or loss of credibility. The decline has fueled a growing sense of division and disillusionment across the nation, prompting many to seek out figures or movements that embody their desire to tear down institutions they view as corrupt and no longer capable of serving the public trust. While many government institutions are undoubtedly in need of reform, figures like Donald Trump and his associates often lack both the experience and the interest required to understand how to make them more effective.

Ironically, while the public longs for someone to restore credibility in government and other institutions, those who hold the highest positions of power often share the same elite status once associated with the old patrician class. This includes Trump and many members of his administration, educated at elite institutions such as Harvard, Yale, and the University of Pennsylvania, and going on to amass significant wealth through industries like banking, technology, and real estate. However, there is a notable difference between today's leadership and the generation that mentored and shaped George Bush and other members of the traditional WASP establishment.

Bush and his generation adhered to a fundamental moral code that inspired them to consider the needs of the less fortunate. While they gained wealth and prominence in the private sector, they were neither dismissive of nor intimidated by the complexities of government and public service. They understood that true competence required both expertise and experience to achieve the highest level of success. Bush, along with many of his contemporaries, also recognized that serving the nation represented a privilege as well as a sacred responsibility, one that entailed preserving the confidence in government institutions.

Despite the criticism of the insularity and detachment displayed by Bush and his contemporaries, they possessed a genuine empathy for those they were appointed or elected to serve. Analyzing the life of George Bush doesn't offer a direct solution to the issues currently facing the nation, but rather serves as a commentary on what we, as a society, have lost by abandoning the principles that shaped his life and made it an example for others. While the late president, like all of us, possessed some personal flaws, the values he sought to uphold and embody can still inspire those who aspire to help the nation move closer to its goal of a more perfect union.

ENDNOTES

Introduction

1 Jon Meacham, *Destiny and Power: The American Odyssey of George Herbert Walker Bush* (New York: Random House, 2015), 425.
2 George Bush and Brent Scowcroft, *A World Transformed* (New York: Alfred A. Knopf, 1998), 318.
3 Meacham, *Destiny and Power*, 425. Bush and Scowcroft, *A World Transformed*, 302.
4 Meacham, *Destiny and Power*, 421. George W. Bush, *41: A Portrait of My Father* (New York: Random House, 2014), 298–299. Bush and Scowcroft, *A World Transformed*, 302.
5 Mark K. Updegrove, *The Last Republicans: Inside the Extraordinary Relationship Between George H. W. Bush and George W. Bush* (New York: Harper, 2017), 220–221.
6 Meacham, *Destiny and Power*, 431. Herbert S. Parmet, *George Bush: The Life of a Lone Star Yankee* (New York: Scribner, 1997), 449. Updegrove, *The Last Republicans*, 220–221.
7 Meacham, *Destiny and Power*, 431.
8 Bush and Scowcroft, *A World Transformed*, 318.
9 "Oral History: Margaret Thatcher, The Gulf War," Frontline, Public Broadcasting Service.
10 Meacham, Destiny and Power, 426.
11 "Oral History: Margaret Thatcher, The Gulf War," Frontline.
12 George Bush and Brent Scowcroft, *A World Transformed*, 340–341. "Remarks and an Exchange with Reporters on the Iraqi Invasion of Kuwait," August 5, 1990, Margaret Thatcher Foundation.
13 "The First Gulf War," Office of the Historian, https://history.state.gov/departmenthistory/short-history/firstgulf.
14 Jeffrey A. Engel, When the World Seemed New: George H. W. Bush and the End of the Cold War (Boston: Houghton Mifflin, 2017), 444.
15 Writer Richard Rovere "popularized" the term "the establishment" in a 1961 article in the American Scholar. The author described those who occupied that position as "that group that gives American society its direction, that fixes major goals and that constitutes itself a ready pool of manpower for the more exacting

labors of leadership...." Geoffrey Kabaservice, The Guardians: Kingman Brewster, His Circle and the Rise of the Liberal Establishment (New York: Henry Holt, 2004), 208. Leonard Silk and Mark Silk, The American Establishment (New York: Basic Books, 1980), 277.

[16] Jean Becker, *Character Matters and Other Life Lessons from George H. W. Bush* (New York: Twelve, 2024), xxvi.

[17] Adam Bellow, *In Praise of Nepotism: A Natural History* (New York: Doubleday, 2003), 12. Meacham, *Destiny and Power*, xxi–xxii. Kabaservice, *The Guardians*, 10. Bush attended Phillips Academy, Baker attended The Hill School, Brady attended The Choate School, and Mosbacher attended St. Marks School. "George Bush, Statement on the Death of John J. McCloy," March 21, 1989, The American Presidency Project. Kabaservice, The Guardians, 11.

[18] Robert Adam Mosbacher Sr. and James Gerald McGrath, *Going to Windward: A Mosbacher Family Memoir* (College Station: Texas A&M University Press, 2010), xi–xii. James A. Baker III with Steve Fifer, Work Hard, Study...and Keep Out of Politics (Chicago: Evanston, Northwestern University Press, 2006), 17.

[19] Bellow, *In Praise of Nepotism,* 12. Meacham, Destiny and Power, xvii.

[20] Peter Schweizer and Rochelle Schweizer, *The Bushes: Portrait of a Dynasty* (New York: Doubleday, 2004),125.

[21] Meacham, *Destiny and Power,* xvii.

[22] Meacham, *Destiny and Power,* xx–xxi.

[23] Meacham, *Destiny and Power,* xxii. Kabaservice, The Guardians, 465.

[24] Kabaservice, *The Guardians,* 465.

[25] David N. Rapp, "Why People Still Think George H. W. Bush Didn't Understand a Grocery Checkout," Washington Post, December 4, 2018. Stephen Hess, "First Impressions: Presidents, Appointments and Transitions," The Brookings Institution, September 18, 2000, 18–21.

[26] Elaine Kamarck, "The Fragile Legacy of Barack Obama," Brookings, April 6, 2018,

[27] Kabaservice, *The Guardians,* 464–465. Richard Brookhiser, *The Way of the Wasp: How It made America and How It Can Save It, So to Speak* (New York: The Free Press, 1991), 80, 134.

[28] Christopher Lasch, *The Revolt of the Elites and the Betrayal of Democracy* (New York: W. W. Norton, 1995), 5.

Chapter 1—Virtues and Values: Family

[29] Kabaservice, *The Guardians*, 10. Silk, *The American Establishment*, 8–9. Aaron M. Renn, "Rediscovering E. Digby Baltzell's Sociology of Elites," *American Affairs* 5, no. 1 (Spring 2021): 149–169.

[30] Silk, *The American Establishment*, 10–11. Brookhiser, *The Way of the Wasp*, 29–30.

[31] Meacham, *Destiny and Power*, 4.

[32] Meacham, *Destiny and Power*, 5.

[33] "Oral History Interview with Prescott Sheldon Bush 1966," Eisenhower Administration Project Oral History Archives at Columbia, Rare Book & Manuscript Library, Columbia University in the City of New York, 2.

[34] Kabaservice, *The Guardians*, 10. Peter W. Cookson Jr. and Caroline Hodges Persell, *Preparing for Power: America's Elite Boarding Schools* (New York: Basic Books, 1985), 3, 5.

[35] Schweizer, *The Bushes*, 21–22. Meacham, *Destiny and Power*, 11–12.

[36] Schweizer, *The Bushes*, 22–23. Meacham, *Destiny and Power*, 11–12.

[37] J. Randy Taraborrelli, *Grace and Steel: Dorothy, Barbara, Laura, and the Women of the Bush Dynasty* (New York: St Martin's Press), 20–21, Schweizer, *The Bushes*, 32. Brookhiser, *The Way of the Wasp*, 2.

[38] Meacham, *Destiny and Power*, 15–16.

[39] Meacham, *Destiny and Power*, 21. Author phone interview with Elsie Walker, May 29, 2024.

[40] Doro Bush Koch, *My Father, My President: A Personal Account of the Life of George H. W. Bush* (New York: Grand Central Publishing, 2006), 10–11.

[41] Meacham, *Destiny and Power*, 21, 28. Author phone interview with Elsie Walker, May 29, 2024. Taraborrelli, *Grace and Steel*, 34. Jean Becker, "Cliff Notes of Great Stories," *41 on 41* transcript.

[42] George Bush with Victor Gold, *Looking Forward: An Autobiography* (New York: Bantam Books, 1987), 23. Schweizer, *The Bushes*, 43. Meacham, *Destiny and Power*, 27.

[43] Schweizer, *The Bushes*, 43. Meacham, *Destiny and Power*, 27. Joe Hyams, *Flight of the Avenger: George Bush at War* (San Diego: Harcourt, Brace, Jovovich, 1991), 20. Taraborrelli, *Grace and Steel*, 46.

[44] Schweizer, *The Bushes*, 54–55.

[45] Schweizer, *The Bushes*, 23, 54–55. Meacham, *Destiny and Power*, 23.

[46] Meacham, *Destiny and Power*, xix–xx, 31–32.

[47] Meacham, *Destiny and Power*, xix–xx, 31–32.

[48] Mickey Herskowitz, *Duty, Honor Country: The Life and Legacy of Prescott Bush* (Nashville: Rutledge Hill Press, 2003), 2. Meacham, *Destiny and Power*, 23.

[49] Parmet, *George Bush*, 28. Schweizer, *The Bushes*, 51.

[50] Schweizer, *The Bushes*, 52. Meacham, *Destiny and Power*, 22–23.

[51] Meacham, *Destiny and Power*, 21. "Oral History Interview with Prescott Sheldon Bush 1966," 11.

[52] Meacham, *Destiny and Power*, 21.

[53] Herskowitz, *Duty, Honor, Country*, 2. Meacham, *Destiny and Power*, 22. Schweizer, *The Bushes*, 52–53. "Cliff Notes of Great Stories," courtesy of Jean Becker, *41 on 41* transcript, 1.

[54] Meacham, *Destiny and Power*, 23, Updegrove, *The Last Republicans*, 28. Kitty Kelley, *The Family: The Real Story of the Bush Dynasty* (New York: Doubleday, 2004), 51. "Cliff Notes of Great Stories," *41 on 41* transcript, 1.

[55] Meacham, *Destiny and Power*, 24–25. Taraborrelli, *Grace and Steel*, 49.

56 Taraborrelli, *Grace and Steel*, 49.

57 Schweizer, *The Bushes*, 56. Taraborrelli, *Grace and Steel*, 13.

58 Parmet, *George Bush*, 34. Bill Minutaglio, *First Son: George W. Bush and the Bush Family Dynasty* (New York: Three River Press, 1999), 34.

59 Meacham, *Destiny and Power*, 23, Updegrove, *The Last Republicans*, 28. Brookhiser, *The Way of the Wasp*, 2.

60 Meacham, *Destiny and Power*, 23, Updegrove, *The Last Republicans*, 28. Parmet, *George Bush*, 34–35. Taraborrelli, *Grace and Steel*, 48–49. Schweizer, *The Bushes*, 61

61 Meacham, *Destiny and Power*, 23, Updegrove, *The Last Republicans*, 28. Parmet, *George Bush*, 35. Dorothy Walker Bush's philosophy was articulated in a bible she inscribed to her son upon his confirmation at age fourteen. "I would be true, for there are those who trust me, I will be pure, for there are those who care, I would be strong, for there is much to suffer, I would be brave, for there is much to dare; I would be friend to all, the foe, the friendless, I would be giving and forget the gift. I would be humble, for I know my weakness; I would look up and laugh and love and lift." Bush Koch, *My Father, My President*. In further comments about his mother, Bush said, "Mother taught us about dealing with life on a personal basis, relating to other people." Bush, *Looking Forward*, 26. "Cliff Notes of Great Stories," *41 on 4*1 transcript, 2. Taraborrelli, *Grace and Steel*, 49.

62 Meacham, *Destiny and Power*, 23, Updegrove, *The Last Republicans*, 28. Parmet, *George Bush*, 35.

Chapter 2—Friends and Mentors: Phillips Academy

63 Walter Isaacson and Evan Thomas, *The Wise Men: Six Friends and the World They Made* (New York: Simon & Schuster, 1986), 180–182. Stimson also spoke at George Bush's graduation on June 12, 1942.

64 Henry L. Stimson, "The World Crises Today: An Address Given at the Graduation Exhibition," June 14, 1940, *Phillips Bulletin* 34, no. 4 (July 1940): 3, Digital Archives, Andover, Massachusetts.

65 John Palfrey, "Honoring President George H. W. Bush, 42," December 1, 2018, Andover website.

66 Peter W. Cookson Jr. and Caroline Persell Hodges, *Preparing for Power*, 8. Isaacson and Thomas, *The Wise Men*, 57–58.

67 Schweizer, *The Bushes*, 62–63. Claude M. Fuess, "Phillips Academy, Andover, Massachusetts," *The School Review* 22, no. 2 (February 1914): 75.

68 *Pot Pourri*, Phillips Academy, Andover, Massachusetts, 1918. Meacham, *Destiny and Power*, 34. Claude M. Fuess, "Phillips Academy, Andover, Massachusetts," *The School Review*, 22, no. 2, February 1914, 77.

69 *Pot Pourri*, 1918. Irish, "Not for Self or Others," Andover website. Frederick S. Allis, *Youth from Every Quarter: A Bicentennial History of Phillips Academy*

Andover (Lebanon, NH: University Press of New England, 1979), 454. Parmet, *George Bush*, 38.

70 "Claude M. Fuess 1962," Oral History Archives at Columbia, Rare Book & Manuscript Library, Columbia University, New York, 25. Fuess, "Phillips Academy, Andover, Massachusetts," *The School Review*, 22, no. 2 (February 1914): 74, 76.

71 Curt Smith, *George H. W. Bush Character at the Core* (Sterling, VA: Potomac Books, 2014), 3. Claude M. Fuess, "Phillips Academy, Andover, Massachusetts," *The School Review* 22, no. 2 (February 1914): 76.

72 Allis, *Youth from Every Quarter*, 462–463. Schweizer, *The Bushes*, 63.

73 Allis, *Youth from Every Quarter*, 462–463, 77–78. Kelley, *The Family*, 64.

74 Allis, *Youth from Every Quarter*, 462–463

75 Cookson and Hodges Purcell, *Preparing for Power*, 48. Axel Bundgaard, *Muscle and Manliness: The Rise of Sport in American Boarding Schools* (Syracuse: Syracuse University Press, 2005), 169. Rita Savard and Alyson Irish, "Point of Light: Looking Back on Milestones and Memories of George H. W. Bush, '42," *Andover* (Winter 2019): 19. Isaacson and Thomas, *The Wise Men*, 46–47. Claude M. Fuess, "Phillips Academy, Andover, Massachusetts," *The School Review*, 22, no. 2 (February 1914): 74.

76 Schweizer, *The Bushes*, 64–65. *41*, director and producer Jeffrey Roth, Home Box Office Documentary Films (New York, 2012).

77 Bush, *All the Best*, 573–574.

78 George Bush to John Kemper, November 19, 1952, Box 4, Zapata Oil File, Personal Alphabetical File, George Bush Presidential Library, College Station, TX (hereafter, GBPL). George Bush to John Kemper, November 28,1952, Box 4, Zapata Oil File, Personal Alphabetical File, GBPL. In 1947, when Bush first learned about a vacancy in the department he had written an equally passionate letter to Phillips Academy trustee, Charles Gage, urging DeClementi's consideration. [Deke's] "popularity with all the boys I ever knew at school, his training for such a job, his knowledge of all phases of athletics and his interest in athletics at Andover…are all strong assets. I won't say any more about Deke, for I know my reasons are tempered by a warm personal regard for him as a friend and as a coach." George Bush to Charles Gage, November 3, 1947, Box 9, Zapata Oil File, Personal Alphabetical File, GBPL.

79 *41 on 41*, directed by Lisa Lax and Nancy Stern Winters; produced by Lisa Lax, Amanda Postel, and Nancy Stern Winters; executive producer, Mary Kate Cary, the George and Barbara Bush Foundation, 2014. Schweizer, *The Bushes*, 64.

80 Meacham, *Destiny and Power*, 34–35.

81 Meacham, *Destiny and Power*, 39. Hyams, *Flight of the Avenger*, 21.

82 Parmet, *George Bush*, 41. *Pot Pourri*, Phillips Academy, Andover, Massachusetts, 1942, 38.

[83] Isaacson and Thomas, *The Wise Men,*181. Godfrey Hodgson, *The Colonel: The Life and Wars of Henry Stimson 1867–1950* (New York: Alfred A. Knopf, 1990), 170.

[84] "Claude M. Fuess 1962," Oral History Archives at Columbia, 85. David Schmitz, *Henry L. Stimson: The First Wise Man* (Wilmington: Scholarly Resources Inc., 2001), 2. "The basic Andover code," said the student Phillipian, "assumes every student is first and foremost a gentleman. Honesty, loyalty, generosity, sportsmanship and modesty...." Richard Ben Cramer, *Being Poppy: A Portrait of George Herbert Walker Bush* (New York: Simon & Schuster, 1992), 20.

[85] Claude M. Fuess, *Independent Schoolmaster* (Boston: Little, Brown, 1952), 247.

[86] Meacham, *Destiny and Power*, 36–37. Fuess, *Independent Schoolmaster*, 248.

[87] "The World Crises Today: An Address Given at the Commencement Exhibition by Henry L. Stimson," *The Phillips Bulletin*, June 14, 1940, 3. "Commencement Exercises Climax Last School Week for Class of 40," *The Phillipian*, June 14, 1940, 1., Phillips Academy Archives, Andover, Massachusetts. *Schmitz, Henry L. Stimson*, 3, 132.

[88] "The World Crises Today: An Address Given at the Commencement Exhibition by Henry L. Stimson."

[89] "The World Crises Today: An Address Given at the Commencement Exhibition by Henry L. Stimson."

[90] "The World Crises Today: An Address Given at the Commencement Exhibition by Henry L. Stimson."

[91] Cramer, *Being Poppy*, 20–21. Michael R. Beschloss, "The Character and Leadership of George H. W. Bush," University of Texas, Lyndon B. Johnson School of Public Affairs, March 27, 1995, C-Span. Claude M. Fuess, *The Andover Way* (Boston: Lothrop, Lee and Shepard, 1926) Fuess's novel tells the story of how the atmosphere and values of Phillips Academy transform a student from a boy into a man. Clifford Smythe, *The Literary Digest International Book Review* 4, no. 8 (July 1926): 538. In a speech delivered at the school in 1989, Bush articulated how much the ideas of the school had impacted him over the course of his life. "For it is in school, as it was for me here at Phillips Academy, that we come to understand real values. The need to help the less fortunate, make ours a more decent, civil world." Mark Walsh, "Bush Pays Homage to Andover Roots," *Education Week*, November 15, 1989.

[92] Cramer, *Being Poppy*, 23. "George H. W. Bush," *The American Experience*, produced and directed by Austin Hoyt, December 4, 2018, Public Broadcasting System. Parmet, *George Bush*, 43.

[93] Allis, *Youth from Every Quarter*, 474.

[94] Allis, *Youth from Every Quarter*, 474.

[95] Meacham, *Destiny and Power*, 38. George Bush, "Remarks to World War II Veterans and Families in Honolulu, Hawaii," December 7, 1991. Public Papers of George H. W. Bush, GBPL. Bush, "My Impressions—World War II," *Life* Magazine, December 7, 1941, Box 26, Speech File, Draft Files, GBPL.

[96] Meacham, *Destiny and Power*, 38. George Bush, "Remarks to World War II Veterans and Families in Honolulu, Hawaii."
[97] Fuess, *Independent Schoolmaster*, 251.
[98] Fuess, *Independent Schoolmaster*, 251.
[99] Bush, "My Impression—World War II."
[100] Fuess, *Independent Schoolmaster*, 251, Meacham, *Destiny and Power*, 39.
[101] Taraborrelli, *Grace and Steel*, 79.
[102] Betty Boyd Caroli, *First Ladies: An Intimate Look at How 38 Women Handled What May Be the Most Demanding, Unpaid, Unelected Job in America* (New York: Oxford University Press, 1995), 280.
[103] Meacham, *Destiny and Power*, 41. Barbara Bush, *A Memoir* (New York: Charles Scribner's Sons, 1994), 16–17. Taraborrelli, *Grace and Steel*, 80.
[104] Cramer, *Being Poppy*, 23. Schweizer, *The Bushes*, 69.
[105] Kelley, *The Family*, 70. The student who introduced Stimson referred to the secretary as "a living and vital representative of our ways and our type of existence, who is out setting an example to the whole nation…living proof that the Andover way is the way of men who guide the fortunes of the nation." Cramer, *Being Poppy*, 19–20.
[106] Updegrove, *The Last Republicans*, 17. Meacham, *Destiny and Power*, 45. Bush, "My Impressions—World War II."
[107] Kelley, *The Family*, 67.
[108] Herskowitz, *Duty, Honor, Country*, 2. Meacham, *Destiny and Power*, 46.
[109] Savard and Irish, "Point of Light."
[110] Bush, "Notes on the Making of an Ambassador," Box 4, United Nations File, GBPL.

Chapter 3—Courage Under Fire: World War II

[111] Schweizer, *The Bushes*, 79.
[112] Schweizer, *The Bushes*, 80.
[113] Schweizer, *The Bushes*, 80. Prescott Bush and Dorothy Walker Bush June 15, 1944, Series: World War II Correspondence, Box 1, GBPL.
[114] Tom Brokaw, *The Greatest Generation* (New York: Dell Publishing, 1998), 329–330. George Bush to Tom Brokaw, March 9, 1998, *41 on 41* interview collection, courtesy of Jean Becker.
[115] Meacham, *Destiny and Power*, 59–60. Kelley, *The Family*, 73–74. Schweizer, *The Bushes*, 70. George Bush, *All the Best*. George Bush, *My Life in Letters and Other Writings* (New York: Scribner, 1999), 24.
[116] Schweizer, *The Bushes*, 70–71. Bush, *All the Best*. George Bush, 28.
[117] Bush, *All the Best*, 45, 49. Bush, Bush, All the Best, 28. Bush, "My Impressions—World War II, Life Magazine Article, Christmas Eve,1944," Schweizer, *The Bushes*, 70. Kelley, The Family, 73–74.

[118] Bush, *All the Best*, 28. Bush, "My Impressions—World War II, Life Magazine Article, Christmas Eve,1944," Box 26, Speech File, Draft Files, GBPL. Schweizer, *The Bushes*, 71. Meacham, *Destiny and Power,* 53. Parmet, *George Bush*, 49. Bush, *All the Best*, 39–40.

[119] Parmet, *George Bush,* "Remarks to World War II Veterans and Families in Honolulu, Hawaii," December 7, 1991, American Presidency Project, 48.

[120] Bush Koch, *My Father, My President*, 29.

[121] Bush, *All the Best*, 42–43.

[122] Bush, *All the Best*, 42–43, 49. Meacham, *Destiny and Power,* 59–60. Kelley, *The Family*, 73–74.

[123] Meacham, *Destiny and Power*, 59–60.

[124] Cramer, *Being Poppy*, 4–5.

[125] Meacham, *Destiny and Power*, 62. Bush, *Looking Forward*, 38.

[126] Meacham, *Destiny and Power,* 65. "Interview with George Bush, Vice President Bush about his experiences in the Navy during World War II," Vice President's office. June 19, 1996, Master Tape # 667, Ronald Reagan Presidential Library, Simi Valley, California. Bush Koch, *My Father, My President*, 22.

[127] Meacham, *Destiny and Power,* 65. "Interview with George Bush, Vice President Bush remarks about his experiences in the Navy during World War II." Koch, *My Father, My President*, 22.

[128] Bush, *All the Best*, 49, 57. Meacham, *Destiny and Power*, 65. Bush, *Looking Forward*, 40.

[129] Meacham, *Destiny and Power*, 63. Bush, *Looking Forward*, 40.

[130] Meacham, *Destiny and Power*, 66–67.

[131] "Bush, My Impressions—World War II." Life Magazine Article, Christmas Eve,1944," Box 26, Speech File, Draft Files, GBPL.

[132] "My Impressions—World War II." Life Magazine Article, Christmas Eve,1944," Box 26, Speech File, Draft Files, GBPL.

[133] Kabaservice, *The Guardians*, 94.

Chapter 4—Young Man in a Hurry: Yale

[134] Meacham, *Destiny and Power*, 74.

[135] Kelley, *The Family,* 91. Bush, *Looking Forward*, 42.

[136] Meacham, *Destiny and Power*, 75.

[137] Meacham, *Destiny and Power*, 75.

[138] "Alan Brinkley, *Henry Luce and His American Century* (New York: Vintage Books, 2011), 267–268.

[139] James Patterson, *Grand Expectations: The United States 1945–1974* (New York: Oxford University Press, 1996), 7–8.

[140] Schweizer, *The Bushes*, 86–87. Kabaservice, *The Guardians*, 99.

[141] Kabaservice, *The Guardians*, 97–98. Parmet, *George Bush*, 63–64.

[142] Kabaservice, *The Guardians*, 100–101.

[143] Kelley, *The Family*, 91. Meacham, *Destiny and Power*, 73.
[144] Kelley, *The Family*, 91.
[145] Schweizer, *The Bushes*, 13–15. Isaacson and Thomas, *The Wise Men*, 61.
[146] Meacham, *Destiny and Power*, 66–67.
[147] George Bush and Jim McGrath, ed., *Heartbeat: George Bush in His Own Words* (New York: Scribner, 2001), 30.
[148] Kabaservice, *The Guardians*, 99.
[149] Bush, *All the Best*, 62.
[150] Bush, *All the Best*, 62–63. Bush, *Looking Forward*, 61.
[151] Kelley, *The Family*, 100.
[152] Kelley, *The Family*, 101.
[153] Kelley, *The Family*, 101. Bush, *All the Best*, 63.
[154] Schweizer, *The Bushes*, 94–95. Schweizer, *The Bushes*, 94–95. Kelley, *The Family*, 98–99.
[155] Bush, *Looking Forward*, 22.

Chapter 5—Triumph and Tragedy: Businessman

[156] Bush, *Looking Forward*, 50.
[157] George W. Bush *41*: *A Portrait of My Father* [New York: Crown Publishing, 2014], 63. Meacham, *Destiny and Power*, 83. Parmet, *George Bush*, 69.
[158] Parmet, *George Bush*, 69–70.
[159] Bush, *41*, 59. Parmet, *George Bush*, 72.
[160] Bush, *41*, 63. Meacham, *Destiny and Power*, 83.
[161] Bush, *41*, 59. Parmet, *George Bush*, 72.
[162] Bush, *41*, 59.
[163] Bush, *Looking Forward*, 55.
[164] Parmet, *George Bush*, 69–70.
[165] Schweizer, *The Bushes*, 99. Parmet, *George Bush*, 69–70, 78. Bush, *Looking Forwar*d, 58.
[166] Parmet, *George Bush*, 79.
[167] Meacham, *Destiny and Power,* 88. Bush, *41*, 72. Tom McCance to George Bush, May 4, 1950, George Bush to Tom McCance, June 25, 1950, Box 4, Zapata Oil file, Personal Alphabetical File, GBPL, College Station, TX.
[168] Bush, *All the Best*, 69–70. Becker, *Character Matters*, 3. In a response to Bush's decision to decline the Brown Brothers Harriman opportunity, McCance viewed Bush's "loyalty to [Dresser] the company and Neil Mallon…understandable, not to say commendable." Tom McCance to George Bush, June 29, 1950, Box 4, Zapata Oil file, Personal Alphabetical File, GBPL.
[169] Bush, *41*, 71–72.
[170] Susan Page, *The Matriarch: Barbara Bush and the Making of An American Dynasty* (New York: Twelve, 2019), 90.
[171] Interview with John Overbey, C-Span, September 11, 1988.

[172] Bush, *Looking Forward*, 60–61. George Bush to Neil Mallon, April 12, 1951, Box 4, Zapata oil file, Personal Alphabetical File, GBPL. Even after Bush began his company, Mallon continued to express his support for the new endeavor. "Some day soon I want to hear in complete detail what you are doing and help in any way I can." Neil Mallon to George Bush, May 22, 1951, Box 4, Zapata oil file, Personal Alphabetical File, GBPL.

[173] Bush, *Looking Forward*, 60–61. Bush, *41*, 60.

[174] Author's phone conversation with Neil Mallon Bush, June 8, 2024,

[175] George Bush to John J. Bush, July 6, 1955, Box 4, Zapata oil file, Personal Alphabetical File, GBPL.

[176] Bush, *Looking Forward*, 67–68.

[177] Meacham, *Destiny and Power*, 98–99. Bush, *All the Best*, 76.

[178] Bush, *Looking Forward*, 69.

[179] Meacham, *Destiny and Power*, 101–102. Bush, *Looking Forward*, 69. Bush, *41*, 81. Bush Koch, *My Father, My President*, 36.

[180] Schweizer, *The Bushes,*109.

[181] Schweizer, *The Bushes,*109. Bush Koch, *My Father, my president*, 37.

[182] Schweizer, *The Bushes,*109.

[183] Parmet, *George Bush*, 82.

[184] Meacham, *Destiny and Power*, 105. Bush, *41*, 93–94.

[185] Meacham, *Destiny and Power*, 106. Parmet, *George Bush*, 84.

[186] Bush, *41*, 95.

[187] Bush, *41*, 95.

[188] Bush, *Looking Forward*, 73.

Chapter 6—The Pragmatic Conservative: Politics

[189] Parmet, *George Bush*, 113.

[190] Bush, *All the Best*, 90.

[191] Geoffrey Kabaservice, *Rule and Ruin: The Downfall of Moderation and the Destruction of the Republican Party, From Eisenhower to the Tea Party* (New York: Oxford University Press, 2012), 10, 12, 14–15.

[192] Isaacson and Thomas, *The Wise Men*, 566, 569, 574.

[193] Kabaservice, *Rule and Ruin,* 10, 12, 14–15.

[194] Kabaservice, *Rule and Ruin*, 13–14. George H. Nash, *The Conservative Intellectual Movement in America Since 1945* (New York: Basic Books, 1976), 253.

[195] Kelley, *The Family*, 115. Schweizer, *The Bushes,*115. Meacham, *Destiny and Power,* 117.

[196] Kabaservice, *Rule and Ruin*, 9.

[197] Kabaservice, *Rule and Ruin*, 9. Laurence R. Jurdem, *Paving the Way for Reagan: The Influence of Conservative Media on US Foreign Policy* (Lexington: University of Kentucky Press, 2018), 9. Herskowitz, *Duty, Honor, Country*, 82–83, 121, 128–129. Kelley, *The Family*, 116. Kabaservice, *Rule and Ruin*, 9.

[198] Herskowitz, *Duty, Honor, Country*, 82–83, 121, 128–129. Kelley, *The Family*, 116.

[199] Schweizer, *The Bushes,*121. In serving as Eisenhower's finance chairman during the 1956 reelection campaign in the predominantly Democratic Harris County, Bush even in this early stage of his political career understood the importance of approaching the campaign in a pragmatic manner. "I feel the reasonability of the committee is two-fold: 1. It must help raise money. 2. It must help attract votes attract votes for Eisenhower. To accomplish these ends, my personal feeling is that we must drop all party partisanship…We must take over the effectiveness that the Democrats for Eisenhower had. We may have a clash or two with our regular Republican organization, but I don't believe we will." George Bush to W. H. Francis, September 11, 1956, Box 1, Personal Alphabetical File, GBPL

[200] Schweizer, *The Bushes,*121. Silk, *The American Establishment*, 268.

[201] Schweizer, *The Bushes,*123–124. Bush, *All the Best*, 77. Herskowitz, *Duty, Honor, Country*, 101.

[202] Parmet, *George Bush*, 83. Meacham, *Destiny and Power*, 107–108.

[203] Herskowitz, *Duty, Honor, Country*, 106, 108, 122.

[204] Schweizer, *The Bushes*, 122–123.

[205] Herskowitz, *Duty, Honor, Country*, 140. In Doro Bush Koch's memoir, the author writes about an interesting encounter she had with her father's 1988 Democratic opponent, Governor Michael Dukakis. In 1954, Dukakis was an undergraduate attending a program at American University. On the day Prescott Bush delivered remarks against McCarthy, Dukakis was watching the proceedings from the Senate gallery. "I couldn't stand the guy," Dukakis recalled of McCarthy. "To have some folks—particularly on the Republican side of the aisle—stand up and say, 'This is wrong,' was very, very important." Bush Koch, *My Father, My President*, 43.

[206] Herskowitz, *Duty, Honor, Country*, 136.

[207] Herskowitz, *Duty, Honor, Country*, 138.

[208] Herskowitz, *Duty, Honor, Country*, 144–145.

[209] George Bush, "Remarks at a Luncheon Commemorating Dwight D. Eisenhower's Centennial," March 27, 1990, Public Papers, George H. W. Bush, GBPL. Bush, *Looking Forward*, 191.

[210] Parmet, *George Bush*, 82. Meacham, *Destiny and Power*, 116–117.

[211] Bush, *Looking Forward*, 81.

[212] Bush, *Looking Forward*, 83. Meacham, *Destiny and Power*, 110. Eisenhower had great respect for Prescott Bush. In another diary entry about potential successors, the president gave Bush "an A." Schweizer, *The Bushes*, 125.

[213] Bush, *Looking Forward*, 83–84. Meacham, *Destiny and Power*, 114.

[214] Wayne Thoburn, *Red State: An Inside Story of How the GOP Came to Dominate Texas Politics* (Austin: University of Texas Press, 2014), 73–74. John S. Huntington, "The Voice of Many Hatreds: J. Evets Haley and Texas Ultraconservatism," *Western Historical Quarterly* 49, no. 1 (Spring, 2018): 65.

[215] Silk, *The American Establishment*, 286–287. Thoburn, *Red State*, 74. Kabaservice, *The* Guardians, 206. Kabaservice, *Rule and Ruin*, 34.
[216] Bush, *Looking Forward*, 85. Meacham, *Destiny and Power*, 114.
[217] Schweizer, *The Bushes*, 144.
[218] Schweizer, *The Bushes*, 145.
[219] Timothy Naftali, *George H. W Bush* (New York: Times Books, 2007), 12. Tom Wicker, *George Herbert Walker Bush* (New York: Penguin, 2004), 15–16.
[220] Meacham, *Destiny and Power*, 116–117. Wicker, *George H. W. Bush*, 16–17.
[221] Bush, *All the Best*, 88. Meacham, *Destiny and Power*, 121.
[222] Meacham, *Destiny and Power*, 123–124. Schweizer, *The Bushes*, 163. George H. W. Bush to Dwight D. Eisenhower, January 7, 1965, Box 3, Dwight D. Eisenhower's (DDE hereafter) Post Presidential Papers 1965, Principal File Series, Dwight D. Eisenhower Presidential Library (DDEPL hereafter), Abilene, KS.
[223] Bush, *All the Best*, 89–90. Nancy Gibbs and Michael Duffy, *The President's Club: Inside the World's Most Exclusive Fraternity* (New York: Simon & Schuster, 2012), 373. Schweizer, *The Bushes*, 164.
[224] Bush, *All the Best*, 89–90. Gibbs and Duffy, *The President's Club*, 373. Schweizer, *The Bushes*, 164. Wicker, *George H. W. Bush*, 18. Kabaservice, *The Guardians*, 216. Richard M. Nixon to George Bush, November 12, 1964, Box 1, George Bush Congressional File, GBPL.

Chapter 7—Listening and Learning: Congressman

[225] Bush, *Looking Forward*, 98.
[226] Meacham, *Destiny and Power*, 143. Bush, *All the Best*, 127. Joe B. Frantz to Lyndon B. Johnson, January 23, 1969, Post Presidential Names file, Box 12, Lyndon B. Johnson Presidential Library, Austin, TX.
[227] Bush, *Looking Forward*, 99. Parmet, *George Bush*, 138–139. Meacham, *Destiny and Power*, 144, 661, footnote 44. Bush, *All the Best*, 121.
[228] Bush, *Looking Forward*, 99–100.
[229] Schweizer, *The Bushes*, 199. Bush, *Looking Forward*, 99–100.
[230] Kabaservice, *Rule and Ruin*, 136.
[231] Parmet, *George Bush*, 114.
[232] Parmet, *George Bush*, 115.
[233] Martin J. Medhurst, ed., *The Rhetorical Presidency of George H. W. Bush* (College Station: Texas A&M University Press, 2006), 10.
[234] Lewis L. Gould, *Grand Old Party: A History of the Republicans* (New York: Random House, 2003), 368.
[235] Gould, *Grand Old Party*, 368, 370.
[236] Schweizer, *The Bushes*, 174–175. Kabaservice, *Rule and Ruin*, 180.
[237] Schweizer, *The Bushes*, 176. Bush, *41*, 117–118.
[238] Schweizer, *The Bushes*, 177–178. Meacham, *Destiny and Power*, 132. Parmet, *George Bush*, 117–118. Kelley, *The Family*, 219. As George W. Bush writes,

"between 1950 and 1960…Houston grew from 600,000 to almost a million. In 1965 Houston's one congressional district split into three." Bush, 41, 79.

[239] Schweizer, *The Bushes*, 174–175. Parmet, *George Bush*, 119, Kabaservice, *Rule and Ruin,* 134.

[240] Parmet, *George Bush*.

[241] Dwight Eisenhower to George Bush, September 13, 1966, Box 25, DDE Post Presidential Papers, DDEPL, Abilene, KS.

[242] Schweizer, *The Bushes*, 178, 183. Parmet, *George Bush*, 121. Bush, *Looking Forward*, 90. Kabaservice, *Rule and Ruin*, 175.

[243] Schweizer, *The Bushes*, 178. Bush, *All the Best*, 95. Parmet, *George Bush*, 121. Meacham, *Destiny and Power*, 130.

[244] Kabaservice, *Rule and Ruin*, 188–189, 191. Gould, *Grand Old Party*, 371.

[245] Meacham, *Destiny and Power*, 134.

[246] Schweizer, *The Bushes*, 183.

[247] George Bush to Gerald R. Ford, November 25, 1966, Box 1, Personal Papers, Congressional File, GBPL.

[248] George Bush to Melvin R. Laird, November 25, 1966, Box 1, Personal Papers, Congressional File, GBPL.

[249] Meacham, *Destiny and Power*, 133–134. Schweizer, *The Bushes*, 183.

[250] Bush, *41*, 125. Bush, *All the Best*, 101.

[251] Bush, *Looking Forward*, 93.

[252] Bush, *Looking Forward*, 93–95.

[253] Bush, *Looking Forward*, 96. Schweizer, *The Bushes*, 184.

[254] Bush, *Looking Forward*, 94.

[255] Patterson, *Grand Expectations*, 630.

[256] Odd Arne Westad, *The Global Cold War: A World History* (New York: Basic Books, 2017), 318–321. "The Wise Men's Meeting of November 1 and Planning to Stay the Course, November–December," *Foreign Relations of the United States, 1964–1968, Volume V, Vietnam, 1967*, Office of the Historian, Document 377, Memorandum from the President's Assistant (Jones) to Lyndon Johnson. Isaacson and Thomas, *The Wise Men*, 643.

[257] Isaacson and Thomas, *The Wise Men*, 678–679. Douglas Brinkley, *Dean Acheson the Cold War Years, 1953–1971* (New Haven: Yale University Press, 1992), 254.

[258] Isaacson and Thomas, *The Wise Men*, 645–646, 654.

[259] Parmet, *George Bush*, 128–129.

[260] Parmet, *George Bush*, 131. Bush, *41*, 127.

[261] Meacham, *Destiny and Power*, 138–139. Bush, *A Memoir*, 71. Kabaservice, *Rule and Ruin*, 216–217.

[262] Bush, *All the Best*, 107. Following a call to Bush's office that threatened his life, Bush said: "That anyone would resort to this kind of talk makes me ashamed I'm an American," Meacham, *Destiny and Power*, 137.

[263] Meacham, *Destiny and Power*, 137. Bush, *Looking Forward*, 91.

[264] Bush, *All the Best*, 109.

[265] Becker, *Character Matters*, 84–85.

[266] Schweizer, *The Bushes*, 185–187. Meacham, *Destiny and Power*, 139. Parmet, *George Bush*, 133–134.

[267] Kabaservice, *Rule and Ruin*, 225, 230.

[268] [44] Ken Hughes, "Richard Nixon: The Campaign of 1968," Miller Center, University of Virginia.

[269] Lewis L. Gould, *1968: The Election that Changed America* (Chicago: Ivan R. Dee, 1993), 5. Gould, *Grand Old Party*, 376.

[270] Richard Nixon to George Bush, July 26, 1968, Box 1, George Bush, Personal Papers, Congressional File, General, GBPL. Schweizer, *The Bushes*, 197. Jeffrey Engel, *The China Diary of George H. W. Bush: The Making of a Global President* (Princeton: Princeton University Press, 2008), 417.

[271] Derek Chollet, *The Middle Way: How Three Presidents Shaped America's Role in the World* (Oxford, UK: Oxford University Press, 2021), 5. During that 1967 meeting Eisenhower told Nixon "that George Bush not only believed in the right conservative principles, but that he had the personality and charisma to win." Parmet, *George Bush*, 135.

[272] Meacham, *Destiny and Power*, 140. Gibbs and Duffy, *The President's Club*, 375. Neil Mallon to George Champion, April 9, 1968, Box 1, Personal Papers, General Congressional File, GBPL. Mallon's campaign to get others to support Bush for vice president resulted in Richard Nixon responding to the following letter of one of Bush's many supporters. "I am doubly grateful for your hearty endorsement of George Bush. I share your high respect for him and…I will certainly be giving his qualifications every consideration…." Richard M. Nixon to James C. Richdale Jr., July 19, 1968, Box 1, Personal Papers, General Congressional File, GBPL.

[273] Bush, *All the Best*, 117–118. Meacham, *Destiny and Power*, 142. Kelley, *The Family*, 246. In a separate note, the younger Bush expressed his appreciation for Dewey's support. "I am most appreciative of [your] interest and help. The wine was a little heady—getting even considered for this post, but I do feel that the efforts made on my behalf were made with taste and in such a way as not to disrupt what I consider are many fine relationships in the Congress. Thanks ever so much for your interest in this Silky Sullivan long shot [a racing term]. Though we finished out of the money, it was a great big plus for me, and I am indebted to you for your interest," Kelley, *The Family*, 247.

[274] Parmet, *George Bush*, 136.

[275] Gould, *Grand Old Party*, 381.

[276] Bush, *All the Best*, 121–122. George Bush to Richard Nixon, May 8, 1969, Box 1, George Bush Congressional Files, GBPL.

[277] Meacham, *Destiny and Power*, 144. Bush, *41*, 134. President Richard Nixon's Daily Diary, Thursday, May 22, 1969, Richard Nixon Presidential Library and Museum.

[278] Schweizer, *The Bushes*, 200.

[279] Meacham, *Destiny and Power*, 150. Parmet, *George Bush*, 144–145. Bush, *All the Best*, 129. Richard Nixon to George Bush, October 27, 1970, Box 1, Bush Congressional File, General, Personal, GBPL.
[280] Meacham, *Destiny and Power*, 144. Peter Baker and Susan Glasser, *The Man Who Ran Washington: The Life and Times of James A. Baker III* (New York: Doubleday, 2020), 50, 55.
[281] Baker and Glasser, *The Man Who Ran Washington*, 54–55.

Chapter 8—An Exercise in Diplomacy: Ambassador to the United Nations

[282] Bush, *All the Best*, 135. Notes on the United Nations, January 19, 1971, Box 4, George Bush, Personal Papers, United Nations File, GBPL.
[283] Becker, *Character Matters*, 19–20.
[284] Becker, *Character Matters*, 19–20.
[285] Meacham, *Destiny and Power*, 151.
[286] Meacham, *Destiny and Power*, 153. Bush, *All the Best*, 132.
[287] Silk, *The American Establishment*, 287.
[288] Silk, *The American Establishment*, 291.
[289] Parmet, *George Bush*, 148–149.
[290] Some notes on the making of a UN ambassador, December 15, 1970, Box 4, George Bush, Personal Papers, United Nations File, GBPL.
[291] Some notes on the making of a UN ambassador, December 15, 1970, Box 4, George Bush, Personal Papers, United Nations File, GBPL. John McCone to George Bush, December 17, 1970, Box 1, Congressional File, Personal, GBPL.
[292] Some notes on the making of a UN ambassador, December 15, 1970, Box 4, George Bush, Personal Papers, United Nations File, GBPL. John Davis Lodge to George Bush, December 14, 1970. Box 1, Congressional File, Personal, GBPL
[293] Some notes on the making of a UN ambassador, December 28, 1970, Box 4, George Bush, Personal Papers, United Nations File, GBPL. Meacham, *Destiny and Power*, 154.
[294] Some notes on the making of a UN ambassador, January 4, 1971, Box 4, George Bush, Personal Papers, United Nations File, GBPL.
[295] Some notes on the making of a UN ambassador, January 4, 1971, Box 4, George Bush, Personal Papers, United Nations File, GBPL. Some notes on the making of a UN ambassador, January 4, 1971, Box 4, George Bush, Personal Papers, United Nations File, GBPL. Some notes on the making of a UN ambassador, December 29, 1970, Box 4, George Bush, Personal Papers, United Nations File, GBPL. Bush also found he had little regard for "the New York establishment," stating, "I have never seen such arrogance and self-assurance-unwillingness to accept criticism etc…there is total arrogance that I simply cannot understand." Some notes on the making of a UN ambassador, Box 4, George Bush, Personal Papers, United Nations File, GBPL. Bush had his own thoughts about the negative *Times* editorial, calling it "not all that bad but snide." Some notes on the

making of a UN ambassador, December 15, 1970, Box 4, George Bush, Personal Papers, United Nations File, GBPL

[296] Some notes on the making of a UN ambassador, January 4, 1970, Box 4, George Bush, Personal Papers, United Nations File, GBPL. Kabaservice, *Rule and Ruin*, 36.

[297] Some notes on the making of a UN ambassador, January 4, 1970, Box 4, George Bush, Personal Papers, United Nations File, GBPL. Some notes on the making of a UN ambassador, January 11, 1970, Box 4, George Bush, Personal Papers, United Nations File, GBPL.

[298] Engel, *China Diary*, 413.

[299] Bush, *All the Best*, 134–135.

[300] Some notes on the making of a UN ambassador, January 28, 1970, Box 4, George Bush, Personal Papers, United Nations File, GBPL. Engel, *The China Diary*, 413.

[301] Some notes on the making of a UN ambassador, January 19, 1971, Box 4, George Bush, Personal Papers, United Nations File, GBPL.

[302] Some notes on the making of a UN ambassador, 1971, Box 4, George Bush, Personal Papers, United Nations File, GBPL.

[303] Some notes on the making of a UN ambassador, Box 4, George Bush, Personal Papers, United Nations File, GBPL.

[304] Bush, *All the Best*, 138. Margaret Heckler to George Bush, April 2, 1971, Box 1, Congressional File—Personal, GBPL. Arranging for Congress to become more familiar with the United Nations was an idea Bush had considered even before he was sworn into the office. "I think we must keep Congress in touch with the UN.... I am determined to get them up there," Some notes on the making of a UN ambassador, December 15, 1970, Box 4, George Bush, Personal Papers, United Nations File, GBPL.

[305] "Exchange of Remarks Between the President and George Bush at the Swearing in Ceremony of Mr. Bush to Be United States Ambassador to the United Nations," February 26, 1971, Box 1, Congressional File—Personal, GBPL.

[306] Some notes on the making of a UN ambassador, January 27, 1971, Box 1, George Bush, Personal Papers, United Nations File, GBPL. Richard Nixon to George Bush, March 22, 1972, Box 1, George Bush, Personal Papers, United Nations File, GBPL. President Nixon also expressed his pride in Bush in a letter congratulating Senator and Mrs. Bush on their fiftieth wedding anniversary. "I welcome the opportunity to tell you personally what you undoubtably hear not only from friends in Connecticut but across the country about the strong leadership that George provides in his sensitive and demanding duties at the United Nations. He is indeed his father's son."

Richard Nixon to Senator and Mrs. Prescott Bush, July 30, 1971, Box 4, George Bush, Personal Papers, United Nations File, GBPL. Jurdem, *Paving the Way for Reagan*, 98–99. But despite Nixon's congratulations, Bush continued to be his own worst critic. "I am beginning to wonder about the allocation of my own time on this new job. How to do all the things right. There doesn't seem to be enough hours in the day," Bush wrote. Box 1, George Bush, Personal Papers, United Nations File, GBPL.

[307] Some notes on the making of a UN ambassador, 1971, Box 4, George Bush, Personal Papers, United Nations File, GBPL. Richard Nixon to Secretary-General U Thant, February 27, 1971, Box 1, George Bush, Personal Papers, United Nations File, GBPL.

[308] Engel, *China Diary*, 414.

[309] Some notes on the making of a UN ambassador, Box 4, George Bush, Personal Papers, United Nations File, GBPL. Engel, *The China Diary*, 417.

[310] Some notes on the making of a UN ambassador, March 28, 1971, Box 4, George Bush, Personal Papers, United Nations File, GBPL. Bush, *All the Best*, 139.

[311] Engel, *China Diary*, 413. Engel, *When the World Seemed New*, 19.

[312] Bush, *All the Best*, 143.

[313] Bush, *All the Best*, 150.

[314] Schweizer, *The Bushes*, 210.

[315] Schweizer, *The Bushes*, 210. Meacham, *Destiny and Power*, 158. Bush, *All the Best*, 152.

[316] Bush, *All the Best*, 149–150.

[317] Bush, *All the Best*, 150.

[318] Meacham, *Destiny and Power*, 159.

[319] Bush, *All the Best*, 153–154. Bush, *41*, 147. Schweizer, *The Bushes*, 210. Meacham, *Destiny and Power*, 159. Jurdem, *Paving the Way for Reagan*, 53.

[320] Some notes on the making of a UN ambassador, November 15, 1971, Box 4, George Bush, Personal Papers, United Nations File, GBPL. Engel, *The China Diary*, 430–432.

[321] "Watching these cabinet meetings and seeing how little decision making goes on there, there is a certain luxury to being out of Washington. You are not under the intense political pressure or fire all the time." Some notes on the making of a UN ambassador, July 19, 1971, Box 4, George Bush, Personal Papers, United Nations File, GBPL. "Because I felt caught between Rogers and Kissinger, I totally changed my mind about whether the U.N. ambassador should be a member of the President's cabinet. The answer is absolutely not." Bush, *All the Best*, 156.

[322] Undated, handwritten note, "Personal, GB," Box 4, George Bush, Personal Papers, United Nations File, GBPL. Bush also had other interactions with President Nixon that he regarded as a "personal touch." That included giving Bush a lift to Maine on Air Force One as well as calling Bush's parents to congratulate them on their fiftieth wedding anniversary. "Nixon does nice, gracious things like this but he gets little credit on that score." Some notes on the making of a UN ambassador, August 12, 1971, Box 4, George Bush, Personal Papers, United Nations File, GBPL.

[323] Schweizer, *The Bushes*, 214. Bush, *All the Best*, 161.

[324] Lyndon Johnson to George Bush, October 9, 1972, Post Presidential Name File, Box 12, LBJ Library, Austin, TX.

[325] Bush, *All the Best*, 161. In a note to his friend Fred Chambers, Bush wrote of his father, "I guess you, probably more than any of our friends know what he meant to me in terms of inspiration in my own life. Wherever I was, whatever I did he was the incentive behind everything," Bush, *All the Best*, 162.

[326] Parmet, *George Bush*, 156.

[327] Patterson, *Grand Expectations*, 761. "The 1972 Democratic Party Platform," July 11, 1972, The American Presidency Project. Ray Taylor, "Peace Is at Hand," November 1, 2022, *Teaching American History*.

[328] Parmet, *George Bush*, 156–157.

Chapter 9—The Dark Side of Politics: Chairman, Republican National Committee

[329] Donald Riegle Jr. to George Bush, July 25, 1972, Box 1, Personal Papers, Republican National Committee, GBPL. Bush, *Looking Forward*, 120.

[330] Bush, *All the Best*, 163. Bush, *Looking Forward*, 119. In a letter to Nixon following the meeting Bush wrote, "Frankly, your first choice for me came as quite a surprise particularly to Barbara. The rarefied atmosphere of international affairs plus the friendships in New York…she is convinced that all our friends in Congress, in public life…will say 'George screwed it up at the UN and the President has loyally found a suitable spot.' Candidly there will be some of this. But—here's my answer—Your first choice was the Republican National Committee. I will do it!" George Bush to Richard Nixon, November 21, 1972, Box 1, Personal Papers, Republican National Committee, GBPL.

[331] Meacham, *Destiny and Power*, 163–164.

[332] Parmet, *George Bush*, 159. Bush, *Looking Forward*, 119. In further comments to Nixon about his wife's view on the position, Bush wrote the president, "My wife's initial reaction is understandable, for she is but a mirror of how the real world views politics. Most people feel it is not the noble calling it should be—not the noble calling like affairs of state. One real challenge lies in enchanting the disenchanted young who view partisan politics with a worrisome cynicism." George Bush to Richard Nixon, November 21, 1972, Box 1, Personal Papers, Republican National Committee, GBPL. Kelley, *The Family*, 313.

[333] Bush, *Looking Forward*, 119.

[334] Parmet, *George Bush*, 157. Bush, *All the Best*, 163.

[335] Schweizer, *The Bushes*, 222. Bush, *All the Best*, 166. Bush, *Looking Forward*, 121. Meacham, *Destiny and Power*, 164–165. "George Bush for the President: Memo: RNC Internal Matters," March 6, 1973, Box 1, Personal Papers, Republican National Committee, GBPL.

[336] Schweizer, *The Bushes*, 222. Bush, *All the Best*, 166. Bush, *Looking Forward*, 121. Meacham, *Destiny and Power*, 164–165. "George Bush for the President: Memo:

RNC Internal Matters," March 6, 1973, Box 1, Personal Papers, Republican National Committee, GBPL.

337 Bush, *All the Best*, 167, 169.

338 A draft op-ed letter, never sent, July 6, 1973, Box 1, Personal Papers, Republican National Committee, GBPL.

339 A draft op-ed letter, never sent.

340 A draft op-ed letter, never sent.

341 A draft op-ed Letter, never sent.

342 A draft op-ed letter, never sent. Engel, *The China Diary*, 433.

343 Bush, *All the Best*, 170, 172.

344 Bush, *Looking Forward*, 120.

345 Donald Riegle Jr. to George Bush, July 25, 1972, Box 1, Personal Papers, Republican National Committee, GBPL.

346 Bush RNC notes, May 8, 1974, Box 1, Personal Papers, Republican National Committee, GBPL. Bush, *All the Best*, 179.

347 Bush, *All the Best*, 180.

348 Bush, *All the Best*, 185.

349 Bush, *All the Best*, 185.

350 Bush, *All the Best*, 181.

351 Schweizer, *The Bushes*, 226.

352 Schweizer, *The Bushes*, 226.

353 Meacham, *Destiny and Power*, 170.

354 Bush, *All the Best*, 189.

355 Bush, *All the Best*, 193.

356 Bush, *41*, 160.

Chapter 10—A Whole New World: China and the CIA

357 Engel, *China Diary*, 427.

358 Engel, *China Diary*, 95. Meacham, *Destiny and Power*, 182–183.

359 Engel, *China Diary*, 95, 405.

360 Bush, *All the Best*, 194.

361 Bush, *All the Best*, 194.

362 Bush, *All the Best*, 192.

363 Bush RNC notes, August 11, 1974, Box 1, Personal Papers, Republican National Committee, GBPL.

364 Bush RNC notes, August 11, 1974. Meacham, *Destiny and Power*, 176.

365 Kabaservice, *Rule and Ruin*, 342.

366 Bush RNC notes, August 11, 1974.

367 Parmet, *George Bush*, 168–170.

368 Bush, *All the Best*, 195–196. In a 1999 C-Span interview, Bush remained matter of fact about not getting the vice presidency. "The day that Ford announced his pick…my phone rang in Kennebunkport, Maine and it was the President and

he said 'I am going in right now to announce, Nelson Rockefeller and I want you to know that it was a hard call for me to make, George,' and he couldn't have been nicer....and to take the time....and here he was calling me because he didn't want to have hurt feelings. So there was speculation flattering speculation, but I didn't expect that." "President George H. W. Bush Interview," November 19, 1999, C-Span.

369 Meacham, *Destiny and Power*, 177–178. Bush RNC notes, August 22, 1974, Box 1, Personal Papers, Republican National Committee, GBPL.

370 Bush, *All the Best*, 197.

371 Bush, *Looking Forward*, 128. George Bush to Reg Murphy, November 14, 1974, Box 1, China File, Correspondence File, GBPL.

372 Parmet, *George Bush*.

373 Engel, *China Diary*, 6.

374 George Bush to Charles Bartlett, October 29, 1974, Box 1, China File, Correspondence File, GBPL.

375 George Bush to Yvonne M. Alford, November 11, 1974, Box 1, China File, Correspondence File, GBPL.

376 Engel, *China Diary*, footnote bottom of p. 36.

377 Engel, *China Diary*, 294.

378 Engel, *China Diary*, 158.

379 Engel, *China Diary*, 349.

380 Engel, *China Diary*, 400, 404–405, 436.

381 Engel, *China Diary*, 403, 412–413

382 Engel, *China Diary*, 430.

383 Meacham, *Destiny and Power*, 190.

384 Naftali, *George H. W. Bush*, 31.

385 Bush, *Looking Forward*, 151–152. Meacham, *Destiny and Power*, 191, 194.

386 Schweizer, *The Bushes*, 246.

387 Bush, *All the Best*, 233–234.

388 Meacham, *Destiny and Power*, 194.

389 Bush, *All the Best*, 241.

390 Bush, *Looking Forward*, 159. Bush, *All the Best*, 242.

391 Meacham, *Destiny and Power*, 196. Bush, *All the Best*, 243. Parmet, *George Bush*, 192.

392 "Swearing in Ceremony of George Bush as Director of Central Intelligence Agency," *Employee Bulletin*, February 2, 1976, Box 1, CIA Files, Events and Appearance File, GBPL.

393 Schweizer, *The Bushes*, 253. Bush, *All the Best*, 251. Bush, *41*, 175.

394 Averell Harriman to George Bush, June 29, 1976, Box 4, CIA Files, Correspondence File, GBPL.

395 Averell Harriman to George Bush, June 29, 1976.

396 Parmet, *George Bush*, 195.

397 Kabaservice, *Rule and Ruin*, 346–347.

[398] Kabaservice, *Rule and Ruin*, 346–347. Ronald Reagan, "Let Them Go Their Way," Second Conservative Political Action Conference, March 1, 1975, *The Greatest Speeches of Ronald Reagan* (West Palm Beach: NewMax.com, 2001) 33–45.

[399] Kabaservice, Rule and Ruin, 347.

[400] Kabaservice, *Rule and Ruin*, 348.

[401] Kabaservice, *Rule and Ruin*, 348–349.

[402] Bush, *All the Best*, 260, 265.

[403] Meacham, *Destiny and Power*, 205. Author's email exchange with Craig Fuller, August 12, 2024.

[404] Bush, *All the Best*, 260, 265. Bush, *41*, 178–179. Following the conclusion of Bush's tenure with the CIA, he received a warm Thanksgiving greeting from President Nixon. Always encouraging, the former president praised Bush for the service he had rendered to the country. "You have taken very difficult assignments and handled each one with high intelligence, great courage and quiet dignity." Richard Nixon to George Bush, November 27, 1976, Box, 1, Post-Presidential Correspondence with George H. W. Bush (1964–1968; 1974–1993). Richard Nixon Library and Birthplace Foundation, Yorba Linda, CA. Meacham, *Destiny and Power*, 205.

Chapter 11—Working with Reagan: Vice President

[405] Meacham, *Destiny and Power*, 259.

[406] Meacham, *Destiny and Power*, 259.

[407] Author conversation with David Q. Bates, October 20, 2024.

[408] Bush, *Looking Forward*, 190.

[409] Patterson, *Restless Giant*, 14–15, 41, 54, 110.

[410] Patterson, *Restless Giant*, 14–15, 41, 54, 110.

[411] Patterson, *Restless Giant*, 124–125.

[412] William Imboden, *The Peacemaker: Ronald Reagan, The Cold War, and the World on the Brink* (New York: Dutton, 2022), 20. Patterson, *Restless Giant*, 122.

[413] Bush, *Looking Forward*, 190–191. Meacham, *Destiny and Power*, 217. Richard Nixon to George Bush, January 9, 1979, Box 1, Post-Presidential Correspondence with George H. W. Bush (1964–1968, 1974–1993). Richard Nixon Library and Birthplace Foundation, Yorba Linda, CA. Bush had agreed with the former president about the importance of limiting the infighting within the GOP. "I couldn't agree more about avoiding a massive blood letting. I know I can campaign so as not to tear down somebody else," Bush wrote at the end of January 1979. Meacham, *Destiny and Power*, 216-217.

[414] Bush, *Looking Forward*, 190–191. Schweizer, *The Bushes*, 280. Bush, *All the Best*, 282–283.

[415] Meacham, *Destiny and Power*, 215. Michael J. Birkner, "The Defining Moment: The 1980 Nashua Debate," *Historical New Hampshire* 42 (Fall 1987): 283–296.

[416] Bush, *Looking Forward*, 198–199.
[417] Meacham, *Destiny and Power*, 230–231.
[418] Meacham, *Destiny and Power*, 232–233.
[419] Naftali, *George H. W. Bush*, 37–38. Meacham, *Destiny and Power*, 236–237.
[420] Meacham, *Destiny and Power*, 237.
[421] Meacham, *Destiny and Power*, 238–239. Bush, *41*, 202.
[422] Bush, *All the Best*, 297.
[423] Bush, *All the Best*, 298.
[424] Meacham, *Destiny and Power*, 228, 235, 242. Bush, *All the Best*, 298. Bush, *Looking Forward*, 205–206.
[425] Bush, *Looking Forward*, 205–206, Bush, *All the Best*, 298.
[426] Bush, *Looking Forward*, 205–206.
[427] Bush, *Looking Forward*, 201, Meacham, *Destiny and Power*, 253.
[428] Bush, *Looking Forward*, 219.
[429] [25] Bush's speechwriter, Victor Gold, suggested the vice president reference Eisenhower during his acceptance speech. "Comments on Bush 1980 VP Acceptance Speech," August 1, 1988, C-Span. Gold also authored Bush's 1984 acceptance speech as well. Author email correspondence with Tom Collamore, August 22, 2024.
[430] Bush, *All the Best*, 300. Meacham, *Destiny and Power*, 258.
[431] Bush, *All the Best*, 302.
[432] Bush, *Looking Forward*, 225–228.
[433] Meacham, *Destiny and Power*, 264. Bush, *Looking Forward*, 225–228.
[434] Bush, *Looking Forward*, 230.
[435] Bush, *Looking Forward*, 230.
[436] Bush, *All the Best*, 303.
[437] Meacham, *Destiny and Power*, 261. Bush, *Looking Forward*, 220.
[438] Meacham, *Destiny and Power*, 261. Bush, *Looking Forward*, 220.
[439] Chase Untermeyer interview July 27–28, 2000, George H. W. Bush Oral History Project, Miller Center, University of Virginia, 27.
[440] Email correspondence with Craig Fuller, August 11, 2024.
[441] Email correspondence with Craig Fuller, August 10, 2024. Schweizer, *The Bushes*, 294.
[442] Email correspondence with Craig Fuller, August 10, 2024.
[443] Email correspondence with Craig Fuller, August 11, 2024. According to Herbert Parmet, Bush also told Fuller, "I can't surrender it like Deaver as Reagan did," Bush told Fuller. But the chief of staff also emphasized that "I'm not here to say that you have to run a staff like Reagan's staff. But I am here to say that if you're serious about trying to achieve an objective, you've got to have a team of people. You're going to have to manage." Parmet, *George Bush*, 339.
[444] "Excerpts of the Reports of the Committees Investigating the Iran-Contra Affair," The American Presidency Project.

[445] Craig Fuller interview, March 12, 2004, George H. W. Bush Oral History Project, Miller Center, University of Virginia, 18–19. Bush, *Looking Forward*, 228–229.

[446] Craig Fuller interview, March 12, 2004, 13.

[447] Email correspondence with Craig Fuller, August 11, 2024. Craig Fuller interview, March 12, 2004, 29–31, 75.

[448] Email correspondence with Craig Fuller, August 11, 2024. Meacham, *Destiny and Power*, 289.

[449] Meacham, *Destiny and Power*, 284–285.

[450] Meacham, *Destiny and Power*, 265. Letter From President Reagan to Soviet General Secretary, Brezhnev, undated, Foreign Relations of the United States, 1981–1988, Volume III, Soviet Union, January 1981–January 1983

[451] Author phone interview with David Q. Bates, August 9, 2024.

[452] Email correspondence with Craig Fuller, August 11, 2024. Schweizer, *The Bushes*, 294. Author's phone interview with David Bates, August 10, 2024.

[453] Craig Fuller interview, March 12, 2004, 14. Meacham, *Destiny and Power*, 272, 275.

[454] Meacham, *Destiny and Power*, 275.

[455] Meacham, *Destiny and Power*, 276–277.

[456] Meacham, *Destiny and Power*, 276–277.

[457] Meacham, *Destiny and Power*, 276–277. Bush, 41, 216.

[458] Meacham, *Destiny and Power*, 276–277.

[459] Meacham, *Destiny and Power*, 276–277. Bush, *41*, 216.

[460] Meacham, *Destiny and Power*, 282.

[461] Bush, *All the Best*, 319.

[462] Bush, *All the Best*, 337.

[463] Bush, *All the Best*, 337–338. Marcus Witcher, *Getting Right with Reagan: The Struggle for True Conservatism 1980–2016* (Lawrence: University of Kansas Press, 2016), 4.

[464] Bush, *All the Best*, 351.

[465] Bush, *All the Best*, 353.

[466] Naftali, *George H. W. Bush*, 43, 45, 49. Meacham, *Destiny and Power*, 300.

[467] Meacham, *Destiny and Power*, 300. Secretary of State George Shultz, who saw the interview and who made notes following a conversation with Bush ally Nicholas Brady, wrote, "VP was part of it.... Getting drawn into web of lives. Blows his integrity. He's finished then. Sh[ou]ld be very careful how he plays the loyal lieutenant role now." Meacham, *Destiny and Power*, 300–301.

[468] Naftali, *George H. W. Bush*, 43, 46–47. Meacham, *Destiny and Power*, 302, 306.

[469] Meacham, *Destiny and Power*, 305.

[470] Meacham, *Destiny and Power*, 301–302. Schweizer, *The Bushes*, 349–350.

[471] Meacham, *Destiny and Power*, 302.

[472] John Sununu interview, June 8–9, 2000, George H. W. Bush Oral History Project, Miller Center, University of Virginia, 11

[473] "George H. W. Bush Presidential Campaign Announcement," October 13, 1987, C-Span.

[474] George Bush, "Remarks at a Question-and-Answer Session at a White House Luncheon for Journalists," March 31, 1989, Public Papers of George H. W. Bush, GBPL.

[475] Kabaservice, *Rule and Ruin*, 370.

Chapter 12—Setting the Tone: President

[476] George Bush, "Remarks at a Question-and-Answer Session at a White House Luncheon for Journalists." Chollet, *The Middle Way*, 5. Bush also mentioned the legacy of Theodore Roosevelt when he addressed the National Organization of Religious Broadcasters in February 1989. In a draft of the speech, Bush alluded to Roosevelt's philosophy of "the strenuous life." Bush spoke of his desire for the American people to take action other than simply focus on their daily lives. "Teddy Roosevelt often talked about 'getting into the arena,' about taking the risk of doing something and not just standing on the sidelines." George Bush, "National Religious Broadcasters," February 1, 1989, Box 1 Speech File Draft Files, GBPL. Speechwriter Mark Davis recalls Bush speaking frequently about Eisenhower. Bush wanted his presidency to reflect the qualities that Ike brought to the White House, which included being a builder and a peacemaker. Author's phone interview with Mark Davis, August 30, 2024.

[477] George Bush, "Remarks at a Question-and-Answer Session at a White House Luncheon for Journalists."

[478] Parmet, *George Bush*, 347.

[479] "George H. W. Bush Presidential Campaign Announcement," October 13, 1987, C-Span.

[480] "George H. W. Bush Presidential Campaign Announcement."

[481] "George H. W. Bush Presidential Campaign Announcement."

[482] Bush and Scowcroft, *A World Transformed*, 17.

[483] George Bush, "Address Accepting the Presidential Nomination at the Republican National Convention in New Orleans," The American Presidency Project. Bush and Scowcroft, *A World Transformed*, 17.

[484] Gould, *GOP*, 442–444.

[485] Meacham, *Destiny and Power*, 339.

[486] "The Legacy of the George H. W. Bush Administration," Council on Foreign Relations, February 17, 2016.

[487] Naftali, *George H. W. Bush*, 61. Meacham, *Destiny and Power*, 342.

[488] Kabaservice, *Rule and Ruin*, 371.

[489] Naftali, *George H. W. Bush*, 61. Kabaservice, *Rule and Ruin*, 371.

[490] Parmet, *George Bush*, 350–351.

[491] Meacham, *Destiny and Power*, 347.

[492] Bush, *All the Best*, 405.

[493] Bush, *All the Best*, 408.

[494] Author's phone interview with David Q. Bates, October 20, 2025.

[495] George Bush, "Inaugural Address," January 20, 1989, the Avalon Project, Documents in Law, History and Diplomacy, Lillian Goldman Law Library, Yale Law School. Catherine L. Langford, "George Bush's Struggle with the 'Vision Thing,'" in *The Rhetorical Presidency of George H. W. Bush* (College Station: Texas A&M University Press, 2008), 26.

[496] George Bush, "Inaugural Address."

[497] George Bush, "Inaugural Address."

[498] Bush, *All the Best*, 412. Bush continued to emphasize that theme of bipartisanship when he addressed the Alfalfa Dinner on June 28, 1989. "We're Democrats and Republicans with different approaches…but really the same goals. We salute the same flag, sacrifice to gain a better life for our kids and comfort for our aging parents. We seem to know that kindness is not a sign of weakness, but rather strength. George Bush, "Presidential Remarks for the Alfalfa Dinner, Capital Hilton, January 28, 1989, Box 1, "Speech File Draft Files, GBPL. Bush and Scowcroft, *A World Transformed*, 16.

[499] Nelson and Perry, *41: Inside the Bush White House*, 149.

[500] George Bush, "Inaugural address."

[501] Bartholomew Sparrow, "Organizing Security: How the Bush Presidency Made Decisions on War and Peace," in *41: Inside the Presidency of George H. W Bush*, edited by Michael A. Nelson and Barbara A. Perry (Cornell: Cornell University Press, 2014), 81. Bush and Scowcroft, *A World Transformed*, 16.

[502] Meacham, *Destiny and Power*, 357–358. Bush, *All the Best*, 428. Assistant Secretary of State Robert Zoellick writes that "not since Thomas Jefferson and James Madison had a president and secretary of state combined talents to create such a productive partnership, although the two pairs reflected different attributes.… Each was self-confident but not arrogant, and they knew how to draw the best from each other. Robert Zoellick, *America in the World: A History of US Diplomacy and Foreign Policy* (New York: Twelve, 2020), 421–422.

[503] Email exchange with Craig Fuller, April 25, 2024. The point is corroborated by John Sununu. "If you remember the climate in Washington was that there was going to be a troika.… The President never had it in his mind, never thought about it, never considered it, never evaluated it, had told them both that they weren't going to be, had made up his mind, and yet the stories persisted." John Sununu interview, June 8–9, 2000, George H. W. Bush Oral History Project, Miller Center, University of Virginia, 19. Bush and Scowcroft, *A World Transformed*, 17.

[504] John Sununu interview, June 8–9, 2000, George H. W. Bush Oral History Project, Miller Center, University of Virginia, 19. Meacham, *Destiny and Power*, 358. Bush and Scowcroft, *A World Transformed*, 32.

[505] Sparrow, "Organizing Security: How the Bush Presidency Made Decisions on War and Peace," 81, 82–83.

506 Sparrow, "Organizing Security: How the Bush Presidency Made Decisions on War and Peace," 82–83. Box 1, George Bush Personal Papers, Republican National Committee, GBPL. Brent Scowcroft interview, November 12–13, 1999, George H. W. Bush Oral History Project, Miller Center, University of Virginia, 11. Bush and Scowcroft, *A World Transformed*, 19.

507 Bush, *All the Best*, 427. Bush and Scowcroft, *A World Transformed*, 18.

508 Sparrow, "Organizing Security: How the Bush Presidency Made Decisions on War and Peace," 83–84.

509 Bush and Scowcroft, *A World Transformed*, 20–21, 30.

510 Sparrow, "Organizing Security: How the Bush Presidency Made Decisions on War and Peace," 81, 86.

511 Brent Scowcroft interview, November 12–13, 1999, 19.

512 Sparrow, "Organizing Security: How the Bush Presidency Made Decisions on War and Peace," 81, 86. Brent Scowcroft interview, November 12–13. 1999, 14.

513 C. Boyden Gray, February 3–4, 2000, George H. W. Bush Oral History Project, Miller Center, University of Virginia, 5–6. David Mervin, *George Bush and the Guardianship Presidency* (London: Palgrave Macmillan, 2016), 62.

514 Sparrow, "Organizing Security: How the Bush Presidency Made Decisions on War and Peace," 81, 86–87. "GB: I wish like hell [Bob Mosbacher] didn't want to do that. I worry about cronyism and about his wife…[James A Baker] spoke the greatest truth when he said, you wouldn't be sitting here making these decisions if Bob hadn't raised a ton of money for you in two campaigns." Chase Untermeyer, *Zenith: Inside the White House with George H. W. Bush* (College Station, TX: Texas A&M University Press, 2016), 36. Brent Scowcroft interview, November 12–13, 1999, 20. Bush and Scowcroft, *A World Transformed*, 35.

515 McGrath, *Heartbeat*, 298.

516 Schweizer, *The Bushes*, 373.

517 Schweizer, *The Bushes*, 374. Author's phone interview with Mark Davis, August 30, 2024. Sununu, *The Quiet Man*, 18.

518 Schweizer, *The Bushes*, 374.

519 Schweizer, *The Bushes*, 374. Parmet, *George Bush*, 380.

520 Schweizer, *The Bushes*, 377–378.

521 Meacham, *Destiny and Power*, 365. Kabaservice, *Rule and Ruin*, 371–372.

522 Meacham, *Destiny and Power*, 365.

523 Meacham, *Destiny and Power*, 365.

524 Kabaservice, *Rule and Ruin*, 371–372. Julian E. Zelizer, *Burning Down the House: Newt Gingrich, the Fall of a Speaker, and the Rise of a New Republican Party* (New York: Penguin, 2020), 4–5.

Chapter 13—A Delicate Balance: The Fall of the Berlin Wall

525 George Bush, "Remarks at the Presentation Ceremony for the Presidential Medal of Freedom," July 6, 1989, The American Presidency Project.

[526] John Lewis Gaddis, *George F. Kennan: An American Life* (New York: Penguin Books, 2012), 672, 674.

[527] Gaddis, *George F. Kennan*, 672, 674.

[528] Chollet, *The Third Way*, 48, 58. Engel, *When the World Seemed New*, 23, 37. Bush and Scowcroft, *A World Transformed*, 39–40.

[529] Gaddis, *George F. Kennan*, 671. "Commencement Address at Texas A&M University," May 12, 1989, Miller Center, Presidential Speeches, George H. W. Bush, Miller Center, University of Virginia. Author's interview with Mark Davis, August 30, 2024.

[530] "Commencement Address at Texas A&M University," May 12, 1989. Bush and Scowcroft, *A World Transformed*, 53.

[531] Bush and Scowcroft, *A World Transformed*, 60.

[532] Bush and Scowcroft, *A World Transformed*, 60. Zoellick, *America in the World*, 438–439.

[533] Author's phone interview with Mark Davis, August 30, 2024. Robert A. Strong, *Character and Consequence: Foreign Policy Decisions of George H. W. Bush* (Lanham, MD: Lexington Books, 2020), 42.

[534] Bush and Scowcroft, *A World Transformed*, 60. Zoellick, *America in the World*, 438–439.

[535] Gibbs and Duffy, *The Presidents Club*, 380–382.

[536] Gibbs and Duffy, *The Presidents Club*, 380–382. Sununu, *The Quiet Man*, 9.

[537] Bush and Scowcroft, *A World Transformed*, 115.

[538] Bush and Scowcroft, *A World Transformed*, 116–125. Sununu, *The Quiet Man*, 30.

[539] Bush, *All the Best*, 433. Bush and Scowcroft, *A World Transformed*, 130.

[540] Bush and Scowcroft, *A World Transformed*, 130.

[541] Bush, *All the Best*, 433–434. Sununu, *The Quiet Man*, 25, 31. Bush and Scowcroft, *A World Transformed*, 133. Bush and Scowcroft, *A World Transformed*, 133.

[542] Tizoc Chavez, *The Diplomatic Presidency: American Foreign Policy from F.D.R. to George H. W. Bush* (Lawrence: University Press of Kansas, 2022), 178–179. Jeffrey A. Engel, "Hippocratic Diplomacy," January 14, 2016, Miller Center of Public Affairs, University of Virginia.

[543] Bush and Scowcroft, *A World Transformed*, 148. Bush, *All the Best*, 442.

[544] Bush and Scowcroft, *A World Transformed*, 148. James A Baker III and Thomas M. DeFrank, *The Politics of Diplomacy: Revolution, War, and Peace 1989–1992* (New York: G. P. Putnam and Sons, 1995), 158.

[545] Bush and Scowcroft, *A World Transformed*, 148–149.

[546] Meacham, *Destiny and Power*, 381.

[547] Bush and Scowcroft, *A World Transformed*, 149. Meacham, *Destiny and Power*, 381.

[548] Bush and Scowcroft, *A World Transformed*, 150–151.

[549] Bush and Scowcroft, *A World Transformed*, 149–150. Becker, *Character Matters*, xxiii.

[550] Bush and Scowcroft, *A World Transformed*, 153–154.

[551] Sununu, *The Quiet Man*, 32. Zoellick, *America in the World*, 438.
[552] Bush, *All the Best*, 444.
[553] Bush, *All the Best*, 444–445.
[554] Bush and Scowcroft, *A World Transformed*, 164.
[555] Bush, *41*, 292.
[556] Engel, *When the World Seemed New*, 297–298.
[557] Chavez, *The Diplomatic Presidency*, 179–180.
[558] Becker, *Character Matters*, 21.
[559] Bush, *All the Best*, 404.

Chapter 14—Not for Self: The 1990 Budget Negotiations

[560] John Robert Greene, *The Presidency of George Bush* (Lawrence: University Press of Kansas, 2000), 83–84.
[561] George Bush, "Second Presidential Lecture," May 6, 1990, Box 57, Speech File Draft Files, GBPL. Greene, *The Presidency of George Bush*, 83–84. Sununu, *The Quiet Man*, 46.
[562] Meacham, *Destiny and Power*, 409, 411. Sununu, *The Quiet Man*, 44.
[563] Meacham, *Destiny and Power*, 361.
[564] Bush, *Looking Forward*, xvi. Meacham, *Destiny and Power*, 360.
[565] [6] Bush, *All the Best*, 408.
[566] Medhurst, ed., *The Rhetorical Presidency of George H. W. Bush*, 10.
[567] Meacham, *Destiny and Power*, 362. Greene, *The Presidency of George Bush*, 95.
[568] Meacham, *Destiny and Power*, 363. Greene, *The Presidency of George Bush*, 80.
[569] Parmet, *George Bush*, 381.
[570] Parmet, *George Bush*, 381. Naftali, *George H. W. Bush*, 97.
[571] Greene, *The Presidency of George Bush*, 83.
[572] Meacham, *Destiny and Power*, 412. Richard Himelfarb and Rosanna Perotti, ed., *Principle Over Politics? The Domestic Policy of the George H. W. Bush Presidency* (Westport, CT: Praeger, 2004), 13.
[573] Meacham, *Destiny and Power*, 412. Dickerson, *The Hardest Job in the World*, 320.
[574] Meacham, *Destiny and Power*, 413.
[575] Meacham, *Destiny and* Power, 412.
[576] Meacham, *Destiny and Power*, 417.
[577] Meacham, *Destiny and Power*, 417. Strong, *Character and Consequence*, 43–44.
[578] Medhurst, *The Rhetorical Presidency of George H. W. Bush*, 8.
[579] Meacham, *Destiny and Power*, 418.
[580] Greene, *The Presidency of George Bush*, 86.
[581] George H. W Bush, "September 11, 1990, Address Before a Joint Session of Congress," Presidential Speeches, Miller Center, University of Virginia.
[582] Greene, *The Presidency of George Bush*, 86.
[583] Meacham, *Destiny and Power*, 445.
[584] Greene, *The Presidency of George Bush*, 87.

[585] Bush, *All the Best*, 481.
[586] Meacham, *Destiny and Power*, 449. Kabaservice, *Rule and Ruin*, 373.
[587] Email correspondence with Robert Zoellick, November 25, 2025.
[588] Bush, *All the Best*, 482.
[589] Bush, *All the Best*, 482.
[590] Kabaservice, *Rule and Ruin*, 373.
[591] Roger Ailes interview, *41 on 41* interview transcript.

Chapter 15—The Triumph of Experience: Operation Desert Storm

[592] Bush, *All the Best*, 496. Bush and Scowcroft, *A World Transformed*, 434.
[593] Engel, *When the World Seemed New*, 44–45.
[594] Engel, *China Diary*, 254.
[595] Bush and Scowcroft, *A World Transformed*, 303.
[596] Bush and Scowcroft, *A World Transformed*, 303.
[597] Bush and Scowcroft, *A World Transformed*, 304.
[598] Engel, *When the World Seemed New*, 382. Meacham, *Destiny and Power*, 422–423.
[599] Engel, *When the World Seemed New*, 385. Bush, *All the Best*, 476. Resolution 660 (1990) adopted by the Security Council at Its 2932nd meeting, on August 2, 1990, United Nations Digital Library.
[600] Bush and Scowcroft, *A World Transformed*, 315.
[601] Richard Haass, *War of Necessity, War of Choice: A Memoir of Two Iraq Wars* (New York: Simon & Schuster, 2009). Bush and Scowcroft, *A World Transformed*, 322. Engle, *When the World Seemed New*, 391.
[602] Strong, *Character and Consequence*, 102. Meacham, *Destiny and Power*, 425.
[603] Parmet, *George Bush*, 455.
[604] George Bush, "Remarks at the Aspen Institute Symposium in Aspen Colorado," August 2, 1990, Public Papers of George H. W. Bush, GBPL. Meacham, *Destiny and Power*, 427. Parmet, *George Bush*, 443.
[605] Schweizer, *The Bushes*, 394–395.
[606] Schweizer, *The Bushes*, 394–395. Bush and Scowcroft, *A World Transformed*, 318–319. Interview notes, Brent Scowcroft transcript, *41 on 41*, 1. Parmet, *George Bush*, 443.
[607] Bush and Scowcroft, *A World Transformed*, 321.
[608] Strong, *Character and Consequence*, 103. Parmet, *George Bush*, 459.
[609] Parmet, *George Bush*, 460.
[610] Bush and Scowcroft, *A World Transformed*, 335. Meacham, *Destiny and Power*, 435.
[611] Bush and Scowcroft, *A World Transformed*, 335. Meacham, *Destiny and Power*, 435. Interview with Robert Gates, transcript, *41 on 41*. The deputy secretary of state recalls one incident when Bush cultivated Mitterrand during a meeting on the island of St. Martin in 1989. In a private meeting with the French president, Bush hoped to develop a closer relationship in the hopes of gaining

the French president's support for the American plan on the future reunification of Germany. According to Zoellick, Bush expressed interest on Mitterrand's geopolitical views on the Middle East. Over the next forty-five minutes the president became the attentive student as Mitterrand discussed his views of the region in great detail. Zoellick later wondered why Bush had not added his own opinions to Mitterrand's analysis. But as Mitterrand departed, Zoellick suddenly understood. Bush had made Mitterrand feel that his views mattered. That what he said was important. Eight years younger than Mitterrand, Bush was showing him the same respect that he had shown to those like Averell Harriman, George Kennan, and elder political leaders. Bush knew that "stroking his colleague's sense of importance" would pay dividends in the future. Zoellick, *America in the World*, 421.

612 Parmet, *George Bush*, 461–462. Bush and Scowcroft, *A World Transformed*, 335.

613 Bush and Scowcroft, *A World Transformed*, 335.

614 Bush and Scowcroft, A *World Transformed*, 34–341, 354. Engel, *When the World Seemed New*, 396–397.

615 George Bush, "Address on Iraq's Invasion of Kuwait," August 8, 1990, Miller Center, University of Virginia.

616 Bush and Scowcroft, *A World Transformed*, 341.

617 In constructing the coalition Egypt's Hosni Mubarak suggested to Bush that he "touch base with these small countries whenever you can just to acknowledge their importance to the United States." Bush and Scowcroft, *A World Transformed*, 341. Interview with Condoleezza Rice, transcript, *41 on 41*.

618 Interview with Brent Scowcroft, transcript, *41 on 41*.

619 Bush and Scowcroft, *A World Transformed*, 343.

620 Bush and Scowcroft, *A World Transformed*, 343.

621 Bush and Scowcroft, *A World Transformed*, 343. "George Bush Public Approval," The American Presidency Project. Bush also had 76 percent approval rating on August 22 that was based on a *New York Times*/CBS Poll, Bush and Scowcroft, *A World Transformed*, 358.

622 Meacham, *Destiny and Power*, 438.

623 Parmet, *George Bush*, 464. Engel, *When the World Seemed New*, 669.

624 Engel, *When the World Seemed New*, 398–399. Author's phone interview with Chriss Winston, September 18, 2024. Parmet, *George Bush*, 471. Bush and Scowcroft, *A World Transformed*, 375.

625 Bush, *All the Best*, 479. Schweizer, *The Bushes*, 396.

626 Meacham, *Destiny and Power*, 438.

627 Bush and Scowcroft, *A World Transformed*, 352. Security Council Resolution 665 (1990) [on implementation of Security Council resolution 661 (1990), especially its provisions related to shipping], United Nations Digital Library.

628 George Bush, "Address Before a Joint Session of the Congress on the Persian Gulf Crisis and the Federal Budget Deficit," September 11, 1990, Public Papers, GBPL.

[629] Bush, "Address Before a Joint Session of the Congress on the Persian Gulf Crisis and the Federal Budget Deficit."
[630] Bush, "Address Before a Joint Session of the Congress on the Persian Gulf Crisis and the Federal Budget Deficit."
[631] Engel, *When the World Seemed New*, 419–420.
[632] Bush and Scowcroft, *A World Transformed*, 371.
[633] Bush and Scowcroft, *A World Transformed*, 372, 379.
[634] Bush and Scowcroft, *A World Transformed*, 382.
[635] Meacham, *Destiny and Power*, 452.
[636] Meacham, *Destiny and Power*, 452.
[637] Parmet, *George Bush*, 472–473.
[638] Meacham, *Destiny and Power*, 452. Bush and Scowcroft, *A World Transformed*, 415.
[639] Bush and Scowcroft, *A World Transformed*, 403–404.
[640] Meacham, *Destiny and Power*, 452. Bush, *All the Best*, 495.
[641] Bush and Scowcroft, *A World Transformed*, 429–430.
[642] Bush and Scowcroft, *A World Transformed*, 434. Becker, *Character Matters*, 45. As Becker notes, Bush typed the letter himself and for whatever reason did not correct the misspelling.
[643] Bush and Scowcroft, *A World Transformed*, 435.
[644] Bush, *All the Best*,499.
[645] Bush, *All the Best*, 500. Meacham, *Destiny and Power*, 455.
[646] Bush, *All the Best*, 500. Meacham, *Destiny and Power*, 455.
[647] Bush and Scowcroft, *A World Transformed*, 446. Bush, *All the Best*, 502.
[648] Bush and Scowcroft, *A World Transformed*, 446. Meacham, *Destiny and Power*, 455.
[649] Bush and Scowcroft, *A World Transformed*, 447–448.
[650] Bush, *All the Best*, 503.
[651] Bush and Scowcroft, *A World Transformed*, 447.
[652] George Bush, "Address to the Nation on the Invasion of Iraq," January 16, 1991, Miller Center, University of Virginia. Strong, *Character and Consequence*, 118.
[653] Bush, "Address to the Nation on the Invasion of Iraq."
[654] Bush, "Address to the Nation on the Invasion of Iraq." Bush, *41*, 306.
[655] Engel, *When the World Seemed New*, 431.
[656] Meacham, *Destiny and Power*, 460.
[657] Strong, *Character and Consequence*, 117.
[658] Bush and Scowcroft, *A World Transformed*, 464, 489.
[659] Meacham, *Destiny and Power*, 464–465. Interview with Brent Scowcroft, transcript, *41 on 41*.
[660] Meacham, *Destiny and Power*, 464–465.

Chapter 16—A More Perfect Union: Domestic Matters

[661] President George H. W. Bush addressed the Annual Boy Scout Jamboree, August 7, 1989, C-Span.
[662] Edward D. Berkowitz, "George Bush and the Americans with Disabilities Act," in *Principle Over Politics?*, edited by Richard Himelfarb and Rosanna Perotti, 144.
[663] Schweizer, *The Bushes*, 73. Bush, *All the Best*, 102.
[664] Schweizer, *The Bushes*, 379. Bush, *All the Best*, 102.
[665] Schweizer, *The Bushes*, 181–182.
[666] Joseph P. Shapiro, *No Pity: People with Disabilities, Forging a New Civil Rights Movement* (New York: Crown, 1994), 119.
[667] Shapiro, *No Pity*, 119.
[668] Shapiro, *No Pity*, 120.
[669] Shapiro, *No Pity*, 120.
[670] Shapiro, *No Pity*, 122.
[671] Berkowitz, "George Bush and the Americans with Disabilities Act," 148. Sununu, *The Quiet Man*, 56.
[672] George Bush, "Address Accepting the Presidential Nomination at the Republican National Convention in New Orleans," August 18, 1988, The American Presidency Project. Berkowitz, "George Bush and the Americans with Disabilities Act," 148.
[673] Berkowitz, "George Bush and the Americans with Disabilities Act," 148. Sununu, *The Quiet Man*, 56.
[674] Berkowitz, "George Bush and the Americans with Disabilities Act," 149.
[675] Himelfarb and Perotti, *Principle Over Politics?*, 156.
[676] Michael Riccards, "George Bush and the Last Whig Presidency," in *Principle Over Politics?*, Himelfarb and Perotti, 314.
[677] "Remarks at the University of Michigan Commencement Ceremony," Ann Arbor, MI, May 4, 1991, Public Papers of the Presidents of the United States: George H. W. Bush (1991, Book I).
[678] Himelfarb and Perotti, *Principle Over Politics?*, 324.
[679] Himelfarb and Perotti, *Principle Over Politics?*, 327.
[680] Himelfarb and Perotti, *Principle Over Politics?*, 327.
[681] Himelfarb and Perotti, *Principle Over Politics?*, 327. George Bush, "Remarks at a Luncheon Hosted by the New York Partnership and the Association for a Better New York," New York, June 22, 1989, Public Papers of the Presidents, GBPL.
[682] Bush, "Remarks at a Luncheon Hosted by the New York Partnership and the Association for a Better New York."
[683] Himelfarb and Perotti, *Principle Over Politics?*, 324. George Bush, "Statement on Signing the National and Community Service Act of 1990," The American Presidency Project.
[684] Remarks at the University of Michigan Commencement Ceremony in Ann Arbor, May 4, 1991.

Chapter 17—Gracious in Defeat: The 1992 Campaign

685 "Interview notes, President Clinton," transcript, *41 on 41*. Meacham, *Destiny and Power*, 533

686 "The Legacy of the George H. W. Bush Administration," Council on Foreign Relations, February 17, 2016.

687 Gould, *Grand Old Party*, 449–450.

688 Wicker, *George Herbert Walker Bush*, 169.

689 Wicker, *George Herbert Walker Bush*, 170.

690 Naftali, *George H. W Bush*, 142. Parmet, *George Bush*, 502.

691 Parmet, *George Bush*, 503.

692 Parmet, *George Bush*, 503. Bush, *All the Best*, 548. Meacham, *Destiny and Power*, 511.

693 Bush, *All the Best*, 567. Meacham, *Destiny and Power*, 512.

694 Meacham, *Destiny and Power*, 521–522.

695 Meacham, *Destiny and Power*, 525.

696 Bush, *All the Best*, 576. Interview notes, President Clinton, transcript, *41 on 41*.

Conclusion

697 Bush, *All the Best*, 583.

698 Gordon Wood, *Revolutionary Characters: What Made the Founders Different* (New York: Penguin Press, 2006), 24.

699 Adam Bellow, *In Praise of Nepotism: A Natural History* (New York: Doubleday, 2003), 15, 441.

700 Bellow, *In Praise of Nepotism*, 2. In the book *The Hardest Job in the World: The American Presidency*, John Dickerson quotes historian Richard McCormack who states, "The ideal candidate in a republic who, through his dedicated and disinterested public service, acquired a reputation for probity and integrity and accepted the call of his fellow citizens to successfully higher offices.…Bush fit that description." John Dickerson, *The Hardest Job in the World: The American Presidency* (New York: Random House, 2020), 316.

701 Bellow, *In Praise of Nepotism*, 465–466.

702 Aaron David Miller, *The End of Greatness: Why America Can't Have (and Doesn't Want) Another Great President* (New York: Palgrave Macmillan, 2014), 242. Alvin Felzenberg, *The Leaders We Deserved (and a Few We Didn't): Rethinking the Presidential Rating Game* (New York: Basic Books, 2010), ix.

703 Issacson and Thomas, *The Wise Men*, 30.

704 Brookhiser, *The Way of the Wasp*, 29–30, 34–35.

705 Isaacson and Thomas, *The Wise Men*, 30.

706 Brookhiser, *The Way of the Wasp*, 74–75, 80. Henry L. Stimson and McGeorge Bundy, *On Active Service in Peace and War* [New York: Harper Brothers, 1947], 9.

707 Brookhiser, *The Way of the Wasp*, 80–81.

ACKNOWLEDGMENTS

While my name appears on the cover of *41: George H. W. Bush and the End of the American Establishment,* this book would never have come to life without the support and generosity of many others.

First and foremost, my deepest gratitude goes to my wonderful agent, Suzy Evans. Suzy's passion for history, her optimism, and her warm sense of humor make every collaboration a joy. I am equally grateful to my editor, Adam Bellow, for helping me clarify my vision for the narrative, and to everyone at Post Hill Press especially my Managing Editor, Lauren Campbell whose dedication made this book possible.

Many people who knew and worked with President Bush were enormously generous with their time and insights. I am especially thankful to Freddie Ford, chief of staff to the office of President George W. Bush, for kindly introducing me to individuals who were invaluable to my research. I extend my heartfelt thanks to Jean Becker and Tom Collamore for taking the time to speak with me, read the manuscript, and offer thoughtful feedback. I am also grateful to Jean for granting me access to the unedited interview transcripts compiled by Mary Kate Cary for her documentary, *41 on 41.*

My sincere thanks go as well to David Q. Bates Jr., Neil Mallon Bush, Mary Kate Cary, Mark Davis, Craig Fuller, Stephen Knott, Thomas Mackey, Roger F. Pasquier, James Pinkerton, Karl Rove, Curt Smith, Robert A. Strong, Tevi Troy, Elsie Walker, George H. Walker IV, Chriss Winston, and Robert Zoellick. Each contributed their time, perspective, or feedback, and I am deeply appreciative. I am especially thankful to Mr. Walker for sharing his grandfather's privately published memoir with me.

Much of this book draws on the remarkable holdings of the George H. W. Bush Presidential Library in College Station, Texas. I owe a great debt to the dedicated archivists who make a historian's work possible. My thanks to Director Dawn Hammatt, Deputy Director Dr. Robert Holzweiss, John P. Blair, and all the archivists whose guidance and expertise were so helpful to the development of the narrative. My appreciation as well to the staffs of the Dwight D. Eisenhower, Lyndon B. Johnson, and Richard M. Nixon presidential libraries. I also want to express my appreciation to the Scowcroft Institute of International Affairs at Texas A&M for funding my visit to the Bush library.

Finally, my deepest love and gratitude go to my wonderful wife, Jorie Waterman, and our fabulous son, Elliot Jurdem. Thank you for filling my life with love, laughter, and joy every single day.